GOD DAY BY DAY

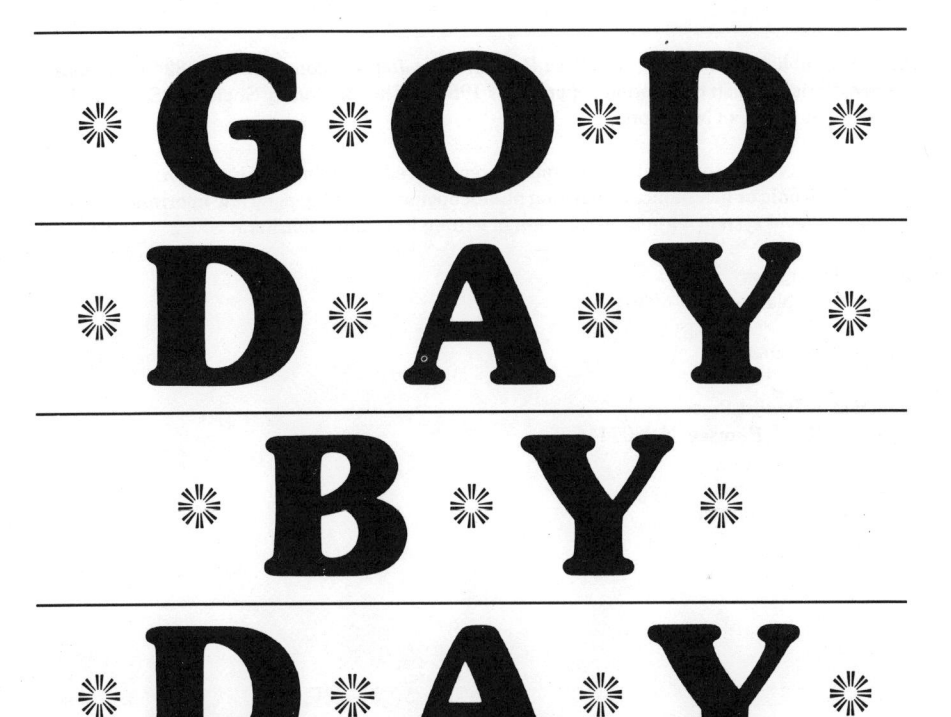

FOLLOWING THE WEEKDAY LECTIONARY

VOLUME ONE

LENT AND THE EASTER SEASON

COMMENTARY ON THE TEXTS
SPIRITUAL REFLECTIONS · SUGGESTED PRAYERS

MARCEL BASTIN · GHISLAIN PINCKERS · MICHEL TEHEUX

TRANSLATED BY DAVID SMITH

Paulist Press • New York/New Jersey

Originally published under the title *Dieu Pour Chaque Jour (1)* copyright © 1982 by Editions Desclée, Paris. English translation copyright © 1984 by The Missionary Society of St. Paul the Apostle in the State of New York.

All rights reserved. No part of this book may be reproduced or transmitted in any form or by any means, electronic or mechanical, including photocopying, recording or by any information storage and retrieval system without permission in writing from the Publisher.

Library of Congress
Catalog Card Number: 84-60391

ISBN: 0-8091-2642-7

Published by Paulist Press
545 Island Road, Ramsey, N.J. 07446

Printed and bound in the
United States of America

CONTENTS

Presentation 1
Foreword by Mgr R.-J Mathen 2
Introduction: The Sacred Time
by M.-D. Chenu 5

KEEPING LENT: CONVERSION AS A CHANGE OF HEART

The Weekday Lectionary of Lent 7
Psalm 51 8

WEEK AFTER ASH WEDNESDAY: MAKE YOUR DAY APPEAR

Wednesday	The Inner Feast 12
Thursday	Nomads on the Way of Life 15
Friday	The Light of Dawn 17
Saturday	Our Heart and Our Practice 20

FIRST WEEK OF LENT: A NEW WAY OF SEEING

Monday	Face to Face 24
Tuesday	God Is God 26
Wednesday	At Once 29
Thursday	Without Tiring 31
Friday	The Future of Man 34
Saturday	To Perfection 36

SECOND WEEK OF LENT: GOING FURTHER

Monday	Without Restraint 40
Tuesday	The Poor Servant Church 42
Wednesday	The Son of Man 45
Thursday	Solitude 47
Friday	Holocaust 50
Saturday	The Heart of God 51

BAPTISMAL LITURGIES: WE ARE BORN AGAIN

Note on the Optional Liturgy

Third Week	Meeting at a Well 57
Fourth Week	Let Your Eyes Be Dazzled 60
Fifth Week	When Our Bodies Rise Again 64

THIRD WEEK OF LENT: CULT AND THE LAW

Monday	Renewal 69
Tuesday	Untiring Forgiveness 71
Wednesday	A Law Engraved in our Heart 74
Thursday	Hardness of Heart 76
Friday	Morning Sacrifice 79
Saturday	Prayer of the Heart 81

FROM THE MONDAY TO THE WEDNESDAY OF THE FOURTH WEEK: BAPTISMAL CONVERSION

The Gospel According to Saint John

Monday	A New Creation 88
Tuesday	Immersed in the Water 90
Wednesday	Like Father, Like Son 93

FROM THE THURSDAY OF THE FOURTH WEEK TO THE SATURDAY OF THE FIFTH WEEK: THE TRIAL OF JESUS

Thursday	God Accused 98
Friday	Testing God 101
Saturday	In Defense of the Stumbling Block 103
Monday	Judgment 105
Tuesday	The Exalted Servant 108
Wednesday	The Son of Abraham 110
Thursday	A Covenant of Life 112
Friday	Sonship 115
Saturday	A Covenant Made in Blood 117

FROM THE MONDAY TO THE WEDNESDAY OF HOLY WEEK: FAREWELL TO GOD

Monday	The Wheat Grain in the Ground 120
Tuesday	The Servant Goes 123
Wednesday	The Hour Is Near 125

CELEBRATING EASTER: A NEW SONG

The Weekday Lectionary for Eastertide
The Acts of the Apostles

THE OCTAVE OF EASTER: THE OTHER PROCESS

Monday	Dramatic Turn of Events 135
Tuesday	"They Have Taken Him Away" 139
Wednesday	Communion 142
Thursday	Peace 146
Friday	By the Name of the One Who Was Crucified 149
Saturday	Bearing Witness 153

FROM THE MONDAY TO THE THURSDAY OF THE SECOND WEEK OF EASTER: NEW LIFE

Monday	Rebirth 156
Tuesday	Together 160
Wednesday	A New Heart 163
Thursday	Bearing Witness 165

FROM THE FRIDAY OF THE SECOND WEEK OF EASTER TO THE SATURDAY OF THE THIRD WEEK: BREAD BROKEN FOR A NEW WORLD

Breaking Bread and Giving Thanks

Friday	For Hunger 173
Saturday	In the Stormy Course of History 177
Monday	God in Flight 179
Tuesday	Manna 182
Wednesday	Growth 184
Thursday	Bread Handed Over 187
Friday	Flesh and Blood 189
Saturday	Freedom 192

FOURTH WEEK OF EASTER: THE LAW OF THE RESURRECTION

Monday	The Gate of the Kingdom 196
Tuesday	Belonging 199
Wednesday	Light 201
Thursday	Love 204
Friday	The Way 206
Saturday	Imitation of Christ 209

FIFTH AND SIXTH WEEKS OF EASTER: THE CHURCH, THE FUTURE OF THE WORLD

Praying with Jesus at the Last Supper

Monday (Fifth Week)	Going Further Than Statistics 215
Tuesday	Our Inheritance: Peace 218
Wednesday	The Vine 220
Thursday	Discipleship 223
Friday	Chosen To Love 225
Saturday	Commitment 228
Monday (Sixth Week)	Memory 230
Tuesday	Counsel for Our Defense 232
Wednesday	Knowledge 235
Thursday	Widowhood 238
Friday	The Body of Christ 240
Saturday	Longing 242

SEVENTH WEEK OF EASTER: CALLING ON THE SPIRIT

Come, Holy Spirit

Monday	The Hour 248
Tuesday	A Testament 251
Wednesday	For the World 253
Thursday	Unity 256
Friday	Love 258
Saturday	Fire 261

PRESENTATION

This book is the first of a set of five embracing the whole of the Church's weekday lectionary. It covers the seasons of Lent and Easter. Many books have already appeared containing commentaries, suggestions and prayers for the Sundays of the three-year cycle of readings. We have been waiting for the initiative to be taken to provide books for the weekdays similar to those already existing for Sundays, and now we have the first of them.

The structure and method of presentation are quite straightforward. The authors have followed the order of the days of the week, but have grouped certain days together according to liturgical periods or within homogeneous wholes, each of which is preceded by an introductory note.

Under each day, the following three elements will be found:

1. A short commentary on the readings and the Psalm. A biblical expert has drawn a clear, simple and firmly based message from the sacred texts.

2. A spiritual text, intended to provide material for private meditation, the preparation for the homily and other purposes outside the Eucharist itself, both by individuals and by groups.

3. Suggestions for prayer, which can be used to extend meditation, for example, by thanksgiving. These prayers can also be used throughout the rest of the day. Their language and thought is strongly biblical.

The authors do not intend any of these three elements to be used to replace the texts and prayers of the liturgy itself. The very reverse is true. Because the authors' aim is to help the reader to prepare for and to extend the liturgical act, their suggestions are above all at the service of the liturgy. They have their origin in the Eucharist and their only intention is to help to make each day holy. To that end, these suggestions are an attempt to stimulate the spiritual benefits of the liturgy to flow as from a source of life-giving water.

The Editor

THE VOLUMES IN THIS SET

Lent and Easter
Ordinary Time: Matthew
Advent and Christmas

These books are the result of ministry and pastoral experience in the parish of Saint-Denis in Liège, Belgium. The parish church is at the center of a neighborhood, that is dominated by trade, administration and leisure, and the local community that has grown up there is always in a state of movement. The church is visited every day by a very great number of people living and working there. It is that aspect of the church that the authors have also tried to present in the pages that follow.

FOREWORD

When the decision was taken at the Second Vatican Council to provide a lectionary for use during the days of the week that were not special feasts, the seed was sown for a rich harvest in the future. We were given the opportunity to meditate on the word every day and allow it to penetrate into our lives and fashion them in accordance with the Spirit of God. The word of God is, after all, life, and it never returns empty to its source without having made our soil fertile (Is 55:10). It is the bread of life for anyone who takes the time to eat it.

That seed has in fact already borne fruit. We would, I believe, not be wrong in thinking that the great biblical renewal in the Church owes something to the daily presence of Scripture in the Christian liturgy. It is, of course, not possible for everyone to take part each day in the Eucharist, but the scope of a liturgical book can never be restricted simply to its use in public worship. The tree can and indeed must also bear other fruit.

We should not be led astray by the strictly liturgical use of the lectionary. It is not simply within the liturgy that it can provide food for the Church. Its usefulness goes much further than that. It can be used in meditation, prayer, and examination of our lives as Christians, and as a means of animating groups and movements. Like the missal, the lectionary is rapidly becoming a bedside book, and if it is not already, it should be in every Christian home.

The word can never truly live, however, if it is not internalized, shared and transfigured in prayer. It is the source of daily conversion, and the inner voice speaking in the text tells us, as it told Saint Augustine while he was still hesitating: *Tolle, lege!* Take and read! So we should take the book, become very familiar with it, and in it listen to the God who is speaking to us every day.

But taking the book in this way is not just getting to know the text. It is much more than that. It is what the prophet Ezekiel called "eating the Word" (Ez 3:1)—making it our own, becoming one with it until it leads us and fashions us. We shall, of course, never fully reach that stage, but we have to strive toward it again and again. That is why the word has to return to us again and again if we are to learn how to live in it.

This is precisely what justifies the existence of the homily (in the liturgy), the commentary (both verbal and written), and our prayer, based on the text and enabling it to rise up again to God in thanksgiving and intercession. Scripture has, on the one hand, to be explained on the basis of solid scientific criteria, and, on the other, it also calls for a spiritual, meditative commentary that will make it a present reality in our lives. We have certainly always to guard against reading into the text what we want to find in it, and to remember that it is leading us. At the same time, however, it is necessary to personalize it by commentary, and this procedure is not alien to the word of God so long as we remain humbly subject to the Spirit.

We have to personalize Scripture even if this means that each of us has to internalize it individually in his or her own life. But, although no one can put himself or herself in another's place, we are also members of the body of Christ and therefore of each other, so that, when one is aware of Scripture, the others can all benefit from this and we are all built up. It is a work of edification in the best sense of the word.

One remarkable aspect of the process of becoming aware of the word in the liturgy is that the texts throw light on each other. In "ordinary time" especially, each reading seems to follow its own course without any intentional relationship with the others, but, if we are at all familiar with the depths of the Bible, the countless facets of the one treasure can be seen to reflect each other in a single great interplay of light that draws attention to the freedom of grace. There is no need to speak of biblical "themes" in this context. These are often too precise and at the same time too abstract. We can perhaps think of the harmonics that can be heard in the same symphony. That is why a commentary that is inspired by these harmonics can be so suggestive. The old and the new covenants both question and complete each other. The Gospels are developed in the apostolic Letters. The Psalms echo the word of God with words that are themselves inspired.

Christians are being invited more and more urgently to pray without ceasing and to go back to the source of their spiritual life in dialogue with the Lord. There is therefore every reason to be very pleased about the publication of this series of books. We need instruments to help us explore the depths of the word, and the authors have done well in venturing to offer us some of the fruits of their own meditation. They know better than anybody how it is possible to go on searching, questioning and being questioned and to let the Spirit pray continuously within us, but they also know that this is not sufficient reason for putting off the task until tomorrow.

We have therefore to thank and congratulate most warmly the three authors, Fr. Ghislain Pinckers, who is a member of the Belgian Interdiocesan Commission for Pastoral Care and the Liturgy (CIPL), Fr. Marcel Bastin, and Fr. Michel Teheux for the initiative that they have taken. Their books will help many Christians to enter into the riches of Holy Scripture, appreciate more fully the beauties of the word of God, and pray with words suffused with the vitality of the Bible.

I should like this series of books to be disseminated as widely as possible among Christians. It will undoubtedly help both priests and lay people to prepare for the daily Eucharist and to celebrate it with greater devotion. It will also help them to pray with greater inspiration both individually and together with others.

R.-J. Mathen
Bishop of Namur
President of the CIPL

THE SACRED TIME

God day by day—this is one way of describing the Church's liturgy, both as a sharing in the word of God and as a making present of the mystery of the resurrection in the mystical body of Jesus Christ. Time is an essential ingredient in both, as it is when we address the "eternal and omnipotent God" in prayer.

This does not mean that private prayer, in which we are in communion with the living God in a God-oriented concentration of faith, hope and love, is without value. Contemplation is, after all, the beginning of the beatific vision. But we have also to be careful not to minimize the value of public worship with its rites and symbols, since, in so doing, we are dehumanizing the divine life in the presence of the fact of the incarnation and we are at the same time risking making our day-to-day existence trivial at the expense of the "Lord's day."

The Sunday missal is designed to be employed within the framework of the creation, in which that Lord's day takes its place at the end of the six symbolic days of creation, with all the various meanings that it has in the Genesis story, from the idea of weekly rest to that of the ultimate glorification of God. We should above all not forget the supreme significance that the Lord's day has in the Christian tradition as the day of the Lord's resurrection. This is clearly a way of making time present as a rhythm in religion and as the virtue of the creature with regard to the Creator.

The missal and the weekday lectionary, as they are presented here, provide a recapitulation of the whole of God's dealings with man, fulfilled in his being incorporated into the body of Christ as a reality taking place day by day. What we have here is not a purely natural rhythm measured out according to the division of the hours, but the stages of a history in which time has more than simply a cosmic dimension and is the bearer of a liturgy which makes it holy rather than merely sacral. It is through that liturgy that the divine mystery lives day by day in man's history.

It is obvious that the elements brought into play in the carrying out of this divine plan originated in the history of man—his sacred history. The texts of the Old and New Testaments, which are so carefully scattered throughout the renewed liturgy of the Church, form the principal fabric of that history. This can be grasped if we understand the fundamental principles of biblical exegesis, and that knowledge will help us to avoid those laboriously constructed and sternly moralizing treatises which were for so long the scourge of religious instruction. The doctrinal content of that history is found within the framework of a homiletic meditation and a prayer, which is both flexible and homogeneous in accordance with our needs and desires, and each day is presented by the authors under a very suggestive heading. That, then, is the instrument which they have given us so that we can become aware of the sacral dimension of time within the mystery of the incarnation.

M.-D. Chenu O.P.

KEEPING LENT
CONVERSION AS A CHANGE OF HEART

"When I was very young . . . " Older people will remember quite well the severity of Lent each year, with its penances carefully counted. But now we can even eat meat on Fridays, in some countries at least—a pity in some ways.

We still have Lenten offerings and appeals for the third world. But people are dying of starvation every day of the year, and many are not even aware that the time for Lent has come.

Many people say that fasting is not the essential aspect of Lent, that it is not what we eat or do not eat that counts. One is bound to ask whether they are not delighted that the Lenten fast has disappeared and that it is sufficient just to love. But love is less demanding.

Should the fast be restored? Perhaps it should, since it is true that we desire more when our stomachs are empty. But that desire has to be directed toward God. We often fast just because we want to look more attractive.

Lent is a time of conversion and change of heart, and our penances are valueless if they do not lead to that. In the past, people ate fish in order to share the life of the poor—wholeheartedly.

The liturgy of the forty days of Lent unfolds like a long retreat, a period spent in the desert and then a going up to Jerusalem, with baptism in the background. It reflects a return to the truth, to essentials.

What is that truth for us today? Is it not above all the rediscovery of God, the living God, the Father revealed in Jesus Christ, finding him again in the depths of our heart, which urges us to stake everything we have on him?

Fasting? Well, yes, so long as Lent makes us hungry to share with those who have nothing and to do that because God has always been on their side and his voice is not heard when we are too prosperous.

Rich food and material wealth have paralyzed us so much that we have lost heart. We have become closed to the poor and at the same time closed to God. However many sacrifices we might make in Lent, they would be valueless if we did not begin by doing without what has made us deaf to God and to the cry of the poor.

We have to learn how to live differently, to breathe with a different rhythm and to sink down again into the Gospel. Unfortunately we have been taught to do penance without having been taught to go outside ourselves and welcome the Other—the one who is both God and the poor.

THE WEEKDAY LECTIONARY OF LENT

The arrangement of the daily readings for the Eucharist during Lent is not at first sight obvious. It only becomes clear from the fourth week onward, when the almost continuous reading from St. John's Gospel points to a "going up to Jerusalem" and the legal action brought against Jesus is intensified. During the week following Ash Wednesday and the first three weeks of Lent, the theme is above all that of penance. It would be very artificial to try to find a clear movement forward in this theme, but a fairly general title has been given to each week or part of a week for the reader's convenience.

It should be noted that there is a choice of readings in the third, fourth and fifth weeks. The great baptismal readings from the Gospel of John suggested for the Sundays of Year A—the Samaritan woman, the man born blind and Lazarus—can be used together with a reading from the Old Testament. These three sets of readings have been included under one heading—"Baptismal Liturgies"—between the second and the third weeks of Lent.

Both the rubrics and our own discretion will tell us that, if we do not follow all the readings at the daily celebration of the Eucharist, we can choose for ourselves those which are most fruitful. For those who are in doubt, however, about how to choose, the following suggestions are offered:

During the week after Ash Wednesday, we should perhaps choose Wednesday itself and Friday, when the meaning of our penitential practices is emphasized. Wednesday and Friday in the second week of Lent are also very good, because they stress the announcement of the passion, and Saturday, because of the parable of the prodigal son.

As for the third week, especially helpful are Tuesday (mutual forgiveness), Friday (the commandment of love) and Saturday (the parable of the Pharisee and the publican).

There is a great deal to choose from in the last three weeks, especially if there is a need for baptismal instruction. A particularly good text is that describing the healing at the pool of Bethesda on the Tuesday of the fourth week.

In the group of days from the Thursday of the fourth week to the end of the fifth week, of special value are the Friday in the fourth week and Tuesday, Friday and Saturday in the fifth. All these readings are excellent sign-posts on the way to a meditation about Jesus' trial.

It hardly needs to be added that the first three days in Holy Week are very fruitful and almost indispensable.

PSALM 51

This is pre-eminently a Lenten Psalm. It is well worth pausing here for a while to consider the symbolism and the theology contained in it. It is one of the Psalms of individual supplication and was composed at the end of the period of the monarchy.[1] It was clearly written to form part of a penitential liturgy presided over by the king, but it is obvious that it expresses the prayer of countless people who were sufficiently religious to be able to recognize themselves in it.

The direction that this prayer follows from the very first verse is quite striking. No attempt is made in this Psalm to exonerate the author from his guilt, as is the case in so many complaints. The psalmist turns straightaway in supplication to God and appeals to his mercy and love. Man is a sinner and his salvation is entirely in the hands of God, who is radically defined by love. The psalmist is aware that God is just and that he wants man to have truth and wisdom in his heart, but he also knows that God's "justice" is made manifest in the forgiveness that he grants to the sinner. It is, as it were, a question of his honor, because the sinner who is forgiven will bear witness to God. He will teach the way of truth to sinners and those who have gone astray will return to him. This recognition of sin, then, has a prophetic dimension. It forms part of the "confession" of God's works.

So the psalmist is quite straightforward in recognizing his guilt and he is not afraid to look at his sin, which is always before him. He has it "constantly in mind." Is this an exaggerated sense of sin, or is it simply a literary device? It is neither. That deep sense of sin is only present in the mind of the psalmist so that he can grasp more fully the dimensions of God's forgiveness. It is only against God that man has sinned. He has undoubtedly committed many faults against his fellow men, but, in the liturgical act of confession, the accent is placed on God, who is at the source of everything that is good, including forgiveness and the ultimate significance of sin. It is here above all that God has revealed himself to be completely at one with us in our lives and in the conditions in which we live.

The psalmist has such a sensitive conscience that he knows that he was "born guilty" and a "sinner from the moment of conception." It is hardly necessary to look in these words for an explicit theology of the doctrine of original sin and even less for an explanation of the way in which it has been transmitted. The author of the Psalm is speaking here at a completely existential level, in the knowledge that he belongs to sinful mankind and that neither he nor any other person can escape from that weight of misery. That conviction is quite clear from his appeal to God the Creator to save him from his fault. His consciousness of sin greatly exceeds the apparently fair proportion that a judge might measure out in accordance with man's responsibilities and extenuating circumstances. It is simply a question of man's existence in the presence of God. Israel is a holy people and sin is always an obstacle between Israel and God.

Verses 2, 7, 10 and 12 are particularly interesting. The first two probably contain an allusion to a purification rite involving washing, whereas the second two internalize the procedure and suggest that the rite is no more than the visible aspect of a profound renewal in man. The Psalm is therefore another one of the many documents within the great movement which began with the disciples of the prophet Isaiah and culminated in the evangelists and which defined in baptismal terms the restoration of man and the cosmos.

Let us briefly review the stages in that movement. Third Isaiah (65:17) proclaimed the "creation of new heavens and a new earth." Jeremiah spoke of the restoration of God's people and of the individual, announcing a new era when the law would be engraved in men's hearts and in this way stressing the deep communion that was to unite the new mankind with God (32:39ff).

Ezekiel, following the same train of thought, spoke of a new creation and a new spirit (36:25–27). He was perhaps the most explicit among the prophets in making a link between water and life. In his preaching, he recalled the river which, according to Genesis, rose from the ground and flowed over the entire surface of the earth. He believed that the day would come when, in the new Jerusalem, a spring would rise and make the desert fertile, becoming a fast-flowing stream with wonderful fruit-trees growing on its banks (Ez 47). The return of Yahweh, then, would be marked by great abundance, symbolized by living water. Later, this same theme was taken up again by the fourth evangelist, who applied it to the body of Christ, the new temple.

Water is therefore the source of life. When the psalmist asks God to wash him, he is asking for life and renewal. From that time onward, he can imagine forgiveness to be a dance of resurrection and a hymn of praise (cf. Ez 37). If it is true that, in wiping away man's sin, God creates a new heart in him, then forgiveness can be seen as a renewal of the entire work of creation. The new time made manifest in the gift of the Spirit is a time of resurrection and feasting. "Confession" is an act in which the God of life is made manifest.

Confronted with this, what else can man do but simply be astonished and thank God? He can also proclaim God's justice, but not in acts of worship which may be hypocritical, because man is not totally committed to them with all his heart. The psalmist warns us against sacrifices offered in the old way. Man must know that he cannot buy God's forgiveness, which goes far beyond every human measure. The only offering that is pleasing to God is a "broken spirit," a "crushed and broken heart"—in other words, a converted heart in man who at last knows what he is and does not want to assert himself in the presence of his Creator.[2]

WEEK AFTER ASH WEDNESDAY

MAKE YOUR DAY APPEAR

The forty great days of Lent begin with the sound of the trumpet. All the people are called to fast as a Church, a holy assembly. At the end of the fifty days of Eastertide, the prophet Joel will proclaim the pouring out of the Spirit on all flesh (Pentecost). The Lenten fast is not an act of individual ascesis, but a long shared celebration when the Church calls on us to let our hearts be renewed by the Spirit. We shall be reborn from the dust of our ashes to a festival of life.

Today, however, we have to set off, rediscover our nomadic origins and follow the path of life. That path is the way of the cross, of humility, inner austerity and stripping away and of justice and love for our fellow men. It is the path followed by the Church in search of her Bridegroom who has been taken from her, a path followed in the silence of the desert and the truth of the heart. But faith knows that the cross announces the resurrection and that night always ends with the dawn of the Easter rising again. Sinners are already invited to the messianic table by the one who came to call the sick, not those who are well.

Should our fast not be a eucharistic fast in the strict sense of the words? Should it not be a stripping away of everything in us that prevents us from sharing in the happiness of the table of reconciliation, the table at which the Bridegroom already gives us the new wine of the feast? Even while he is doing penance, the Christian knows the inner peace of life and forgiveness and he goes into the desert because it is there that God can speak to his heart. In that silence and absence, our desire can be deepened.

■

It is good to fast for you, God our life,
   and to let hunger deepen in us
   our desire for a much greater love.
Following Jesus, we will go into the desert
   and from our daily stripping away
   will be born again a new humanity,
   the work of grace and poverty.
Blessed are you, Lord, for your table of broken bread,
   where those who give themselves to you unreservedly
   are reconciled with you and with each other.
Blessed too is the day
   when your Church will know
   the tenderness with which you loved her
   when she walked along the rough paths of the cross.

ASH WEDNESDAY

THE INNER FEAST
Joel 2:12–18: "Let your hearts be broken, not your garments torn." It is so tempting to seek refuge in external rites. All the prophets warned Israel again and again: Circumcise your heart, not your foreskin. We have to remind ourselves of this every day. Our ashes can so easily become a talisman.

"Sound the trumpet in Zion." May the sound of that trumpet be heard in all the villages of Judah. May everyone come together on this great day for Yahweh and his people. Today is a day of holy assembly. Today is the beginning of a fast for the Lord. Let everyone be in sackcloth and ashes today and refrain from all pleasure.

Conversion, stripping away, austerity and commitment—Joel announces the day of Yahweh. He goes ahead of the God who is coming. At the end of Eastertide, on the day of Pentecost, there will be another reading from the Book of Joel, but then the ancient world will have given way to a purified world, inhabited by the Spirit.

Psalm 51 is a song of the distress of the "poor," the sick and the persecuted whose lives or possessions are threatened and of the hope of the man who trusts in God. Who will change my heart of stone into a heart of flesh? The Lord will do that.

2 Corinthians 5:20—6:2: The phrase "ministry of reconciliation" meant a great deal to the Corinthians, since it called to mind an event in the history of their city. When Corinth was being rebuilt in 44 B.C. Caesar sent settlers from Greece and the whole empire there. These were people with a bad record, but the consul wanted to give them the chance of a new life.

What the Apostle Paul is saying is: God acts in the same way. He also calls everyone to build the new Jerusalem, and Christ came as an ambassador for the ministry of reconciliation. The time of the Church is pre-eminently the time of conversion, because it makes reunion between Jews and pagans possible and necessary. It is therefore important not to let it just slip by, especially since the price paid by Christ acting as our ambassador was more than any man can imagine. "For our sake God made the sinless one into sin, so that in him we might become the goodness of God."

Matthew 6:1–6, 16–18: Almsgiving, prayer and fasting were three important Jewish practices, but, in carrying them out, the pious Jew ran a serious risk. Their real end was God, but it was all too easy to lose sight of this and use religion to glorify oneself, becoming caught up in the actions of the game and forgetting why one is playing it. It was, after all, because he wanted to be like God that Adam ate the forbidden fruit.

What we do in almsgiving, prayer or fasting must be done "in secret," that is, in truth, in the presence only of the Father who tries our "minds and hearts." And "when you pray, . . . shut your door," because the Lord likes to speak in the hollow of your silence. And "when you fast, put oil on your head," because God is calling you to take part in a feast.

■

What is the feast for which we are singing? It is true that many Christians are not aware of a feast on Ash Wednesday. Yet God's

words are unequivocal: "Proclaim a solemn assembly, call the people together, summon the community."

Today the whole of the Church is called to take part in a feast, the main dish of which is fasting. It is a very strange feast. But are we still able to celebrate a feast at all nowadays? In our modern world, in which everything tastes of ashes, can we still experience joy—can we still sing? It may be because Easter is no longer the most blessed of days that Lent has become so gray, sad and misty.

"When you fast, do not put on a gloomy look . . . . Put oil on your head." Fasting is creating a vacuum in oneself. Our hearts are heavy with so many useless things. We have to empty ourselves in a radical stripping away. We have to rediscover poverty and let God find a place in our innermost depths. The true feast takes place, after all, within us. The Spirit initiates it in our hearts, so long as they are ready to welcome him. To do that, however, we have to fast. We must be hungry if we are to recognize our desire for him, and we have to get rid of all the dross if we are to go to the source of life. It is in silence that the sound of that feast with God will come to us. It is in humility that our spirit will become open to the breath of the Holy Spirit. In fasting, we can take part in the feast of the poor—a feast at which the smallest things can suddenly have the taste of eternity.

"Make your day appear." Can you not see it coming? It is coming, that feast day, but it is coming in secret, in your innermost depths. Shut your door. We are all called to be silent. May there be room for the Spirit at our solemn assembly.

■

We thank you, Lord our God,
  because you are calling your Church today
  to discover the way of peace
  in the unity of a single heart converted to your word.
We bless you for Jesus Christ.
  In him the hope of a new day
  appeared for us,
  the hope of a day of feasting and light.
We bless you too for his Spirit of life and holiness.
  When man's heart is ready to be possessed by him
  he creates it anew in silence and poverty.

*With all the saints in heaven and on earth
   we bless you and praise you unceasingly
   throughout this time of grace.*

1. See E. Lipinski, "Psaumes," *Dictionnaire de la Bible, Supplément,* IX, col. 66 (Paris, 1974).
2. Verses 20–21 are an exilic addition, made in the hope that the temple would be restored.

THURSDAY AFTER ASH WEDNESDAY

NOMADS ON THE WAY OF LIFE

Deuteronomy 30:15–20: Deuteronomy originated in the northern kingdom of Israel. It was written during the second half of the eighth century and began with the preaching of a group of Levites whose task was to deepen the traditions of the covenant.

The people of Israel were troubled by a religious problem of a special kind. Their religion, Yahwism, was a religion of a nomadic people, but they had adopted a settled way of life and their religion was hardly adapted to this. Confronted with farming techniques that they could only with difficulty make their own, they increasingly sought refuge in forms of nature worship.

Deuteronomy recalls the conditions of God's covenant with his people. For making his people leave Egypt and giving them a share in the promised land, he expected them to worship him and him alone. Two ways were open to Israel—the way of idolatry, which led to death, and the way of faithfulness to Yahweh, which led to happiness and the peaceful possession of the land that he had given them.

Psalm 1 is a paraphrase of an ancient hymn of congratulation. It is very similar to a fable in the Book of Jeremiah (17:5–8) and also to a passage of Egyptian wisdom ascribed to Amen-em-Opet. Before the exile, a scribe rewrote it so that it reflected the contrast between the two ways.

Luke 9:22–25: Death can lead to life. Jesus told men about God's desire to save them, but he only encountered skepticism and hatred. A suffering

Messiah—that was not what Israel was expecting, nor was it what Jesus himself was hoping for. Yet, when the time came, he resolutely followed the way to Jerusalem. Circumstances forced him to do that and salvation was achieved through suffering and failure.

Every day—we have to give up our lives every morning. Every morning we are confronted with the choice between the two ways, one leading to nothingness, the other to transfiguration. Every day we have to take part in the game of love, in a spirit of unconditional faithfulness to the will of God.

■

On Psalm 1
Happy is the man who goes straight ahead along his way
and does not listen to scoffers.
Happy is the man who keeps God's law
and is anxious to do his will.
Like a tree planted in good soil,
he will yield fruit a hundredfold
and his name will be blessed among the brethren.

■

Grace is offered to us every morning, when God calls us to go further along the road. Yet how many mornings are dark and how many times everything seems to turn away from us! We know how tempting it is to live by clinging stubbornly to the past, protecting what we have acquired. The way ahead in the morning so often seems to lead to death. We are conscious of the cross outlined on the horizon and want to turn back, but we have to go on in faith and hope, because the grace that we are offered each day anew is paradoxical and it points forward.

"Anyone who wants to save his life will lose it." Our lives are in the hands of God. We are bound to him by a covenant in which he has absolute priority. God's ways are not always our ways. He does not reveal the future to us. He commits himself to it and is our guarantee that, however steep and rough the climb may be, it will lead to a full life. But we have to follow our way in faith. It is the way of the cross. It may not be a way of suffering every day, but it is always a way that is absolute and a way of renewal.

The disciple cannot remain where he is. He is always on the way, going resolutely ahead with Jesus. He may be tempted from time to time to stop, but he knows that the apparent security can only draw him down into death. Life is always in the future—like God.

∎

God of life,
  morning born again and again anew,
do not let us follow
  the easy path that leads to death.
Let us, with your Son Jesus,
  go resolutely further and further
in hope that will never be disappointed.
  For we know
  that every cross is the sign
  of an unexpected resurrection
  in Jesus Christ, your beloved Son.

∎

We pray for those who lose their lives
  in gathering what is useless—
  let them discover the grace of poverty.
We pray too for those who have nothing,
  who lack even what is necessary for life—
  let them have the helping hand of a brother.
We also pray for ourselves,
  that we may go forward without hesitation
  and bear the yoke of your love together.

FRIDAY AFTER ASH WEDNESDAY

THE LIGHT OF DAWN
Isaiah 58:1–9a: Walk with your head lowered . . . Dress in sackcloth and lie down in ashes . . . A disciple of the Second Isaiah speaks out against the

hypocrisy of the people of Jerusalem in a ceremony of penance. They think they are beyond reproach. They are surprised by God's silence. 'Why should we fast', they say, 'if you never see it?'

How far they have come from the prophet Isaiah, who spoke of the passion of their God! When they did penance, the Jews wanted God to respond to their devotion, count their merits and reward them. They only gave to him in the expectation of receiving something back! They did not really need a God who forgave them and was overwhelmingly kind to them. A God who can be held responsible is a God of human dimensions, whose qualities can be measured . . .

A God who does not see might be better! A God who sees judges men's hearts and where are we then? 'The sort of fast that pleases me', says God, is that you, whose backs have been bent beneath the Babylonian yoke, should now 'let the oppressed go free and break every unjust yoke' and do even more than this: begin to build the kingdom of God, 'share your bread with the hungry and shelter the homeless poor'. If you do this, the God of Israel declares, 'your light will shine like the dawn'!

Psalm 51: see above, p. 8.

Matthew 9:14–15: So long as Jesus is among them, the disciples do not need to fast. There is feasting when God is present. But God has been put to death and today you may fast so that you can deepen your hunger for his word. Do not forget to "put oil on your heads"—Easter morning is here already, today.

■

On Psalm 51
Do not try to hide your sin from God,
for he is tenderness and mercy.
Do not be afraid of his justice and truth,
for he can cleanse you.
Go down into the depths of his mercy
and, with a crushed and broken heart, say:
Have mercy on me, O God, in your love.

■

Where is our world going? Will it be overshadowed forever by night and darkness? God seems to be enclosed in silence and his light no longer shines on and warms our ruined paths. Where is our God?

The resurrection of Christ is hidden in a hollow of the earth. It is a dawn, but hardly visible, and those who keep their hearts awake in faith and in fasting and prayer throughout the long night are particularly blessed, because they will be there when the new day dawns.

Yet in fact the dawn has already come. Whether or not it sheds light on the world of men and women depends on you. If you never try to get away from your fellow men, if you share with them without counting the cost and if you are active in the cause of freedom, you are already like God, and his day can dawn through you.

God has made a covenant with you. He is the Bridegroom. The wedding songs are often difficult to hear. The Bridegroom has been taken from us. But our hearts are ready and we are awake and waiting. We know that he is still alive. So let your heart fast and get rid of all your useless belongings. Then, desiring God and loving your fellow men, you will know that the feast is still being celebrated. The table is laid and at it the Bridegroom is sharing his own life with us. The dawn of the resurrection is already there.

■

*You, Lord,
are the light of mankind
and the freedom of the oppressed.
Put your Spirit in us
so that the light of our love
may be in the world
as the dawn of the new day
that you have made appear
in the resurrection of your beloved Son.*

■

*Giving freedom to the oppressed
and breaking unjust fetters—
that is the sort of fast that pleases you.
Lord, make us active in the cause of justice.*

*Sharing our bread with the hungry
and sheltering the homeless poor—
that is the sort of fast that pleases you.
Lord, make us hungry for charity.*

*Following you to the cross
and living your Word that is always new—
that is the sort of fast that pleases you.
Lord, lead us and save us.*

SATURDAY AFTER ASH WEDNESDAY

OUR HEART AND OUR PRACTICE

Isaiah 58:9b–14: The Jews came to regard the keeping of the sabbath as a holy day as very important during their exile in Babylonia, because this practice distinguished them from the pagan people among whom they were scattered. There was, however, a very real danger that a fundamentally good practice would be transformed into a scrupulously kept obligation that simply salved their consciences.

When Jerusalem was restored, this movement spread and the prophets reacted against it. It was well worthwhile to give new life to the sabbath, but only if it was made a day that was really acceptable to the Lord, a day on which man would remove himself from the world and business and give new life to his soul. If it ceased to be a visible expression of a life turned toward God, the practice of the sabbath was no more than hypocrisy.

Psalm 86: This is a prayer of supplication, proclaiming God's forgiveness.

Luke 5:27–32: "What I want is mercy, not sacrifice." The Pharisees were scrupulous in their fasting, but they refused to invite the publicans to their tables, because of the lowly profession that the latter practiced. The Pharisees fasted, but their hearts remained arid.

Jesus came to save sinners, and that is what we all are. He knew that the sinner's heart can only begin to live again when it is made warm, so he invited the publicans to his table and spoke words of reconciliation to them. The Pharisees could be in no doubt about that.

Our religious practice is only meaningful if it comes from a heart that is converted. When that happens, it becomes a sign of our openness to God and our fellow men. Otherwise, it is only a sign of coldness and rigidity. Therefore let us be converted.

■

On Psalm 86
You who feel poor and needy,
let your heart be turned toward the Lord,
for he is good.
He watches over the one who calls on him
and fills the heart of the one who invokes him with joy.
He is full of love and tenderness
and never fails to respond to every cry.
He is the God who saves us.

■

The day was not far ahead when he would himself lay the table for sinners and give up his life as the sacrament of salvation. Throughout the whole of his way through life, Jesus invited the poor to share his table, and in so doing he gave meaning to the Last Supper before it took place, that Eucharist during which the blood of the Son of Man was to be shed for the "remission of sins." He was sent by God to heal and to save and until he died he acted as the good physician who calls the sick to conversion and to health, going so far as to give his life for them.

Levi was a sinner. He was a sinner by profession. That at least was what those who kept the law called him and all publicans. They were not entirely wrong in their judgment, of course, since it was common knowledge that the publicans were for the most part very oriented toward making a profit for themselves and they also collaborated with those who occupied their country, the enemy. What, then, are we to think of the Messiah agreeing to sit down at a feast with a great number of publicans?

What happened, of course, was that Levi gave up everything and followed Jesus. He was converted, and it is certain that others were also converted by Jesus as he went about and came into contact with his fellow men. It is also certain, however, that our faults follow us and Levi was not able to overcome his bad reputation overnight. Everyone knows, moreover, that converts cannot really be trusted—the fire of their new faith is often hidden beneath ashes and not all fire is good. When they have finished attending to their patients, doctors always wash their hands.

At the Last Supper, Jesus was to wash the feet of sinners. He had come from God and he knew that wounds are not healed instantaneously. His disciples, he knew, would hardly wait until the Supper was over before denying him. But he also knew, with an even deeper conviction, that man's salvation was in love, a love that can only be effective if it shares in man's condition to such an extent that he is able to trust it totally. That was precisely what righteous people could never understand. They would never be able to accept the idea of eating with sinners. But what, then, did they want to do at the Lord's table?

■

You who came to call sinners—
set us free from our self-sufficiency,
open our eyes to the evil that consumes us.
   Lord, have mercy!

You prepare for us the table of forgiveness
while we persist stubbornly
in justifying our behavior.
   Christ, have mercy!

We are also publicans and cheats,
but we have been fascinated and overcome by your love
and want to live with you.
   Lord, have mercy!

FIRST WEEK OF LENT

A NEW WAY OF SEEING
"Be holy, for I, the Lord your God, am holy." "You will be a people consecrated to the Lord, as he has promised." God is holy and his holiness

is radical and decisive. He is God. He is like none other. He is transcendent. And yet he calls us to that holiness. He does not call us to acquire a few more virtues—he calls us to be totally recreated in our hearts. Jesus said: "You must be perfect just as your heavenly Father is perfect." Perfection and holiness are above all a grace, a gift, and the result in us of the word that is always effective and similar to the rain that makes the soil fertile. If we are indeed a holy people, it is because the times have been fulfilled in Jesus, in whom the decisive sign of the Kingdom of God has been given to us.

A new law has resulted from that new identity, a law that goes far beyond the minimum of the Commandments and appeals to us as free and responsible persons. It is a law of perfection that can only be grasped on the basis of a new way of seeing. "I was hungry and did you give me food?" Did you recognize me? This new way of seeing distinguishes between those who can see and those who cannot—between those who ask for signs and those who trust. The hour of judgment has come. In Jesus, God makes his Kingdom come. There is an urgent need to be converted. That conversion is to behave as "saints" and to welcome God's grace.

The great sign of that new law is God's forgiveness. "Love your enemy." But that forgiveness is linked to prayer—immediate prayer as an act of faith in God, prayer which raises us to the level of the Kingdom of God and enables us to say in faith: "Forgive us as we forgive others." In that way, the name of God is really "hallowed," that is, known to be holy.

∎

Holy God, love without imperfection,
you see our selfishness, our idleness—
   forgive us and give us your Spirit.

Perfect God, infinite mercy,
you see how divided and malicious we are—
   make us one and give us your Spirit.

Living God, Word of fire in the hearts of men,
you hear our prayer of supplication—
   make us holy and give us your Spirit.

MONDAY OF THE FIRST WEEK

FACE TO FACE

Leviticus 19:1–2, 11–18: The Book of Leviticus is a collection made from various traditions, some of which are extremely ancient. This collection was edited after the exile at a time when the priesthood enjoyed a very high reputation. Chapters 17 to 26 are among the oldest parts of the book and are known as the Law of Holiness.

God is the "Other" who is quite different—the Holy One. He is radically different from anything that man can ever think about him, but he is also the One who has made a covenant with man. He wants man to share in his holiness: "Be holy, for I, the Lord your God, am holy." Consecrated by Yahweh, Israel had to make God's holiness appear in all the circumstances of the people's life.

The rhythm of this liturgical passage in the Book of Leviticus is determined by the statement "I am the Lord," and it sets out how the holy people of God should behave. What emerges above all is a deep respect for one's fellow men, especially the workers and the handicapped members of society. The *lex talionis* of ancient society was so harsh that it is quite astonishing to discover a law of this kind: "You must not call for the death penalty against your neighbor."

Psalm 19: This is a proclamation of Israel's faithfulness to the law of Yahweh.

Matthew 25:31–46: The apocalyptic discourse ends with the parable of the last judgment. The scenario is the evangelist's, but he has taken the content of the judgment from the theme of the "two ways," especially in connection with the list of good works.

It was first edited in Aramaic and was contemporary with Jesus and Christianity. The theme of the two ways, one leading to life and the other to death, is found for the first time in *Deuteronomy* (see the Thursday after Ash Wednesday, above).

Matthew records Jesus as saying in the Sermon on the Mount: "It is not those who say to me 'Lord, Lord' who will enter the Kingdom of heaven, but the person who does the will of my Father who is in heaven." Here he is even more concrete in his statement, for he says that the true disciple can be known by his feeding the hungry, giving a glass of water to the thirsty, welcoming the stranger and caring for the "least of these brothers of mine."

■

What a face to face! The Son of Man judges man according to his way of seeing. "When, Lord, did we see you?" Both ask the same question—those who are blessed and those who are cursed. But the blessed, letting their hearts be moved in the presence of misery, have in faith seen the one whom they can now see face to face. "Happy are the pure in heart!" "Be holy, for I, the Lord your God, am holy."

It is not a question of preserving one's purity in the presence of the world's misery, but rather a question of sharing in the holiness of the one who showed that he was on man's side when he became man—and particularly on the side of the poor, the strangers, the prisoners, the rejected. The holiness of God has, for us, one especially important aspect which fills our everyday experience with an eternal dimension. By becoming man, God broke through the barrier between heaven and earth. Man's salvation is no longer a flight into what lies beyond this life. He is saved by being able to see what lies beyond in the face of his neighbor, who at first sight seems so remote from the divine.

■

Holy God, our Lord and our God—
heaven sees you in the infinity of your glory,
but you have taken on a human face
and have shared the misery
of the poorest and the most abandoned of men.

Let us one day be counted among your blessed.
Make our hearts holy with the fire of your word,
so that we may recognize your presence
in the hand that is stretched out
and the eyes that beg for our love.

For you will judge us according to that love
when the day of judgment comes.

■

Do not judge and you will not be judged.
Let us, Lord, see your face
in the face of the man who is scorned and rejected.

Do not seek revenge and you will not be condemned.
Let us, Lord, look for peace
in those places where the world is seeking war and division.

Do not slander others and you will not be punished.
Help us, Lord, to love in our brethren
the hidden good and the seeds of progress.

Do not exploit the weak and you will live in the light.
Make us, Lord, active in the cause of justice
and let us work for reconciliation and the future.

TUESDAY OF THE FIRST WEEK

GOD IS GOD

Isaiah 55:10–11: Chapter 55 marks the end of the oracles of Second Isaiah. His writing is closely related to that of the Deuteronomist, and he takes up various themes from the beginning of the book, such as the proclamation of a new exodus.

In vv. 10–11, the word of God is personified and anticipates the Word who, in Jesus Christ, will visit this earth. The comparison is above all concerned with the fact that the Word of God is effective. Like the rain coming down from heaven and going back there, the word of Yahweh does not return without bearing fruit. Surely there can be no more striking proof than this of the imminent end of the exile? Did the prophet Jeremiah not say very much the same: "For Yahweh says this: Only when the seventy years granted to Babylon are over will I visit you and fulfill my promise in your favor by bringing you back to this place" (29:10)?

Psalm 34 is an alphabetical Psalm. Vv. 10–22 contain teaching of the type found in the Wisdom literature. The preceding verses are fundamentally a thanksgiving, although they also express trust in Yahweh and a conviction that Yahweh answers prayer.

Matthew 6:7–15: The pagans thought that they could exert pressure on the deity by praying at great length. The prayer of the disciples, on the other hand, is striking because of its great simplicity. It is addressed to the Father and it expresses the hope felt by the sons of God. The apparent triumph of evil in the world did not deter the disciples from asking God to reveal his sovereign power. May the day come, they implore him, when the transcendence of the name of God is recognized by all men. Asking for "daily bread" and for wrongs to be righted also looks forward to the coming of the Kingdom of God: "Give us today our daily bread and forgive us our debts." May these fundamental aspects of the Kingdom be experienced today in our own lives—the bread of life and the forgiveness of God. As for the final petition of the Lord's Prayer, it is not so much directed toward our everyday temptations as toward the great test experienced by every disciple—that of doubting and denying the Master, as Peter did toward the end.

■

God is not deaf, nor is he tired, so we do not need to pray with many words to him in order to overcome his obstinate resistance. Our God is not an idol. The Christian is urged to pray without ceasing, but that prayer is first and foremost an act of faith toward God, who first spoke to us—and in what an incomparable way, since he spoke to us in his Son Jesus, in whom he has given us everything. His word is more effective than the rain on the soil, since it is from our earth that a Savior arose. We are sons of the Father and our prayer should never deny what we are.

Too many Christians say the Our Father as though, by repeating it again and again, they will eventually obtain what they are asking for: "Thy Kingdom come! And let us make a great effort, so that we do not have to wait too long."

No, God is God. He did not wait for us to make his Kingdom come. He raised Jesus from the dead. Why pray, then? We pray, surely, because God's presence on our earth is so great that we cannot cease praying. And we say "May your Kingdom come" and "Blessed is your Kingdom that is coming" because, although the Kingdom of God is there, it is hidden and can only be contemplated by those who look at

the world with a new way of seeing and with hearts that have been made new. We therefore have to pray in order to make that new way of seeing more acute and to make our hearts more open to the translucence of the Spirit of God.

That is why the Christian who prays without forgiving others is speaking in a vacuum. He has not risked leaping into the new world. He does not yet know that, in Jesus Christ, God has paid all his debts. So he will not relent, with regard to others and to himself. The only prayer that God really hears is the cry of faith.

Our Father in heaven,
only you are holy
and only you are transcendent.
You are tenderness and mercy.
We bless your name.
Continue with the work of your hands
and make yourself known for what you are.
May your Kingdom come
and may men discover your presence,
for you are a faithful God.
Give us today the bread of life,
your Word and your Son,
your grace and your light
on our way today.
We bless you,
who have paid all our debts
and saved us through Christ Jesus.
We ask you to forgive us again today,
as we have forgiven all those
who have offended us.
Forgive us in the peace of your grace.

Father,
do not let us undergo the great test.
Keep us in faith and hope
and let us never deny your name and your Word.
Protect us from the adversary,
for you alone are our God—
holy God and merciful Father.

WEDNESDAY OF THE FIRST WEEK

AT ONCE
Jonah 3:1–10: Written after the exile, the Book of Jonah is fundamentally a long parable. The hero of the book sums up in his own person the experience of every prophet. Emulating Jeremiah, he expresses the inner conflict of the man who has to go in the opposite direction to that of his contemporaries, sometimes risking his life. He also expresses the greatness of the prophet's call, since what the prophet says may be disturbing, but only he can provide the world with that soul without which it cannot survive. And finally, the conversion of the Ninevites points to the universal dimension of God's salvation.

The readiness of the pagan people to be converted in the Book of Jonah is contrasted with the "stiff-necked" attitude of the Jews in many rabbinical texts, the authors of which also place great emphasis on Jonah's time in the belly of the whale as an example of the salvation of the just man after the catastrophe.

Psalm 51: see above, p. 8.

Luke 11:29–32: The sign of Jonah—in the light of the rabbinical texts, this sign is first and foremost an anticipation in cryptic language of Jesus' suffering and triumph. Matthew interpreted it in this way (12:38–41), seeing Jesus' destiny in that of Jonah.

But the sign of Jonah is also preaching to the pagans. On the day of judgment, the Ninevites and the queen of Sheba, who have listened to the words of the men sent from God, will rise up against the unbelieving generation and will act as witnesses for the prosecution.

■

On Psalm 51

Against you and against you alone I have sinned,
for I have my sin always in mind
and I know how it has darkened my heart.
But you are the Creator, the faithful God.
Only you can create a new heart in me.

Only you can renew me with your Spirit.
O God, do not banish me from your presence.
Let me live, Lord, in the light of your face,
and a song of praise will rise
from my sorrowful heart.

■

What more do you want? The man who is always asking for signs so that he can believe is clearly lacking in faith. Faith is a vital movement from the heart, an illumination of the spirit in the presence of God. Its only guarantee is an appeal or a grace. Jonah begins to proclaim the word of God, and Nineveh, that great city, is converted. Is it a fairy tale? Faith itself looks very much like a fairy tale, although the fairies are replaced by the living God, whose ways are not our ways—foolishness for the wisdom of this world. Those who base everything on reason call for signs.

Jesus came as the Son of Man and he ended on the cross. If he were to come again now to our towns and villages, the same thing would happen again. A handful of exceptional people would believe in him and follow him. And if he were to rise again from the dead, all the scientists and thinkers would want to study the phenomenon very cautiously, taking their time and looking for additional miracles and further information.

Faith that analyzes itself in this way is not really faith, because God cannot be analyzed. He says simply: "Come—at once!" He passes by and tomorrow it is too late. At another time and in another place, men have discovered the Gospel and given themselves to it without discussion or analysis. To us they seem as strange and remote as the queen of Sheba. God grant that they do not rise up again and confound us!

■

We pray for the prophets that God is sending to us now:
  May they stress that we should be converted at once.
We pray for those who are bogged down in subtle reasoning:
  May they be converted at once to a more simple faith.
We pray for those who have discovered the power of the Gospel:
  May they lead us forward with the vigor of their faith.

We worship you, God of the universe.
  You do not remain angry with us,
  but raise up prophets
  who proclaim your will to save us.
Now, Lord, in our own times,
  do not let mankind be swallowed up by evil.
  Show your tenderness to those in power
  so that they will discover the strength of your love.
Then everyone, great and small,
  will turn toward you
  and bless you with one voice.

THURSDAY OF THE FIRST WEEK

WITHOUT TIRING

Esther 14:1, 3–5, 12–14: This is a prayer of petition—greatly discredited nowadays. But it is a form of prayer with an excellent pedigree, since most of the Psalms are, after all, prayers of petition. In fact, they form a real school of prayer. They are healthy and vital prayers, expressing what is in the depths of man's heart and reflecting both the light and the shade of his existence. His goodness, his need for tenderness, his complaints and even his desire for revenge are all expressed in them. So many of the Psalms are a cry, a protest or simply a question: "Why are you asleep, Lord? How much longer will you be angry with us?" What the Psalms so often make heard is the cry of the man who is not able to accept what happens to him as God's will, the cry of the man who is scandalized by God's silence.

But the believer who can express feelings of that kind in his cry to God is someone who knows that God is completely at one with him. In the course of the history of the community to which he belongs and throughout his own personal history, he has been able to measure God's faithfulness. This is clear from the fact that the last word in almost all the Psalms is one of trust and confidence. Esther's prayer is similar. In it, she appeals to God's justice and recalls the faithfulness of God as reflected in the history of God's people.

Psalm 138 is an individual act of thanksgiving. The believer thanks God for a favor that he has obtained, but at the same time he also recalls a time of distress in the past.

Matthew 7:7–12: Jesus did not reject the cries of his fellow men. He did not despise their petitions. He may perhaps have given the prayer of petition a rather different orientation—toward a realization of God's dream about mankind. Be that as it may, he was always very close to the poor, the unimportant and those who had nothing but their suffering and their complaints. He asked the Father too not to disappoint the faith of his disciples and to forgive his enemies.

(It is worth noting that the responses to two of the three prayers in Matthew 7:7 are not rendered very well in most modern translations. The Greek passives are a circumlocution and point indirectly to God, with the result that these petitions should have more direct replies: "Ask and God will give you . . . knock and God will open to you.")

∎

On Psalm 138
You, God, call yourself love.
You are eternal and faithful Love
and the power of tenderness.
We thank you with all our heart.
We owe everything that we are to you
and our future is assured because of your promise.
Continue with the work of your hands.

∎

Praying is asking, seeking and knocking at the door, night and day and without tiring. We have to "pray constantly," to such an extent that prayer becomes, not simply an occasional practice, but a state of being. Praying is a mode of being in the presence of God. But there are two ways of persistently asking. One is the way of the troublesome and insistent man; the other is the way of the lover. The first is only thinking of himself; the second is fascinated by the object that he loves and would give everything to possess the treasure that

he has found. Could God keep the door closed to such a man? God wants us to pray in that way because he reveals himself to us as the most precious treasure and as the most faithful of all friends. A love that is sold at a low price or just given away is not really love.

Listen, then, to Esther: "My Lord, our King, the only one, come to my help, for I am alone and have no helper but you. . . . Remember, Lord. . . . I have no one but you, Lord and you have knowledge of all things." She knew how to set about it, and she pleads on her own behalf with words that will move God. Should we say nothing or only a few cautious words because God knows what he is going to do for us before we ask him? That is not what is required. Our not asking shows a lack of love. It is pride to do without another's help. Asking God for nothing is often the sign of hidden pride.

We have to go on asking without tiring. If we capitulate too soon, it only shows that we are not sufficiently trusting. God wants us to ask and to seek—he always goes beyond anything that we can ever expect. He makes us knock at his door and go on knocking, because his door opens on an infinity that we can never fully reach. The best attitude that we can have toward God, the attitude of prayer in our life, is that of the beggar who knows that he is loved and called to Life—begging for oneself and for God.

■

You are the only God
  and you know all things.
  No one who has called on you
  has ever been rejected.
We seek you, but we bless you,
  because you have already come to us.
Hear our cry and give us
  what is best for us—
  your love and faithfulness,
  because it is the love of your name
  that makes us say without ever tiring:
  You are our God, our only God.

FRIDAY OF THE FIRST WEEK

THE FUTURE OF MAN
Ezekiel 18:21–28: For a very long time, Israel saw the individual, both as he was and as he might become, in terms of the community. He only existed in relation to the social group of which he formed a part. He was a member of his community, and, if he sinned, all his people were responsible.

With Jeremiah, the idea of personal individuality entered the teaching of the prophets. Preaching to exiled Israelites, who believed that they were paying for the sins of their ancestors, he proclaimed the abolition of collective punishments. "Each is to die for his own sin," he cried. "Every man who eats unripe grapes is to have his own teeth set on edge" (31:30). Even before the time of Jeremiah, however, there were temple priests who examined the behavior of each member of a group of pilgrims going up to the temple and who had the right to admit an individual to or exclude him from the liturgy.

Ezekiel went even further. He separated the individual entirely from the destiny of the nation and insisted that each man was treated according to his own personal behavior. At the same time, he stressed the effectiveness of personal conversion. Yahweh does not, in other words, keep a man imprisoned in his sin, but reveals a future to him. If he turns away from evil, he will enter into life.

Psalm 130, closely related to the Psalms of individual supplication, is a song of ascents which was used by pilgrims as they "went up" to Jerusalem. In the Christian liturgy, it is employed above all as a "penitential Psalm," but it also expresses hope and the need for vigilance: watching for the dawn.

Matthew 5:20–26: "It was said" (= God said) is contrasted here with "I tell you." Is Jesus setting himself up against God? No, not against God, but against the interpretation of the law imposed by the scribes. In fact, Jesus went much further than the rabbinical schools of his own time by situating himself at the level of love. Keeping strictly to the law so often means condemning oneself to a minimum that is lifeless. That minimum can never be love; it can at the most be only a caricature of love. The Christian who is satisfied with the righteousness of the Pharisees—and that is really quite considerable—has not yet discovered the way of the Kingdom of God. The law forbade murder, but Jesus condemns the mere fact of anger against our brother. He goes even further and says that it is not enough simply to make an offering of expiation—we have to be reconciled with our brother. How can we come to the table of reconciliation if our heart is still full of resentment? The Kingdom of God is with us, and when the Judge comes we must not be found in conflict with our brother.

The people of God consists of men and women. "You have not chosen me," says the God of the covenant. "I have chosen you." If we are a holy people, it is because of God's grace, and if God made a covenant with us, it is because he wanted to give us life and give it to us, his creatures, in abundance. "I do not want the death of the sinner," the Lord says. No, God wants us to live.

But there is always a risk that sin will kill us, not simply because of our fault, but even more because of the weight of our remorse, so heavily does it rest on our shoulders. What are we to say if a fault is handed down from generation to generation? If we do not have the right to be converted and to be radically forgiven, because we belong to a sinful generation, it can only lead to despair and death in the short term. When the prophet stresses personal responsibility, he is disclosing to each individual a possible future and offering him freedom and a return to life.

The way that the holy people of God behaves can only be derived from God himself. The fact that we have to be reconciled with each other before worshiping God shows that our freedom has priority in God's plan. Jesus placed himself firmly at the level of love, and that is man's only way toward the future. He did not encourage the expression of anger or urge men to insult or curse each other. On the contrary, he condemned such behavior, not in order to add weight to the law, but rather to open our hearts to a love that would allow us to go forward in freedom. God wants us above all to live, and he wants us therefore to be a source of present and of future life for each other.

From the depths I call to you, Lord.
   You cannot let me sink down into the fatal pit.
If you remember our faults,
   who will survive?

But with you there is forgiveness,
  grace and a future.
With all my soul I hope for you.
  More than a watchman waiting for the dawn
  I know that you are life and light.
With you there is full deliverance.
  You set your people free
  from all their faults.
You are a God of men.

SATURDAY OF THE FIRST WEEK

TO PERFECTION

Deuteronomy 26:16–19: This passage is the work of the Deuteronomic school and was written as an introduction to the accounts of the renewal of the covenant of Shechem. What we have here is not so much a contract between two equal partners as two parallel declarations, each drawing attention to the part played by the two parties. Yahweh agrees to be Israel's God and in return insists on obedience to the law. Israel, on the other hand, promises to be Yahweh's people and in return expects to be protected by him.

Psalm 119 is a very long meditation on the law as the source of life. It is an alphabetic Psalm consisting of twenty-two strophes.

Matthew 5:43–48: Here, too, Jesus goes much further than the scribes. We read, for example, in the Book of Leviticus: "You must not exact vengeance, nor must you bear a grudge against the children of your people. You must love your neighbor as yourself" (19:18). There was no question here of hating one's enemies. There is no such Commandment anywhere in the Old Testament, although it is reflected in the sectarianism of Qumran. Jesus called for more than simply a renunciation of revenge and taught that evil had to be overcome by good.

Jesus therefore pointed to a future for man. If we hate, we want our enemy to be eliminated. If, on the other hand, our enemy is overcome by goodness, he may give up his evil ways and become good himself. Good will in this way has overcome evil. Forgiveness creates freedom in revealing a logic that is quite different from that of evil.

■

On Psalm 119

Happy is the man who walks on a straight path.
At the crossroads of the covenant
he will be at one with his brothers.
Happy is the man who tries to live like God.
In dark days
he will know the joy of light.
Happy are the people who follow the word.
Along the ways of this world
they will make hope dawn.

■

"Be perfect just as your heavenly Father is perfect." Applying the Gospel to perfection—is this not a task inviting discouragement? Who can possibly go as far as that, especially if we think of the perfection of God himself as a motionless and impassive serenity, fixed in an eternity without movement and protected from all error? But if we think this, then we do not know God at all. He is certainly not like the gods of pagan mythology, who are as flawed as they are powerful. God's perfection is that of love, and love is not at all impassive.

The image of the sun shining on all men, bad as well as good, is a very fine one. What kind of situation would be created and what would happen to us if God were to punish his "enemies" every time? Underlying the idea of punishment, there is the *lex talionis,* the kind of justice that calls for "an eye for an eye and a tooth for a tooth," reparation being made for a fault by a comparable sanction. But God is not like that. He does not punish. He converts. He does not dwell on what has happened, but goes straight to our hearts.

"Be perfect." And perfection is made concrete in forgiveness, which is pre-eminently giving. Yes, for-giving is giving, recreating, setting free, believing in the other person, pointing out to him the possibility of a new life. Will he hear us every time we forgive him? If we forgive them, will all our enemies become our friends? It is hardly likely, but what we are asked to do is to behave like God toward each other. The future is his. Let us not close the door in our hardness of heart. The history of God's dealings with man bears it out. When love is entirely disarmed, it becomes disarming. That is a new law—a law of the Kingdom of God. It presupposes a new way of looking at the world, and it cannot be understood without faith, but, at that level, it is the most effective law imaginable—the law of the living God.

∎

God, you make your sun rise on all men.
We bless you and thank you for your Son,
who came into our world
like a sun of grace and love.
In his light,
sinners imprisoned in the darkness of their past
were set free.
In his warmth,
men paralyzed by the hardness of their hearts
were reconciled to each other.
And when the sun darkened
as he died on Golgotha,
he revealed to us the possibility
of life and renewal
by forgiving those who had nailed him to the cross.
You, God, raised him up
at the dawn of a new day,
and now your Son shines on our earth
as a source of freedom and hope.
With all those who drink deeply of his light,
we praise you, God our rebirth.

SECOND WEEK OF LENT

GOING FURTHER

"He led them up a high mountain, where they could be alone" (Second Sunday). The whole of Lent is going up. We have followed the Easter road, which leads both to Golgotha and to the mountain of the transfiguration. On Mount Tabor, Jesus spoke with Moses and Elijah about his passion (Luke). Back on the plain with his disciples, he tells them: "Now we are going up to Jerusalem and the Son of Man is about to be handed over." He is the only Son and he will be put to death, as the landowner's son was killed by tenants of the vineyard who wanted to take over his inheritance. The Lord's passion was the way that he had to go to find life and what lies beyond.

Beyond! Not so much what lies beyond time and this world, but what can transfigure time and history because it is the hidden presence of the new passover. Beyond for men who have been driven to the point where they can only suffer and be despised. Beyond too for the prophets who were rejected and badly treated because they proclaimed the surprising word of God. Jeremiah, Joseph and countless men throughout history have prophesied in this way. They have been witnesses to a Church that is poor, ready to serve and always willing to drink to the dregs the cup of the Son of Man, who came "to serve and to give his life as a ransom for many," a Church stripped of every means of dominating men, unlike the scribes, who imposed heavier and heavier burdens on the shoulders of the poor in order to deceive them more easily. Care for the poor forms an integral part of Easter and salvation. In Abraham's bosom, the poor Lazarus is at last recognized in the dignity of his humanity.

Beyond—and transfiguration. That is addressed to the sinner, whom Jesus welcomes to the extent of eating with him. The parable of the Father of the prodigal son shows us the divine source of forgiveness without restraint. God is mercy and tenderness, and when he welcomes the repentant but uneasy sinner, he recreates him and raises him up again. Forgiveness is a creative act and we are invited to be creative in the same way toward our brethren: "Be merciful as your Father is merciful." On the first and the last day of this second week of Lent, two great litanies of forgiveness direct our hearts toward the God who "throws our sins to the bottom of the sea" because he always keeps his covenant and never ceases to love.

There is no difference between having our lives made spotless again and treating the poor justly, because Christ has included us in his resurrection by becoming poor in the midst of us.

MONDAY OF THE SECOND WEEK

WITHOUT RESTRAINT
Daniel 9:4–10: Anyone who wants to gain a better understanding of the confession of sins that John the Baptist required as a preliminary to the baptismal rite should read this prayer in the Book of Daniel. It appears in the context of a meditation. Daniel is preparing himself before consulting the oracle of Jeremiah (25:11–14), according to which the fall of Babylon and the deliverance of Israel would take place at the end of a symbolic period of seventy years.

This prayer is in fact older than the Book of Daniel itself, and it can be found also in the Books of Nehemiah and Ezra as well as in Baruch. This is confirmation of its cultic character. It opens with an invocation addressed to the God of the covenant and then goes on to enumerate the various groups of people who have broken God's commandments: kings, princes, heads of families and "all the people of the land."

Breaking the covenant led to exile in Babylonia. But Yahweh is a God of mercy and forgiveness. He does not look back at the past. He looks toward the future.

Psalm 79: The whole nation invokes God in this Psalm. Do not remember our past faults, the people are saying, but forgive us. Your honor is also at stake, since, if you do not forgive us, our neighbors, the pagans, will laugh at us and ask: "Where is their God?"

Luke 6:36–38: Matthew used the legalistic language of the Jewish community and wrote: "Be perfect just as your heavenly Father is perfect." Luke prefers to call God "merciful," and that may have been the word which Jesus himself used. If God is merciful, then man, who is created in his image, must also be merciful. Then we read: "Give and God will give you a full measure, pressed down, shaken together and running over." The measure that God will use is the one employed in trading. The measure belonging to one's partner in trade was used to measure wheat or barley to be bought or sold.

■

On Psalm 79

God, we cannot go on any longer.
Our past is suffocating us
and we are imprisoned in it.
Will you go on forever reproaching us
for faults committed in the past?
God, show us your forgiveness
because among men you are called
the faithful God, the God of tenderness.
The honor of your name is at stake.

Forgive! Give without restraint—a full measure, running over. Jesus is urging his disciples to accept a new life-style, a way of life that is revolutionary in terms of human justice. He goes straight to the point, as radically as God himself, because he shares in the act of creation. Forgiving—what is it but an attitude of absolute renewal and recreation? Only God can forgive, and man can only succeed in forgiving if he is as merciful as God himself.

Why is it that so many religious people cannot forgive? Is it perhaps because the spiritual life has enclosed them in an anxious search for perfection which ends by making them too inward-looking? They may be holy and beyond reproach, but they only look outward in order to weigh the good and the bad in the lives of others.

How do we break out of this attitude? Only by looking at God and his full measure, which is running over and measureless, without restraint, because it is love and tenderness. "To the Lord our God, mercy and forgiveness": God's heart forgives us not like a judge who weighs the pros and the cons, but like a father who commits his life to the future of his children. We have to accept God's measure and then live the life of faith as love that is measureless and without restraint. As soon as we know how much God loves us, because he

forgives us so magnanimously, we shall be able to forgive others, in the conviction that God can give us back to each other and that the future is always open to us.

■

We have been rebellious
   and have turned away from you.
But you, Lord,
   are a God of mercy,
   always faithful to your covenant.
Give us your forgiveness
   and change our hearts.

We have been torn to pieces
   judging our brothers.
But you, Lord,
   condemn no one.
Gather us together in your mercy
   and change our hearts.

We have calculated precisely
   and have measured out our forgiveness.
But you, Lord,
   give without restraint.
You make all things new.
Fashion us in the image of your Son
   and change our hearts.

TUESDAY OF THE SECOND WEEK

THE POOR SERVANT CHURCH
Isaiah 1:10, 16–20: Sodom and Gomorrah—two towns defiled with sin and cursed by God. But acts of worship can also be defiled when they are tainted with religious hypocrisy, and the people of God performed many such acts: sacrifices, pilgrimages, offerings, sabbaths and solemn feasts (vv. 11–15). And of what value is an act of worship if it does not lead to a change in one's inner life?

But all will be well so long as the people are converted. "Let us talk this over," God says. Let us look at your thoughts and your attitudes. And he reveals his heart in the words: "Though your sins are like scarlet, they shall be as white as snow."

Psalm 50: Yahweh calls heaven and earth to witness and, listing their many faults, judges his people. Here, too, he accuses them of hypocrisy. The whole Psalm should be meditated, since the verses contained in the liturgy for today do not provide a full picture.

Matthew 23:1–12: The scribes had the very responsible task of following Moses in interpreting and completing the written law of God. They worked within a long tradition and most of them were very serious men. But their work was valueless when the law simply became a burden on men's shoulders and became distorted as a result of their skill and knowledge.

A tree is known by its fruit, and the Pharisees liked their obedience to the law—obedience at least in the material sense—to be seen. They wore wider phylacteries (those little boxes containing short texts from the law and attached to their arms or foreheads) and they lengthened the tassels of their cloaks to recall the divine Commandments. They also insisted on taking the place of honor in the synagogues. They were, in other words, zealous so that others would honor them. But there is a big gulf between desire and reality. Many priests, for example, like to be called "Father" in the Church of Christ. But this "pharisaical" phenomenon can be observed at every level.

■

On Psalm 50

God judges us. He is not deceived.
It is useless to offer more and more sacrifices
when your hearts are wallowing in lies.
God judges us. Appear before him,
you who call upon him.
It is useless to plead innocence
when he came to change everything.
At the judgment of his love,
all sorrowful hearts will be transfigured.

■

"They say and they do not do . . . . Woe to you hypocrites." Words themselves are often very revealing. We know, for example, that, in the ancient world, the word hypocrite meant the soothsayer as an actor, that is, the man who said words that did not come from himself. Under the influence of Aramaic, however, it soon came to mean, in the Bible, the man who was only playing a part without committing himself.

Has this perhaps always been the case with masters in religion? Have they always imposed burdens on others, while refusing to do anything at all themselves? What is certain is that Jesus was not in any way like this. What he said came from himself, and all that he taught was at the very heart of his own activity. His infinite greatness is revealed in every aspect of his service of his fellow men.

It is difficult if not impossible to "manage" a religion systematically. Sooner or later, it becomes a legal or a doctrinal system, and those in a position of leadership have to adorn themselves with special titles in order to have their system and themselves accepted. Is there any system that can ever save mankind without again and again calling its own truthfulness into question?

We have only one "master." We have only one Teacher, and that is God and his Son, Jesus Christ. The Church does not try to "manage" a system of revelation. It lives rather in the presence of the Spirit, and that presence is always new. The Church's tradition is moreover renewed again and again by that Spirit. What would lords or masters do in that Church? Even the title "Father" is not adequate in the matter of faith, since, in the presence of God, we are all each other's brothers and servants and we are all subject to the word and the movements of the Spirit. No one has a "part" to play; each one of us has his own life and has to use this to bear witness on behalf of his brothers. No one is a soothsayer acting a part, and no one can claim a monopoly of prophetic inspiration. Each one of us is a servant and none can take a place of honor. The highest place of all is the one which calls for total service.

■

God our Father, our only Lord,
  take away from us all sense of superiority,

for we are all brothers in Jesus Christ.
Give those who are at the service of the Word
   the grace to be the first to live in conformity with it.
You who are tender and good
   will not allow your poorest people
   to be weighed down with burdens
   without letting all of us share in the carrying.
For, in your Son Jesus,
   you have mapped out the one way of salvation—
   the one which brings us all together
   in the same poverty, guided by your Spirit.

WEDNESDAY OF THE SECOND WEEK

THE SON OF MAN

Jeremiah 18:18–20: "You have seduced me, Yahweh, and I have let myself be seduced" (20:7). While he was still quite young, the prophet was called by the Lord to be a prophet, and from that time he was never again allowed to rest. He was a prophet, but he was also a man. If only he had been permitted to proclaim oracles of happiness and success! If only he had been allowed simply to flatter his listeners, as so many false prophets had done! But the word of the Lord is a two-edged sword, and the prophet had a mission "to tear up and to knock down, to destroy and to overthrow, to build and to plant" (1:10).

Jeremiah was committed to fight for God, and in that struggle he often encountered skepticism and sarcasm. He was still a man, and he protested, criticizing God for having thrown him so violently into public life. He even demanded that his enemies should be defeated. Here, in this passage, he is expressing his complaint in the form of a lament and calling on God to punish those who are persecuting him. We are still a long way from Christ's cry from the cross: "Forgive them, for they do not know what they are doing" (Lk 23:34).

Psalm 31: When he is surrounded on all sides by enemies, the righteous man has only one refuge: God. This Psalm is a cry from a deeply wounded heart. The author appeals to God to be angry with those who are against him and at the same time praises the one who has not deserted his friend when he was put to the test.

Matthew 20:17-28: "Alas for you, scribes, who build the tombs of the prophets, the men your ancestors killed" (Lk 11:47). On more than one occasion, Jesus violently denounced his adversaries. It was clear that nothing had changed since the time of Jeremiah. Tombs were built for the dead prophets—men who had been effectively silenced—and now the decision had been taken to put the prophet Jesus to death. The die had been cast. The Son of Man had certainly come to give his life as a ransom for many.

In this passage in the Gospel, Jesus informs his disciples about what will happen. They are incapable of grasping this revelation of a suffering Messiah and protest indignantly. There is nothing in Scripture to indicate what Jesus is telling them. The figure of the suffering servant had become almost completely obscured in first century Judaism, and so Jesus' disciples were hardly conscious of that prophecy.

The mother of James and John dreamed of glory for her sons, as they themselves did. She asked him if they might sit in important places in the Kingdom of God. Yes, Jesus replied, they will have places, but only when they have learned that the way to glory has to follow the way of the cross. "The disciple is not superior to his teacher" (Mt 10:24) and the Master "came not to be served, but to serve."

∎

"You do not know what you are asking." But how could they know, when they still did not know who the Son of Man was who was leading them? Before they could know, there would have to be the crucifixion and the morning of Easter, the flight in panic and baptism in the Spirit as well as the meal shared in memory of the one who had died and the cup of the Kingdom and so much more besides. And even now we do not yet know. Which one of us has not dreamed of having a special place in the Kingdom of God?

Since the first day, the Church has been faithful even though its members may not always have understood and the bread and the cup have been shared. The cup of wine—it at once calls cheerfulness, life, resurrection and the coming Kingdom to mind: "I will drink the new wine with you in the Kingdom of my Father" (Mt 26:29; cf. Mk 14:25; Lk 22:18). He drank it to the last drop. At the Last Supper he offered it to them, and "all drank from it" (Mk 14:23). Every Communion commits us to follow the Servant: "Can you drink the cup that I am going to drink?"

Drinking that cup, the Church drinks at its source and to its salvation, but cannot do this without becoming what Christ was and serving all men—handed over for the salvation of all men. No one can receive Communion without at the same time serving his fellow men to the end. Can we do that? For men it is impossible, but everything is possible for God. We do not have to be stronger than the Son of Man. After all, he knew fear and he wept in the Garden of Olives. We do not have to save the world. What we have to do is to let ourselves flow in that stream of love that can renew all things. We have to drink that cup in all humility and then let ourselves be led by Christ, to share in the destiny of the Lord day after day, until the end.

■

God, you know how impatient we are.
Teach us how to go forward
　at the pace of your Son Jesus.
The cup that he puts in our hands—
　let us drink it with him
　to the last drop,
　borne up by hope.
We believe that, if we hold out with him
　when we are put to the test,
　you will let us taste the new wine
　at your table in the Kingdom,
　forever and ever.

THURSDAY OF THE SECOND WEEK

SOLITUDE
Jeremiah 17:5–10: Two ways are open to man. One leads to perdition, the other to happiness. This has been a recurrent theme in human wisdom

since the earliest times. Amen-em-Opet, an Egyptian scribe, had already drawn attention to the happy fate of the man who trusted in his god, and the blessed state of the man who "never follows the advice of the wicked" is, for example, contrasted in Psalm 1 with the bad end of the sinner. The wicked man is compared with "chaff blown away by the wind," whereas the wise man is "like a tree planted by water streams."

Man, then, can choose between two ways. The first is the way of trust and self-abandonment. On this way, the righteous man can build his house firmly founded on rock. The second way is apparently easier to follow, but it is unstable and ephemeral. It is the way of the man who places all his trust in his fellow men and it leads to disillusionment. The prophet says that the man who follows this way is "like dry scrub in the wastelands."

Luke 16:19–31: Is it possible that even a miracle—a resurrection—would change a man who has such security in his many possessions that he is made blind by it? His heart is, in the words of Jeremiah, a "salt land, uninhabited." There were special arrangements in the Mosaic law which favored the poor. One of these laws, for example, stated that the man who took another man's cloak as a pledge had to give it back to the owner before sunset, because "it is all the covering he has; it is the cloak he wraps his body in" (Ex 22:25–26).

The prophets frequently spoke out against luxurious living, and what they said about this is too little known nowadays. Amos, for instance, wrote: "Lying on ivory beds and sprawling on their divans, they dine on lambs from the flock and stall-fattened veal; they bawl to the sound of the harp ... they drink wine by the bowlful and use the finest oil for anointing themselves" (6:4–6).

■

On Psalm 1

At the crossroads of each man's life,
two ways lie before him:
the wide road of luxury and unconcern
and the arid path of love and the cross.
These two ways never meet.
The first is an effortless descent into ruin,
the second is a hard climb up to life.
From time to time,

*God comes and offers man the chance to change.
But who would leave the easy downward slope
for the painful ascent to Golgotha?*

■

A rich man who is not deliberately bad in his attitude toward the poor, but is just unconcerned—perhaps he was born in a splendid and comfortable house and he just takes it for granted that he should have magnificent food to eat every day. For him, the poor are simply part of the countryside, of the light and shade in the landscape that one sees every day without really seeing it. He is unconcerned. But it is not just wealth that leads to unconcern. Who can really be concerned when confronted with so many familiar situations even if they are not in accordance with human dignity? Most of us have long ago capitulated to the fatality of our experience of the world. And how can we really see ourselves as guilty when no one feels responsible? Each one of us keeps himself to himself, remains isolated, protects his own interests, and remains blind.

Then this rich, unconcerned man dies. He has to die before he can become really aware, and now he sees things with the inner eyes of eternity. He is conscious of the frightening abyss that separates him from the blessed, the great gulf that cannot be crossed, and knows that he allowed himself to be led into it while he was still on earth. Now he wants above all to have his brothers warned—after all, his hell began on earth, but he did not know it. But it is a waste of time because even the most solemn warnings have never changed anything in the world.

Hell is an abyss in which everyone is lost in total isolation and without any communication with others, yet knowing that no one can survive without communicating with others. What tragic knowledge! Everyone wants to go on living, but in this hell no one can. It is moreover no longer even possible to plead: "I did not know," since concern for others is a cry from the heart, heard by everyone who does not close his heart by isolating himself from others.

The story of the rich man is a parable about all who are poor and in solitude and those who are secure but eternally isolated from life. It is tragic but true that hell can begin on earth, both for the rich and for the poor. Hell is simply putting the world the right way up.

When our hearts become closed by unconcern,
   open our eyes, Lord,
   and do not let us lose our lives
   in the abyss without hope.
When the poor hold out their hands to us,
   open our hearts
   and give us the joy of communion
   in sharing our goods.

FRIDAY OF THE SECOND WEEK

HOLOCAUST
Genesis 37:3–4, 12–13a, 17b–28: Here is a story of family jealousy—the youngest son whom the aging father likes better than his other children, a boy who does not take part in the work the others do (with a tunic with long sleeves) and who irritates the whole household with his boasting. So the older sons plan to get rid of him. They decide to kill him and throw his body into a well—a horrible case of fratricide in which Joseph's mortal remains are to remain unburied. Finally, they decide to sell him to a caravan on its way to Egypt.

But is there not a deeper reason underlying this implacable hatred of the young Joseph? We should not forget that he was a "dreamer" and that his dreams were interpreted as prophecies. In the ancient world, it was believed that a prophecy could only be effective if it was proclaimed. What need did Joseph have to tell his prophetic dreams to others? It was necessary to suppress the prophet if the effectiveness of the prophetic word was to be suppressed.

Psalm 105, in the form of a hymn, recalls the great deeds performed by Yahweh in Israel's favor.

Matthew 21:3–43, 45–46: Jesus was also received as a prophet. His pronouncements against the temple and the law upset very many people, and those who opposed him finally decided to put him to death. In his own discreet but very meaningful way, he warned his fellow countrymen.

Israel had rejected God again and again in the course of history, but God had remained consistently faithful. He had sent many prophets and now he was sending his own beloved Son. This was Israel's last chance, but the people did not take it. This is vividly illustrated in the parable of the wicked husbandmen. When the Son comes to them, they decide to suppress him and seize the inheritance themselves. What, then, was to be the fate of faithless Israel? When Matthew had finished editing the parable, the Roman legions had already taken Jerusalem and had destroyed the temple. Was that perhaps not a clear sign of God's judgment? Judaism had had its life, and its privileges were transferred to the new Israel, the Church.

■

Did you not forbid the clouds, Lord,
  to make rain fall on our neglected land?
We bless you because you cannot see an unhappy man
  without wanting to raise him up.
Make sure that we shall not leave you
  by increasing our longing for your love.
May we also bear fruit
  as you expect us to when you give us grace.

SATURDAY OF THE SECOND WEEK

THE HEART OF GOD
Micah 7:14–15, 18–20: "However great the number of sins committed, grace was even greater" (Rom 5:20). It is hardly possible to count the number of times Israel was unfaithful to the covenant, just as it is impossible to know how many times man has sinned. But God is in love with man and no lover can ever take stock of his love. God loves. It pleases him to bestow grace. He does not want to enclose man in a sterile past. He simply "throws all his sins to the bottom of the sea."

Psalm 103 is a hymn of praise to the Lord who protects the weak and forgives the sinner.

Luke 15:1–3, 11–32: This too is a hymn—to the tenderness of God. It is also a plea that we should behave like Jesus, who did no more than simply imitate the Father. The Pharisees understood quite well what Jesus was doing when he was at table with publicans and sinners. For the Jews, table-fellowship meant a community of life, and when he extended the messianic table to sinners, Christ was proclaiming their forgiveness and making it a reality. That forgiveness was total in the manner of God himself.

When the prodigal son returned to his father, he had no need to justify himself. The father went out to meet him, threw his arms around him and raised him up. God the Father's forgiveness is no different: when God forgives, a feast is celebrated. The table is set, there is singing and dancing, and the one who is forgiven wears the finest garment, a ring and sandals. There is a resurrection.

But the elder son does not understand. He has never broken a Commandment (like the Pharisees) and he refuses to eat at table with the sinner. We should not, however, throw stones at him. Who, after all, can understand forgiveness if he has not experienced misery and love? We would be misunderstanding this parable if we were not to recognize that we are the elder, pharisaical brother every time we refuse to welcome the prodigal or rather every time we say or think with scorn: "That son of yours!"

Reconciliation is always a shared process in the Church which is only effective if the Father succeeds in reminding us that "that Son of his" is really "our Brother."

∎

We may have in one sense or another followed the way of the prodigal son. We may not, of course, have led a disordered life or spent all that we have on girls. But have we, for example, never claimed our inheritance from God in order to live in what we may have believed was freedom—free from grace and mercy? It is wearying to have to depend all the time on God, the God of love. Adam found that out. Who has never wanted to live a roving life in the freedom of the open air? But those of us who do often end up with the pigs. We cut ourselves off from the source and, whatever we may call it, all that is left is depravity.

"I am dying of hunger"—the prodigal son's conversion begins with his empty stomach. He has humility and knows that he "no longer" deserves anything. But the fact remains that he has still not learned anything, because it is never a question of deserving. He is taking the right road, even though he does not know where it will lead him, any more than we do, with our deep remorse, our sense of guilt and our protestations of worthlessness, treating God as the supreme arbiter of justice.

But our God is the Father in the purest sense of the term. He is a Father who lives exclusively from fatherhood, that is, he lives by giving himself gratuitously and in tenderness. He does not listen to the choice of words in our carefully prepared confession. He runs so quickly to meet us that he almost falls over his long garment. He is not afraid of what would make almost any "righteous" man sneer: effusiveness and feasting. The sinner who returns to him is a prince and the profligate who comes back is reborn. "My son has come back to life."

What is it that prevents us from understanding that the essence of reconciliation is not to be found in our confession, but in the heart of God himself? Let us put ourselves for a moment in the place of the elder son. Does he understand? For years he has never complained and he has never once dreamed of going out on a celebration with his friends (or maybe he has). Then, quite suddenly, he finds that he is full of envy, anger and obstinacy. His whole religious world is upset by the return of the wanderer, in other words, by the revelation of the heart of God himself. He cannot understand God at all, because he is enclosed within his own strict and distributive sense of righteousness, his own merits and his own generosity which is firmly based on the expectation of receiving something back.

Only the prodigal son can really understand God. Only he has experienced the tenderness of God's forgiveness, the foolishness of a resurrection and the feast of renewal. Only he, the sinner, the one who was lost, has been through that.

There are things in the Gospel that are very difficult for right-minded people to believe, things that are often shocking. The blessedness of sinners is perhaps the most difficult of all: "There is more rejoicing in heaven over one repentant sinner than over ninety-nine virtuous men who have no need of repentance." The prodigal son is, let us be honest, likeable—he is, after all, alive. How can we really understand love if we have never been anything but good, obedient children, doing our duty and never suspecting that our true relationship with God does not begin until we go beyond duty?

■

We bless you, God,
  because you like to forgive
  and you reveal yourself in forgiving.
You run to meet the sinner.
  You throw his sins to the bottom of the sea.
  You crown him with love and tenderness.
We bless you, Lord, for this table,
  at which your only Son gave his body and blood
  to bring together your scattered children
  at a feast in which all things are renewed.
Unwearying God, Father of mercy,
  we thank you
  and proclaim your faithfulness.

BAPTISMAL LITURGIES
WE ARE BORN AGAIN

Note on the Optional Liturgy

There are, apart from the special formulae provided for each day, several optional readings in the weekday lectionary for Lent in years B and C. These are the great pericopes suggested for the Sundays of Lent in year A: the woman of Samaria (Jn 4:5–42), the man born blind (9:1–41) and Lazarus (11:1–45).

The restoration of these passages to the last three Sundays of Lent marks a return to the early catechumenical tradition, evidence of which is found in

Rome from the fourth century onward, the Gelasian Sacramentary being the best example of this. Before they were baptized, adult catechumens were submitted to a severe "discipline," the intention of which was to demonstrate their conversion. This moral preparation took place before the final dogmatic instruction, in which the catechumen had to study the creed. This *traditio symboli* occupied the last part of Lent. The new Christian learned about the sacraments only after he had been baptized, since that was, as it were, the revelation of what he has experienced in the sacramental rites themselves.

It cannot be denied that these Johannine pericopes have a baptismal significance. T. Maertens observed, for example, in his impressive study of the history and pastoral significance of the rites of the catechumenate and of baptism: "The choice of formulae is powerfully determined by the desire to illustrate the conversion of the catechumens, their transition from one world to another, their entry into a new creation and their new understanding of things.... A complete movement of conversion, following the rhythm of Easter itself, is in this way made explicit in these formulae and conversion is at first seen as being hungry and thirsty.... It is also worth noting that each of these formulae is concerned with one of man's senses.... We may sum up by saying that this represents the process of man's re-creation."[3]

It is also important to add that the choice of formulae draws attention to the fundamental relationship between baptism and Christ himself. It is not simply a question of giving man's conversion a sense of direction by making him aware of his hunger, his thirst or his blindness. On the contrary, these passages present him with the Lord himself as light, life, living water and the bread of life. In other words, man's condition may provide the fundamental material for baptism, but it is Christ, the new man, who gives it its ultimate meaning. The newly baptized person has put on Christ and it is by grace that he has been saved.

∎

Source of life and unfailing light,
God and Creator of the universe,
we bless your name.

From the very beginning,
you have made all things
as praise flowing from your love.

*You know how blind man can become
when he turns away from your grace.*

*And death can end
by plunging your creature into the night.*

*But you are a God of the living.
You are faithfulness and tenderness.
How, then, is it possible for us
to think that you are far from us
when an infinite desire to live
makes us look for you every day?*

*We have looked for you where you were not,
but you have found us;
your Word of mercy
has been a sign to us
at the crossroads where we went astray.
Your Word made flesh
came to our earth
to recreate what was lost
and to give life to those
who were without a soul.*

*May he give us without restraint
the living water that will make our desert fertile
and the light that will bathe our eyes.
May he pronounce over us
the word of resurrection,
so that we may live forever in him.*

*May his Spirit be the breath
of all those who have been plunged
by the same baptism into the death of Calvary
and into the eternal light of the new day.*

*With our brothers and sisters
who are born again in your grace,
we worship you,
God and Creator of hope.*

OPTIONAL DURING THE THIRD WEEK

MEETING AT A WELL
Exodus 17:1–7: Countless commentaries have been written by Christians on this well-known text. The theme of complaining, which can also be found in the story of the manna in the desert, was taken up again by the fourth evangelist in order to characterize the opposition of the Jews to Jesus (Jn 6), and Paul made the rock the symbol of Christ present in the midst of the Hebrews in 1 Corinthians 10:4.

Chapters 16 and 17 of the Book of Exodus are evidence that the Israelites reflected about their sojourn in the desert. They were used to a comfortable life in Egypt, and the climate in the desert made them suffer, so that they began to quarrel with God, to challenge him and to insist that he intervene on their behalf. We are told in v. 7 what was really at stake in the exodus—their faith was being put to the test. "Is the Lord with us or not?"

Christians are bound to read this passage in the light of Paul's teaching: water from the rock is the grace of Christ which satisfies man's thirst. Paul, however, also warned Christians that being open to grace presupposes a real thirst and an unwearying search for God. There is, in other words, no assurance of salvation either in the privileged state of Judaism or in the Christian sacraments.

Psalm 95: Yahweh accuses his people of having become idolatrous and of having broken the covenant. Vv. 1–7 were clearly intended to be sung in the procession to the holy of holies, where Yahweh would denounce Israel's sin. In vv. 8–11, Israel's challenging the Lord of Meribah is recalled in particular.

John 4:5–42: Water changed into wine, the temple destroyed and rebuilt, Jacob's well contrasted with living water, and ancient forms of worship replaced by worship "in spirit and in truth"—all these point to a rebirth. We are in fact born again, as Jesus told Nicodemus, "through water and the Spirit."

Here the water is in the first place the spring flowing at the bottom of Jacob's well. In the rabbinical traditions, it is also the Torah which can quench man's thirst and purify him. That water, however, has been replaced by the new wine of the Kingdom. In the prologue to the Fourth

Gospel, we read that Moses gave the law, but grace and truth came through Jesus Christ.

The temple is, of course, the holy of holies in Jerusalem, but Jesus threatened to replace that temple with the temple of his own body. Orthodox Judaism with its center in Jerusalem, the syncretical forms of worship practiced in Samaria, and all the Gnostic heresies had to be destroyed and replaced by a cult that included the whole reality of God. It was that cult which Jesus taught his disciples when he invited them to pray: "Our Father."

The Samaritan woman went back to her fellow believers and told them about the stranger she had met at the well and how he had revealed her past to her. Surely he must have been a prophet or perhaps even more than that? In fact, the one who could satisfy man's thirst also had at his disposal a food that was not known to his disciples—that of doing the will of the Father. The final harvest had begun with Jesus, and the Samaritans who came out to meet him were the first-fruits of that harvest. Jesus was and is the Savior of the world.

It was, it should be noted, midday. That is the time of full light.

■

She came to draw water. He was thirsty and had sat down on the curbstone of a well. He had come from elsewhere and was going through the country, proclaiming that the time had been fulfilled.

She had come to draw water—ordinary, everyday water of the kind that was necessary for life. She had come, in other words, to draw life. "Give me some of that water, so that I may never get thirsty."

Instinctively she had expressed the same complaint as the one made by the people of Israel in the desert: "Give us water to drink." She had come to draw the water that would make the desert green. She also hoped to quench her thirst and at the same time she also had in her a longing which made her want to live. "I know that the Messiah is coming. When he comes he will tell us everything."

Thirst and longing—rain is a companion or friend who seizes hold of us. Are we still moved, our hearts still stirred, when such words as water, thirst, spring, well and desert are mentioned? We do not really know what thirst is. We often die nowadays without ever experiencing

deep thirst. Our longings are too quickly satisfied and our lives are spent aimlessly. Our aspirations are very close to the ground. We seem to be quite content with stagnant water. Why, then, does this longing return again and again to trouble us? Why do we have this impression of emptiness in our lives? "Why did you bring us out of Egypt? Was it so that we should die of thirst with our children and our cattle?"

"If you only knew what God is offering. He would have given you living water." If you had only known. Let the thirst that you are trying in vain to dismiss become deeper in you and you will discover in yourself unfathomable hope. Deepen your longing—life is found hidden in those depths. Cease living on the surface of life. Your aspirations can never be too high. God has always had such dreams before you had them. He longed for six days before deciding to fashion man as the work of his heart from the dust of the ground. "If you had asked me for that water," God says, "I would have given you living water." God dreams for you and he dreams of a future. God's longings are the crazy longings of youth. He thinks he will change the world and the world is changed. So you must let yourself be gripped by a renewal that will not stand in the way of the past. You have five husbands, but the secrets of the Kingdom have been revealed to you.

Let yourself be overcome by thirst. Longing is, after all, being born to something new and different. Be open to what God wants to do with you. God is, after all, not enclosed in the prison of what we call "reality." He believes that it is always possible to long for everything. He cannot be contained within the framework of Mount Gerizim and Jerusalem, since nothing can contain flowing water. Our meeting with God, then, is at a well.

■

We are hungry and thirsty
for freedom and holiness,
   for love and life.
May your love come to us, Lord,
   like water that quenches our thirst.
May your word nourish our hope
   as we wait for the coming
     of the Kingdom.

■

*You come to us, Lord,
to quench our thirst.
May we, when we receive you,
ourselves become a source of living water
and bear witness to the good news
among those who are looking for you.*

■

*"You will draw water joyfully
   from the springs of salvation."
Here is living water
   to satisfy the world's thirst,
      the body handed over for the life of mankind.*

■

*"I am thirsty."
Jesus said this twice—
to make a woman thirst for the Spirit
and share with her his own thirst for life,
and to give that same Spirit to men
by handing over his own life to them
to the point of death.*

*If you are thirsty for life,
drink the cup of wine, the blood of love.
If you drink to the end that wine of the Spirit,
you will really be thirsty to give your life
to those who say with Jesus: "I am thirsty."*

OPTIONAL DURING THE FOURTH WEEK

LET YOUR EYES BE DAZZLED

Micah 7:7–9: How deeply Israel trusted in the Lord! The people were very conscious of their sinfulness, but they were always ready to risk everything on the faithfulness of their God. Yes, they had sinned against Yahweh and had to bear his anger against them, but was he not light and salvation? God is tenderness and truth, and darkness cannot prevail against his light.

Psalm 27 is a declaration of man's trust in God. The crowd listens to the psalmist as he affirms that he will "see the goodness of Yahweh in the land of the living."

John 9:1–41: "He was the true light . . .
coming into the world.
He was in the world
that had its being through him
and the world did not know him.
He came to his own domain
and his own people did not accept him.
But to all who did accept him,
he gave the power to become children of God."

The triumph of light over darkness—that is the sign that emerges from the healing of the man born blind. From the moment of his birth, he had been an outlaw. Had his parents sinned? But he was a man of upright heart and Jesus cared for his eyes with his own spittle and sent him to wash in the pool of Siloam. (John points out that the name means "sent.") After this, the blind man was able to see. The water used for purification had been changed into wine, the dead water in the well had become living water, and the water in the pool was filled with a curative value by the one sent by the Father.

But already the judgment was proceeding. The trial was taking place and the man who had been blind was defending the cause of light. He recognized that Jesus was a prophet with an extraordinary power, a man of God of a kind unknown in Israel in the past. The final step was taken by Jesus himself when he revealed himself to the man who had placed his faith in him as the Son of Man.

Persecuted by the Pharisees, the man pleaded on behalf of Jesus. In fact, however, Jesus had to defend himself, and although he died as one who had been accused, his death accused others. Isaiah had prophesied with regard to Jesus' adversaries that they could look in vain, but would not see. Because their works were bad, they preferred darkness to light. They were thieves and brigands. They were bad shepherds. They drove the man whose blindness had been healed by Jesus from the flock and scattered the sheep that Jesus had come to gather together.

Jesus himself is the true shepherd who gives his life for his sheep. "Now sentence is being passed on this world . . . .While you still have the light, believe in the light and you will become sons of light" (Jn 12:31, 36).

■

Eyes that had always been closed—a night that no star had ever crossed and a day that had never dawned. Man can only wander aimlessly and hopelessly. He can only continue in eternal solitude. Marked by life, he can only enclose himself in night. Sin has always clung to us. Darkness grips us and despair encloses us. In which direction should we go? Everywhere we encounter injustice or indifference, disunity or unconcern, exploitation or economic gain. How are we to share with and to love one another? Will our darkness last forever? "As he went along, he saw a man who had been blind from birth."

Jesus declared: "As long as the day lasts, I must carry out the work of the one who sent me," and he added: "As long as I am in the world, I am the light of the world." Do not, my enemy, rejoice in my misfortune. I live in darkness, but the Lord is my light. I am watching and waiting for him, my Savior and my God.

"The light shines in the dark—a light that darkness could not overpower" (Jn 1:5). That light is in this case made of mud formed from a little earth and spittle—fertile mud from which the vine grows and the harvest is obtained. The Light tells the blind man to wash himself. He goes off through the streets of the town, already enlightened by the hope that is in him. He goes because a man has looked at him and told him where to go and which path to follow. He goes because he is already enlightened by the hope that is at last in him. He goes, but he already knows how he will come back. The light is already in him.

Let your eyes be opened. Let light bring about truth in you. "It is for judgment that I have come into this world," Jesus proclaims, "so that those without sight may see and those with sight turn blind." Later, men will believe that they have extinguished God's light, when darkness covers the hill of Golgotha. But later still, the embers hidden in the ground will blaze into a fire of joy in the morning of Easter.

It is true that light has come into the world and that darkness has not been able to overcome it. Since that Easter morning, your eyes have been dazzled by such a clear light that you can no longer say: "Who are you, Lord, so that I may believe in you?" You may still hesitate as you walk, like a man who does not yet dare to believe his eyes, but you can now go forward in the clear light of God.

∎

Blinded by our night,
a long way from God,
we cry to him:
  Open my eyes, Lord,
  to the wonders of your love.
  Heal me. I want to see you.

Lost in the world
with no horizon in sight,
we cry to him:
  Put me on the path
  that leads to the Father.
  Heal me. I want to see you.

With hope dwelling in us
and eager for the encounter,
we cry to him:
  You have washed me with life-giving water.
  Heal me. I want to see you.

∎

Lord, you know how blind and selfish we are.
Do not go past without stopping.
  Show us your love.
  Let us receive your salvation.

You can see where our world is going—
it is coming to a bad end
and is in the grip of fear.
Do not go past without shedding your light on us.
  Show us your love.
  Let us receive your salvation.

*You can see further than we can.
Do not forget those in despair
and those who suffer or are lost.
Do not go past without raising us up.*
  *Show us your love.
  Let us receive your salvation.*

*You blind those who claim to see.
Do not let your Church live
with certainties that are illusions.
Do not go past without questioning us.*
  *Show us your love.
  Let us receive your salvation.*

OPTIONAL DURING THE FIFTH WEEK

WHEN OUR BODIES RISE AGAIN

2 Kings 4:18b–21, 32–37: The stories about the prophet Elisha all come from popular circles and contain marvelous elements. One of the underlying intentions in these stories is to transfer the prestige of the master Elijah to the disciple Elisha.

Like Sarah during the age of the patriarchs, this woman of Shunem had been promised a son in return for her hospitality to Elisha. One day, however, the boy fell sick and died. His mother laid him on the bed of the man of God, in a gesture of hope. Her son did not revive and she went herself to fetch Elisha, who prayed at great length to the Lord and then applied a very strange treatment—he lay down on top of the boy's body and warmed it. The child sneezed seven times. This is symbolic in two senses. Sneezing indicated a return to life and the figure seven pointed to a complete return to life.

Psalm 17: The psalmist implores Yahweh to deliver him from his enemies, because he has remained righteous.

John 11:1–45: "In him was life.
To all who did accept him

*he gave power to become children of God,
to all who believe in his name."*

To the Jews who criticized him for healing the paralytic man, Jesus said: "The hour is coming when the dead will leave their graves at the sound of the voice of the Son of Man" and they "will rise again to life" (Jn 5:28–29). Lazarus heard Jesus' voice and came out of the tomb.

Martha and her family must have shared the hope that had developed in those Jewish circles that had been influenced by pharisaism, but Jesus' words transcended time. Whoever places his trust in Christ will never know death. Life is a gift from Christ. If we eat his body and drink his blood, we have eternal life and Christ will raise us up on the last day.

"Lazarus, come out!" Jesus called the dead man to life while he himself approached death. When he decided to go back to Judea, his disciples had reminded him of the attempt to put him to death that he had avoided (8:59). Now, at Bethany, Thomas insisted: "Let us go too and die with him." When he went to "waken" Lazarus, Jesus began the process that was to lead to his own crucifixion. It was immediately after the incident at Bethany that the chief priest held a meeting at which the decision was taken to put Jesus to death (11:46–53). He also made use of the prophetic charism of his sacred office, although he did not know this himself, when he made the mysterious pronouncement that Jesus had to die "to gather together in unity the scattered children of God." Jesus had himself said that the true shepherd had to give his life for his sheep and that he had to bring in the sheep that were not yet in the fold so that there would be only one flock.

Jesus, then, gives his life, and God's glory is manifested in the Son. Death is definitively overcome. Lazarus and all who, in the darkness of the tomb, hear the voice of Christ can come out. They are awakened to new life and "there is no more death" (Rev 21:4).

∎

It was a very good funeral. It took half an hour to walk from Jerusalem to Bethany. Many friends had come to show their sympathy to the two sisters. Everything was over now. The stone had been rolled in front of the tomb and the house had been set in order. Martha and Mary had been left alone with their grief. Human history is tragically simple, it would seem. Night is obviously victorious over

day. Who has never thought of accusing God? It is hardly necessary to look far for death—it is at work everywhere and at all times. Then there is man's experience of evil, the absence of love, the barrenness of failure, the destructive effect of suffering, the idiocy of injustice and above all the absurdity of death. Man perishes. His hope is in vain.

But Jesus said: "I am the resurrection and the life. If anyone believes in me, even though he dies he will live." God has accepted our accusation. "This sickness will not end in death, but in God's glory," Jesus had said when he was told that Lazarus was ill. He who was God himself embraced death like someone handing himself over to an enemy and the cold stone of the tomb had closed over him. The wheat grain remains only a single grain unless it falls and is buried in the ground. "I am the resurrection and the life." If the wheat grain does not die, it will not bear fruit (see Jn 12:24). The dead seed rises and produces ears of corn. The harvest is already ripening in the sun. The Lord has said: "I shall open your graves and make you come out." We believe what he has said and that the dry bones will be covered with flesh, for God will not allow death to do its work without preparing for spring and new life somewhere.

We believe that this is possible. Believing in absolute love is believing that there is a guarantee of love somewhere. It is also believing and expecting that it will bring a rebirth of life. If it is true that our successes and failures will rise up to build a new creation and that our positive efforts and our tears of defeat will be gathered in to be sown in eternity, then those early pictures that strike us now as naive may also be true and bodies will really rise from the tombs and be given life again through the spirit.

If the grain of wheat does not fall into the ground and die it will remain a single grain. If anyone believes in me, he will live. It is surely because Life, who presided over the act of creation, has entered time and because he made the tomb which could not hold him open one spring morning that we dare now to believe in Life.

■

May the Lord lead us out of those dead-ends
   into which we are drawn by death.
May he bring us back to the land of the living.

We are living without hope.
Raise us up from the dead.
   Lord, have mercy!

Our hands are closed,
tied by injustice.
Open them and let us share.
   Christ, have mercy!

Our hearts are cold and dry.
Let them be warmed by your love.
   Lord, have mercy!

∎

Lord, our God,
   like a father standing up for his child,
   you rise up in our defense.
Break the diabolical circle
   of our impotence and despair
and let Jesus, your light, grace and life,
   rise above the darkness of our graves.

∎

We thank you, God our Father,
   because you have created us
   for life and not for death.
We bless you for Jesus, your Son,
   because you have, through him,
   put an end to the power of evil.
Thanks to him, truth and joy, love and justice
   and peace and freedom can open
   like ripe fruit.
We bless you for your Spirit,
   who leads us out of the dead-ends
   into which we have been drawn by death.
We may still sow in tears,
   but we bear fruit with hope.
And so with all those who have passed
   from death to life,
   we bless you, God of the living.

THIRD WEEK OF LENT

CULT AND THE LAW

"It is love that I want, not sacrifices," since "the whole of the law is summarized in a single command: Love your neighbor as yourself." Hosea, Jeremiah and all the prophets said this again and again in different words. The only sacrifice pleasing to God is that made by a sincere heart. Love is the horizon of the whole of religion.

Why, then, did Jesus encounter such fierce opposition when he tried to put these fundamental data of faith first? No doubt because he challenged the Pharisees and the priests of the Jewish world. The first had transformed the law of freedom into a set of precepts making every aspect of human behavior a stereotype, while the second made cult a soulless contract. The prophet Jesus had to die before the human heart could be given a central place in religion. His death was love to the end.

God makes all things new, including man's heart. He is the God of the dawn and of the springtime. He gave the leper the skin of a little child and his people a beauty as green and fresh as the hills of Lebanon. But his people was deaf and stiff-necked. They went back instead of going forward and they were, above all, unfaithful, because their love was as ephemeral as the morning mist. They were hard and insensitive to the mercy that their God gave them again and again without restraint.

They refused to welcome the prophet in his own country and they were obstinately blind to the Kingdom of God when the Messiah caused it to burst open upon them. How, then, could God go on making all things new? Here and there a man—a scribe here and a publican there—was aware of that newness. The second sat close to the temple, humbly repeating the heartfelt prayer: "Have mercy on me, a sinner." He understood the priority of love over sacrifices. It was through men such as this that the Kingdom of God came.

That Kingdom was one in which the law was accomplished by being brought back to the simplicity of its fullness, to the point at which it was a law of love and of the heart that could be expressed in thanksgiving. "We put our whole heart into following you, into fearing you and seeking your face once more. Do not withdraw your favor from us. Do not repudiate your covenant." The law comes from the covenant and leads to a "sacrifice of thanksgiving" that is worth more than all burnt offerings. "Israel, come back to the Lord your God! Come back and say to him: We offer you our words of praise."

This is the new cult that transcends the rites and spreads out in the humility and the forgiveness of the publican. The law, then, is accomplished in loving God and one's fellow man. There can be nothing to add to this, since, when man begins to live his religion in this way, God has really made all things new.

3. *Histoire et pastorale du rituel du catéchuménat et du baptême* (Bruges, 1962).

MONDAY OF THE THIRD WEEK

RENEWAL
2 Kings 5:1–15a: In the Bible, water is almost always associated with renewal. It purifies, quenches the thirst and gives life. In the second account of the creation (Gen 2:4b–25), the author speaks of the presence in the middle of Eden of life-giving water irrigating the still barren soil. The prophet Ezekiel dreamed during the exile in Babylonia of water flowing plentifully from the temple in Jerusalem and making the desert around the Dead Sea fertile. Naaman, the general, was invited to immerse himself seven times in the Jordan River so that his leprosy could be healed. Later still, just before the coming of the Kingdom of God, John the Baptist baptized Jesus in the same river and the Son was renewed in the Spirit.

Psalm 42: Like a thirsty deer, the psalmist remains in the entrance to the temple, longing to go in and appear before God to ask him for justice.

Luke 4:24–30: After his baptism, Jesus went into the synagogue at Nazareth and read the passage in the Book of Isaiah proclaiming the year of jubilee. He confirmed the fulfillment of the prophecies to his Jewish listeners, but he was not welcomed by them. No one is a prophet in his own country. Neither Elijah nor Elisha was sent to the Israelites. Elijah was sent to the widow of Zarephath, and Elisha to Naaman the leper. As Paul wrote, "Pagans who were not looking for righteousness found it all the same, a righteousness that comes from faith, while Israel, looking for a righteousness derived from the law, failed to do what the law required" (Rom 9:30–31).

■

On Psalm 42

You who are thirsty—
come to the source, go up to God
and follow the Son of Man to the cross.
From his open side will flow for you
the living water of the Spirit.

■

"My soul thirsts for the God of life." True conversion is based on a great longing to know God. All the rest is still fundamentally selfishness. Naaman was a leper and he was not healed until he had gone beyond being preoccupied with his own healing and had become open to a knowledge of God.

God reveals himself and carries out his work in very simple ways and this makes it possible for man to guard against any temptation to create for himself a god who will be useful to him in all his existential needs. The Jordan is only a river and baptism is simply being immersed in water. The simplicity of the symbolism makes an appeal to faith, and without faith there would be nothing there. Baptism is not administered so that the person baptized can receive useful graces. On the contrary, baptism is an encounter with the Lord, from whom the baptized person begins to live as the source of a great longing.

The words spoken by Jesus of Nazareth are also marked by the same disarming simplicity. Not only does he say very simply: "This word is being fulfilled today even as you listen"—he also presents himself as the one whose task is to renew human history, in that he is himself only a man among men, a fellow citizen.

It is here that the great evangelical renewal is to be found: a faith firmly rooted in man's heart and based on signs as fragile as a man without any power or a symbol of living water. This is because what

God wants to renew is man's heart. Confronted with the Gospel story, we are bound to ask: Will he succeed in the presence of those masters in Israel who have constructed a closed system of laws and rites in which the heart has no place? Now it is the people of Nazareth who shrug their shoulders, but he only has to throw the lesson of the Scriptures back in their faces, and they are at once enraged and want to put him to death by throwing him down a cliff.

"But he slipped through the crowd and walked away." He went on his way—the way of the cross, the only way along which God was able to renew the heart of man.

■

Our souls are thirsting for you, the living God.
　Our souls are looking for you, night and day.
Open our eyes to your light,
　revealed in your Son, a man among men,
　so that it will shine on our way,
　the way of life,
　and, following Jesus up to the top,
　we shall see your face and your glory.
You are a faithful God
who makes all things new.

TUESDAY OF THE THIRD WEEK

UNTIRING FORGIVENESS
Daniel 3:25, 34–43: After the death of Alexander the Great, the government of Palestine passed first into the hands of the Ptolemies of Egypt and was finally taken over by the Greek Seleucids. One of the latter, Antiochus IV Epiphanes, tried to unite his huge kingdom by imposing Hellenistic customs and cultic forms on all the inhabitants. The Jews disliked him, particularly when he had an altar in honor of the Olympian Zeus erected in the temple of Jerusalem in 167 B.C.

The author of the Book of Daniel clearly aimed to encourage the Jews in their courageous resistance to the one who had profaned their temple. To add authority to his message, he called to mind another invasion, that of the Mesopotamian ruler Nebuchadnezzar, whose great empire had already become lost in the mists of time. In Chapter 3, the author exalts the virtue of faithfulness to the true God, and he does so by describing the courage shown by Daniel's young companions in the fiery furnace.

This chapter is full of liturgical elements: the song of Azariah (vv. 26–45) and the famous canticle of the creatures (vv. 52–90), both of which are very representative of Jewish prayer. In the name of the people, the leader confesses the sins of the whole community and asks God to intervene, suggesting that he should at least look after his own reputation among the pagan nations.

Psalm 25 is an individual lamentation in which not only themes that are peculiar to this literary genre, but also specifically Wisdom writings—themes such as that of the antagonism between the righteous and the evil man—are developed. It is an alphabetical Psalm.

Matthew 18:21–35: Again and again in the Gospels, Jesus insists on the need to forgive. In the Our Father, for example, he made it an explicit requirement. In his eyes, it was clearly the condition sine qua non of all prayer (see Mt 6:14–15). This is vividly illustrated in the Matthaen parable that concludes the "discourse on the Church" in the First Gospel.

The enormous sum of money owed by the servant shows that his situation was quite desperate and that he could only be saved by the mercy of his master. That, of course, is our situation in the presence of God who forgives us. The king, however, is merciful and cancels the whole of the servant's debt after the latter had pleaded for a little time in which to find the money.

But why, then, was the servant whose debt had been cancelled so cruel toward a colleague who owed him only a small amount of money? Did this unworthy servant not recognize that he was, in behaving in this way, preventing God's grace from acting in him? Man's relationship with God is destroyed when he has no true relationships with his fellow men. The Church is always shaken by bad and unforgiving relationships. God will measure his grace and favor to us with the measure that we use when dealing with our fellow men.

We are angry with the bad servant, just as his master was. His unforgiving attitude calls to heaven for vengeance. But should we not apply this parable to ourselves? Are we not bad servants in the same way? Surely what is really wrong with that heartless servant is precisely that he is heartless. We cannot help wondering whether he ever really understood the king's mercy toward him. It is certainly difficult to believe that any master could be so merciful.

But how can a heartless person understand mercy and forgiveness? The master cancelled his debt, and for the servant the affair was settled and he just went off confidently to settle his own affairs. The story is always the same: God forgives, but men make contracts. Business is business. It suits me very well if I can get out of a mistake without harm to myself. As for others—remember the splinter in our brother's eye and the plank in our own.

God is forgiving. He is so merciful that he cancels without hesitation a debt of ten thousand talents—quite a fantastic sum of money, an exaggeration. But does not everything take on an infinite dimension in the case of God? If God had been simply justice and not mercy, nothing more would have been heard of us for a very long time, even without taking the monstrous acts committed by men against God and their fellow men into consideration. Even if we confine ourselves simply to our everyday faults, can any one of us say he is not a debtor when confronted with the infinite love of God? But God expresses that love as grace and forgiveness, tenderness and mercy, a mercy that is, above all, creative, in that, by untiringly forgiving us and cancelling our debts, he gives us new life.

So, if we ask Peter's question "Lord, how often must I forgive my brother?" we are simply asking: "How many times am I going to live again?" If we cease to be untiring in our forgiveness of others, without counting the number of times we forgive, we cease to live. We can only be thrown out. But how is it possible to live without experiencing the grace and forgiveness that saves us every day? That is a gratuitous experience of life itself, because it takes us to the very source of life. Wholeheartedly forgiving our brother is making our own the infinite movement of love which goes back to the origin of man, whom God took from his own heart.

For the love of your name, Lord,
  do not forsake your humiliated people.
We have sinned against you.
  Be merciful to us.
  Give us a new heart.

WEDNESDAY OF THE THIRD WEEK

A LAW ENGRAVED IN OUR HEART

Deuteronomy 4:1, 5–9: This passage is composite in character and is written in the style of the Wisdom literature. It expresses Israel's pride in possessing the Mosaic law. The people have no need to envy their neighbors in Mesopotamia or Egypt and no reason to run after other gods. They have a law which makes them the envy of other nations and a God who is closer to men than the other gods are.

Psalm 148 is a hymn to the glory of God's power. There is no other god equal to Yahweh.

Matthew 5:17–19: Even in the early Church, v. 17 gave rise to controversy, some Christian teachers claiming that Jesus said precisely the opposite of what is in the text, namely: "I have not come to fulfill the law, but to abolish it."

Whatever the case may be, Christ's words in their present form mean that he was, in his person, the fulfillment and realization of the prophecies of the old covenant. He gave the law its true meaning by taking its demands to a much deeper and more human level.

But which law? According to Jesus' words and the "treatise of the two ways," the law is simply the Decalogue with its rules concerning man's attitude toward his fellow men summed up in the Commandment to love. But these "ten words" provide a great deal of scope for creativity, because they are in each case no more than a negative definition of the characteristic signs of the people of God and leave the door open to that almost unlimited sphere in which man is able to create everything that he needs in order to live in love. We should never forget that Israel received the law, not as a burden, but as a blessing. Yahweh gave Israel the Decalogue and, in so doing, gave the people the chance to live.

■

On Psalm 148

Celebrate God by singing for him,
you people of his love,
you who know his words.
Be the sign of his presence
at the heart of the world.
Our God is peaceful—
be active in the cause of his peace.
Night and day,
summer and winter—
recount the wonders of our God.

■

The law—it has a bad name among Christians. Do we have to blame St. Paul for that, because he judged and condemned it without an appeal? But there are so many laws and interpretations of the law, and often the only function of the law seems to be to serve our rulers or to justify a rigid and inflexible tradition. The law is destined to die. Péguy's God said: "When you have experienced what it is to be served by free men, slaves bowing down before you means nothing." That goes without saying.

But God's law is an inner word that shows you the way and appeals to your creativity. "Even if we were so burnt by love that we were to die of it, we would still not love enough. Love is everything that is God."

A law that shows us the way—but we need signals and parapets on that way. The psalmist says: "The commandment of the Lord is clear, light for the eyes" (Ps 19:8), and indeed the way of the Decalogue is very simple and one which men can follow together with infinite respect for each other in the light that God sheds on us. We are free people. We have been set free in order to learn how to live together without fear, without withdrawing into ourselves and without seeking weapons or possessions. We can follow the way of God's law with all the enjoyment that comes from loving.

The law is only fully lived ("fulfilled") when men begin to discover love—the love of God and neighbor. That was how Jesus himself fulfilled the law in his own person—by living love to the very end. His attitude was often in complete contrast to that of the world. He forgave those who put him to death. He suggested the love of poverty to the rich young man, who had never stolen or killed. He designated gentleness, mercy and longing for justice as blessed. Has there ever been on our earth a God who was closer to men? Is there any law that can give life more perfectly than the Gospel? Those who are radically simple can understand that law, and for them the Lord's words are sweeter than honey. The law has really been fulfilled in Christ.

■

Your words, Lord, are truth
  and your law sets us free.
Blessed are you for the one Commandment
  in which all things are fulfilled in love.
Give us hearts that are pure and simple,
so that, with your Son Jesus,
  we may live from your words
  and for the joy of creating a happy world
  in which man may live in peace,
  seen by you,
  the God who is very close to us.

THURSDAY OF THE THIRD WEEK

HARDNESS OF HEART
Jeremiah 7:23–28: In 608 B.C., at the beginning of the reign of Joiakim, Jeremiah pronounced a famous discourse at the entrance to the temple in which he denounced the Israelites for their blindness in boasting that they

possessed the temple, but in failing to keep the religious laws of the covenant. The covenant was above all concerned with faithfulness to God's word and not with ritual sacrifices. The latter were only the external sign of that faithfulness. Jeremiah was not opposed to worship, but he insisted again and again on the need for inner religiosity, for only that could give meaning to cultic observances.

Psalm 95: This has often been used in the first office of the day to invite believers to pray. It is a composite Psalm, the first seven verses consisting of a pilgrimage chant and the last four of a list of accusations of Israel's faithlessness. It was probably sung as the procession approached the holy of holies, where it was believed that Yahweh pronounced judgment.

Luke 11:14–23: "Every kingdom divided against itself is heading for ruin." Jesus drove out demons and he was accused of practicing magic. As an exorcist, it was claimed, he invoked the prince of demons. Satan, then, would be doing himself a great disservice by driving out his own allies. The accusation is all the more unacceptable in that the Pharisees themselves also drove out demons. This is a clear case of wrong faith.

No, Jesus drives out demons, he says, "through the finger of God." Satan—the "strong man"—can defend his own domain by means of arms, but "someone stronger than he is"—this is what John the Baptist called Jesus (in Lk 3:16, for example)—can defeat him. The Egyptian pharaoh eventually recognized the hand of God in the miracles worked by Moses. In the same way, the Pharisees finally accepted the sign given by Jesus. As the new Moses, he expelled demons by his own power. The Kingdom of God had entered the world of men.

■

On Psalm 95

Do not close your heart
and do not challenge love.
Bow down in front of God
and receive everything from him.
In the desert of everyday life,
only he can give you life,
so long as you are ready
to share his love.

■

"Sincerity is no more; it has vanished from their mouths." This is a terrible accusation. It is terrible because faithfulness—and faithfulness is perhaps a better word here than "sincerity"—to God is at the heart of biblical religion. That faithfulness is moreover active and creative. Those who wanted to explain Jesus' activity as based on a pact between him and the prince of demons did not understand that being in agreement with God meant entering into the movement of his revelation and being close to man. So that they could preserve what they believed were God's laws, they "refused to face God and turned their backs on him." In rejecting Jesus, they became unfaithful to God. They were divided and therefore ruined.

We should not think that the drama of unbelief that is enacted throughout the Gospel is the result of a rejection in opposition to Christ. If Jesus had healed sick and possessed people without claiming any special relationship with God on his part, he would have been congratulated—there are never people in the world with the gift of healing. And if he had performed an additional miracle to give them a "sign from heaven," he would have been carried shoulder high. But he never agreed to take part in such a competition. All he ever wanted to be was the Son of the Father, and he called for a faith in himself that would not be subjected to any test other than that of trust. He called on those who were faithful to take a decisive step forward. It was not possible to step aside, since "he who is not with me is against me."

Many believed that he had been defeated when he was crucified. He refused to come down from the cross and went to the very end, dying. Faithfulness to God presupposed acceptance of that dark pit in which nothing is open to human understanding. Since then, Christ's resurrection has not been a more decisive argument than the signs given during his life. If we are to be faithful to God and go forward on the way of life, we must believe in the one whom we shall not see until we ourselves cross over into death and beyond. Every day our faithfulness has to recreate the conditions of trust in the Holy Spirit at work among men and women. That is something that is quite different from hardness of heart, however religious that may appear to be.

■

Your Kingdom has come as far as us, Lord,
  and men are giving their lives
  to drive evil out of our world.
May your Spirit enlighten us
  so that we may recognize them
  as ambassadors of your salvation.
We shall be faithful to you
  because you are a God who is always at work
  in the almost imperceptible signs of your love.

FRIDAY OF THE THIRD WEEK

MORNING SACRIFICE

Hosea 14:2–10: "Israel, come back!" Offer no more sacrifices to idols that can do nothing for you, Turn away from Assyria and the horse that will not help you in flight. Come back to God and offer him the sacrifice of your lips. "My sacrifice is this broken spirit. You will not scorn this crushed and broken heart."

So Yahweh will heal you. You will be reborn to new life. The fields will be covered with lilies and the mountains of Lebanon will be fragrant with incense. The exiles will come back and begin to cultivate the land once more. It will be the springtime of God.

Idols are powerless. Yahweh is the only true God of fertility, and he will enable Ephraim, the "fertile" one, to be fruitful again.

Psalm 81: The trumpet calls Israel to celebrate the Feast of Tabernacles in this Psalm, which also contains a list of Yahweh's accusations against the people.

Mark 12:28b–34: "Listen, Israel! The Lord our God is the one Lord." Only he is able to evoke the deepest effort of which man is capable. And man, the true icon of God, also has a right to the love that everyone has of himself. There was a great deal of discussion among the rabbis about the relative importance of the various Commandments, but Jesus went straight to the heart of the matter.

At the same time we should not forget that his trial had already begun. He had just driven the dealers from the temple and the authorities called on him to explain where his authority came from: "What authority have you for acting like this? Or who gave you authority to do these things?" Rather than engage in heated controversy, Jesus told those who were questioning him the parable of the wicked husbandmen. But, for a little while, the Kingdom of God was very close. In the name of Judaism, a scribe accepted Jesus' explanation.

∎

On Psalm 81

You are weighed down by a heavy burden
and are wondering which god to serve.
Turn to the only God, the Most High!
His hands will take the weight from your shoulders
and you will learn from him
how easy the yoke of love is.

∎

Keeping a great number of Commandments and taking part in a great number of acts of worship may give the impression of deep fervor and total obedience, but the heart soon tires as these observances are increased. Is there not one single commandment and one simple liturgy in which all this is concentrated—not so much in order to make things easier as to make everything more truthful? This desire for unification and simplification is at the heart of every sincere religious intention, and there is a perfect example of it in the Bible. When Jesus was questioned by one scribe, he simply went back to the teaching of the old covenant and repeated the text that summed up the whole of the law: "You must love."

But that love is not just any kind of love. If it were, the concentration of the law in the single commandment to love could be used as an alibi for easiness. We are above all to love God as the only God and to love him with the whole of ourselves. God cannot share man's worship of him with anyone or anything. He is also not willing to accept fear or respect that does not come from within man's heart. He has to be loved absolutely. All the rest is no more than an explanation of this first love.

Together with this first Commandment, however, there is the second that is parallel and similar: "You must love your neighbor as yourself." Our God is one with man. It is only possible to love man if his full dignity is recognized and every man is a son of God. Cult itself is required by God, but it is only meaningful if it helps to make man live fully as a son of the Father.

So Jesus told this scribe who had questioned him and accepted his explanation that he was "not far from the Kingdom of God." He was on the right way, but he had even further to go—he had still to learn that the two Commandments to love were only one in the death and resurrection of the Son. Having loved his own to the end, Jesus was then able to say to the Father: "I have accomplished the love that you have given me," and that was, of course, worth more than all offerings and sacrifices. When Easter dawned, Jesus celebrated the morning sacrifice in which man, born again, was one with his God.

∎

Loving you above everything else
  is worth more than all sacrifices.
  Accept the gift of our love, Lord.
Loving our neighbor is discovering your face.
  Let us go on loving, Lord,
  to the very end.
May all our strength and understanding
  be enlightened by love,
  so that we shall enter your Kingdom
  in which all men are your children,
  through Jesus, your beloved Son.

SATURDAY OF THE THIRD WEEK

PRAYER OF THE HEART
Hosea 6:1–6: Even when they go to the temple, the hypocritical people of

God do not speak truthfully, and it would be foolish to hope that they will be repentant. They think of Yahweh in terms of Baalism and believe that salvation is as automatic as the rain that falls every springtime. When will they understand that the Lord wants love, not external sacrifices? "What am I to do with you, Ephraim? What am I to do with you, Judah?"

Yahweh will go on castigating you with his prophets until you are truly converted, and then he will heal you. He will bandage your wounds and bring you to life again. He will act very quickly—on the third day he will raise the righteous man.

Psalm 51 is a typical penitential Psalm. The psalmist asks God to forgive him and then speaks about the true meaning of sacrifice as something that is only valuable if it is accompanied by inner conversion.

Luke 18:9–14: The evangelist presents us with a case of another man who has understood nothing in his conviction that acts of worship and liturgical performances are effective in themselves. Although this Pharisee is so wrong, we cannot help liking and admiring him. He fasts twice a week and gives ten percent of his salary to the poor. Let the person who does as much as that throw the first stone! Like so many other Pharisees, he practices the counsels of piety and virtue common to his group.

Yet we criticize the Pharisees because they are so self-assured. They do so many things for God that they are able to do without him altogether. Yahweh is for them an accountant who assesses their efforts and their merits. They no longer see him as what he really is—the source of salvation.

The publican, however, has a true understanding of God. He has faith in God and he is aware of his own wretchedness. So he stands at the entrance to the temple and calls out in his distress. He is like all of God's poor. He relies exclusively on God and cannot defend himself. And God justifies him.

■

There will always be Pharisees in our midst. Happy is the man who sees clearly that he is also a poor Pharisee, because the man who claims that he is not will become one simply by virtue of that claim. A caricature is a deformation of the reality, and everyone thinks that it does not apply to him. The Pharisee in the parable is so self-satisfied that we all say: "Stupidity of that kind is an exaggeration." Yet, in our

hearts, are we not secretly happy that we are not at all like him? Have we never placed the burden of our own superiority or intelligence on the poor man's shoulders? Which one of us is not a Pharisee?

But what is a Pharisee and what is a publican? Let us reflect for a moment about these words, their development and their irony. A Pharisee is a member of a strict religious sect, a faithful, sincere and practicing member, punctilious in his observance of the forms of prayer common to his group. But, in the Gospel and in the history of the Church, "Pharisee" means "hypocrite." Is there some link between the two words?

A publican, on the other hand, is a public thief, collaborating with the enemy, a man who has become rich by defrauding and plundering the defenseless. Yet we have made this man our model of perfection, and Jesus certainly puts him in first place. What, then, has happened? What is this strange reversal of values that makes the Gospel so surprising? This publican is not the only unexpected figure in the New Testament; we have only to think of Zacchaeus, Mary Magdalene and the good thief.

Two men, then, go to the temple to pray. In prayer, man's heart is exposed. When he prays, the Pharisee stands in the center and God is present only to recognize his claim. The publican stands "some distance away," conscious of his worthlessness and looking at God who can save him. Is there really any one of us who thinks, when he receives Communion, that he is unworthy? "Lord, I am not worthy. . . ." This does not mean that we should stay in the pew and wait until we are worthy. We are never worthy and never will be, but God wants to give himself to our unworthiness. Our hands stretched out toward him should be empty hands.

And that is the danger of the pharisaical attitude. The Pharisee has been taught to avoid sin, to offer countless sacrifices and do many good works, to live according to the holy rule. He has done all this so well that he has become proud of his achievement. He is right with God, who is only there now to do justice to him and not to be tenderness and forgiveness. It is enough for him simply to be just. For his part, the Pharisee can now function as a moral judge and custodian of the moral code. He knows how thankless but very necessary it is for society to have such men as he, who can put right what is wrong and who have suffered in the process of becoming upright.

Two men go into a church to pray. One is upright. The other is perhaps divorced or alcoholic or an ex-prisoner. The second man remains at a distance from his fellow men. He does not congratulate himself on his faults. He knows how much he has suffered from being rejected by his fellow men. Does he also know that God has come forward to meet him and show him tenderness? Publicans, after all, enjoy this privilege; only they know the point at which God is able to be mercy. Will we Pharisees also know that point one day?

■

Have mercy on me, Lord, in your love.
I am only what I am—nothing very much.
But you are tenderness and forgiveness and mercy
for the one who gives himself to you.

FROM THE MONDAY TO THE WEDNESDAY OF THE FOURTH WEEK OF LENT

Baptismal Conversion
Lent is a period of conversion and we should not make any mistake about our change of direction. It is a time of grace, and our conversion should be an immersion in God's eternal plan for us. It is more important for us to discover what we are already by God's grace than to make a great effort to change. It is also a time of baptism, when the whole Church is once again immersed in Christ. He has already set us free and he will make us free again.

Our conversion during Lent should take place so that we become by grace what we are already by character. This means that we are invited to discover our roots and even to discover our root, which is Jesus who died and was raised again and who continues to spring up and grow in our human earth. This permanent root is the work of the Holy Spirit, who enables us to enter into communion with the God of life and love.

Baptism is a unique action in the life of the believer, making it possible for him to be at one with that other action which is the unique sign in human history of the coming of the eschatological era—the death and resurrection of Jesus Christ. What was fulfilled in Jesus is made a reality for every man. As Paul said, "Our former selves have been crucified with him" (Rom 6:6). The great significance of baptism is that it unites us with the Christ who died and rose again in his commitment to the new life. In this way, the meaning of our history is gradually unfolded.

The limitations of which we are conscious and which hold us back are not merely those of our human condition; they are also and perhaps even more importantly those of our "reduced" human condition. Sin reduces and restricts us, but as soon as we try to go beyond its limitations, we become "capable" of God and the Holy Spirit is already working in us. The mystery of human life is that man is both a sinner and saved.

Because Christ rose from the death, the last word that can be said about our life is not sin, but salvation. Baptism does not give a moral significance to our life, as something that is purified from sin. On the contrary, it gives it an eschatological meaning. "The Spirit himself and our spirit bear united witness that we are children of God" (Rom 8:16).

St. Augustine wrote: "The death and resurrection of Christ—that, Christian, is your mystery." Immersed in the water, we are made children once again and reborn. Baptismal conversion turns us toward the future which is, for God, already our reality. Conversion, like baptism, can only live as hope.

A GLANCE AT THE FOURTH GOSPEL

In the past and even until quite recently, the Fourth Gospel was not highly regarded by historians, who thought that it was too "theological" or too "symbolical" and therefore unlikely to provide valuable data. More recent research has, however, put an end to this suspicion by reassessing the historicity of the Fourth Gospel and the symbolism of the Synoptics and showing that John contains first-hand historical information. In this respect, John seems to be better informed about the beginning of Jesus' ministry than the other evangelists. This applies in particular to Jesus' association with John the Baptist and to the choice of the disciples, which is described in the Fourth Gospel (Jn 1:35–51) in a very spontaneous way. Another example is the Last Supper. The Johannine chronology of the events of the passion seems to be better than that of the Synoptics, and this had led scholars to dispute the paschal nature of the Last Supper.

The historical value of the Fourth Gospel, then, has been widely recognized today. However, no solution has been found for the problems raised by its structure and composition. There is only one datum about which scholars are unanimous, and that is the division of the Gospel into two parts. By general consent, the first part consists of the first twelve chapters (The Book of Signs) and the second part of Chapters 13 to 20 (The Book of the Passion). Chapter 21 is generally regarded as an appendix. As for the rest, however, there are as many opinions as there are authors. It is possible to get some idea of their differences if one compares the ideas of C.H. Dodd, for example in his *Interpretation of the Fourth Gospel*, with those contained in the French *Traduction Oecuménique de la Bible*.

Dodd has described the Fourth Gospel as a musical fugue, with many intertwining but powerfully united themes. The *Traduction Oecuménique*, on the other hand, speaks of "a succession of episodes constructed without any strict plan, but with the aim of developing on the one hand the confrontation between Jesus and the world and his difficult progress in the knowledge of believers on the other."

Dodd's Book of Signs contains seven episodes. Leaving aside the intrinsic value of this sevenfold division of the first part of the Gospel, the author's way of looking at the Gospel is also extremely suggestive. In his description of the first episode (Jn 2:1—4:42), for example, which he calls the "New Genesis," he stresses the newness of Jesus' message and draws attention to various factors. These include the replacement of the water by wine at the wedding at Cana, the proclamation of the new temple (the incident of the driving of the merchants out of the temple), the theme of new birth which dominates the conversation with Nicodemus, and finally the contrast, in the episode of the Samaritan woman, not only between "living water" and Jacob's well, but also and above all between the ancient cult of Jerusalem and Mount Gerizim and "worship in spirit and truth."

Generally speaking, greater progress has been made in the interpretation of the composition of the Gospel than in that of its structure. Here, one can only be very glad that the various hypotheses suggesting that certain texts and even whole sections of the Gospel have been shifted from one place to another have at last ceased to appear. There would seem at present to be a general consensus of opinion that there was a Johannine tradition or school, and Raymond Brown has, for example, recently postulated a history of the Gospel in two phases.[4] The first of these is a pre-Gospel stage, dating from about 55 A.D. and still open to the Jewish world. The second, dated about 90 A.D., is the stage when the Gospel was being edited and is characterized by hostility toward the Jews, John the Baptist's disciples and the various Gnostic groups.

Another biblical scholar, A. Descamps, has found traces of a Palestinian theme in the Fourth Gospel together with a double Hellenistic theme. The first, he claims, is one-sided in its insistence on the transcendent nature of Christ, while the second acts as a balance to this transcendent Christology by stressing Christ's incarnation.[5]

A similar flexibility of ideas about the influences on the composition of John's Gospel has also characterized more recent scholarship. At the beginning of the present century, the Hellenistic influences were too strongly stressed. Now, however, it is the Old Testament origins of Johannine thought that are more heavily emphasized, and especially in this respect the influence of the Wisdom literature (water, manna and wisdom itself, for example) and that of the composition and the language of the rabbinical literature. It is also generally agreed that a considerable influence was exerted by Qumran. There is, in other words, a very pronounced dualism in the Fourth Gospel. There has also been awareness in recent years of a Johannine reaction against gnosticizing tendencies. John did not share the Gnostics' pessimism, and his faith in the incarnation made it possible for him to look in quite a different way at man's condition.

Finally, there is the term "sign," and it is difficult to think of a better word than the one used by the author of the Gospel itself to define the miracles. For John, the whole of Jesus' life was a sign. He believed that God made himself manifest in the world through the events that formed the fabric of that life. At the same time, however, that revelation brought about a division between men. On the one hand there were the believers, who had entered into a new life, and, on the other, those who rejected God's revelation. The contrast was as strong as that between light and darkness. But those who rejected were judged, and the most striking events in that judgment were, according to the fourth evangelist, the passion and resurrection of Christ.

MONDAY OF THE FOURTH WEEK

A NEW CREATION

Isaiah 65:17–21: Hear the Word of the Lord. Listen to the judgment that he pronounces on his people: "Now I create new heavens and a new earth." Life is victorious over death and salvation is more powerful than the forces of chaos. There will be joy forever in Jerusalem. There will be no more weeping and cries will no longer be heard in the city, because Yahweh will whisper into the heart of Israel: "My people," and Israel will reply: "My God." Chapter 65 is attributed to Third Isaiah and it is a declaration of judgment—Yahweh is judging his people. It falls into two parts. The first is addressed to the rebels (vv. 1–12), and the second contrasts them with those who are faithful to the Lord (vv. 13–25).

Psalm 30 expresses individual thanksgiving, but it was sung at the dedication of the temple, and this gave it a national status. It therefore came to express the thanksgiving of the whole people of Israel whom Yahweh had restored to life when they were apparently destined to die.

John 4:43–54: "In the beginning was the Word . . . and the Word was life." The water of purification changed into wine, the ancient sacrifices abolished and replaced by worship "in spirit and truth," living water—Jesus initiated a new order of things. He was and still is the way that leads to true life—eternal life.

He gives that life in his word: "Go, your son will live." The man, who is in the service of Herod Antipas, believes in Jesus' word and goes. Later, he learns from his own servants that his dying son has returned to life and that this happened at exactly the same time as Jesus spoke his word. "Whoever listens to my words and believes in the one who sent me has eternal life; without being brought to judgment he has passed from death to life" (Jn 5:24). This happened at Cana, where Jesus had already manifested his glory.

■

On Psalm 30

The enemy was victorious and was mocking,
but you are Lord of the living
and you have brought me up from the pit.

A veil of mourning darkened the earth,
but you are the God of hope
and you have changed our night into day.

You were angry and everything had been reduced to dust,
but you raised your Son up from the dead.

How is it possible, Lord, for us
not to praise you in our hearts?

■

Jesus was the chosen one of God. John the Baptist bore witness to this. Something quite new had appeared in the history of salvation. The new wine of the messianic age had replaced the water of purification. With Jesus, God's plan entered a new phase, a final period that was full of promise. "I will make rivers well up on barren heights and fountains in the midst of valleys" (Is 41:18). The one who gives living water fulfills the expectation of the little ones. The times are fulfilled, as on the first mornings of the universe. God has chosen life.

The word of God does what it says it will. "As the rain and the snow come down from heaven and do not return without watering the earth, making it yield and giving growth . . . so the word that goes from my mouth does not return to me empty . . . without doing what it was sent to do" (55:10–11). On the morning of the universe, God spoke and light appeared. He spoke again and the earth was created, with flowers to rejoice the heart of man and creatures to populate it. God spoke and man came from the breath of his mouth.

Jesus appeared and God once again came as Creator to his earth. His word renews all things. The Spirit, who had become silent with the last of the prophets, spoke again and restored creation to its early beauty. Listen to what he will tell you. Yes, the word of the Lord is: "Now I create new heavens and a new earth . . . . No more will the sound of weeping or the sound of cries be heard, no more will be found the infant living a few days only or the old man not living to the end of his days."

How were we ever able to read the Gospel and yet make Lent a gloomy time? Surely it is a time when God proclaims: "The exaltation that I shall create will be Jerusalem and the enthusiasm will be my people." It is surely a time when we are recreated. Jesus went into Galilee. He returned to Cana, where he had changed water into wine. The wine is overflowing and the wedding has begun. The word will give growth and bear fruit. Keeping Lent is letting God take hold of you. Can you not feel the new wine flowing through the dead parts of your body? Are you not conscious of the mad hope that is seizing hold of you? Get up! The word has been spoken once and for all time: "He is alive."

■

Lord, there is no new wine
and our hearts are dry.
  Have mercy on us!

Come down to us before we die.
  Our hope is faltering.
  Have mercy on us!

Renew our hearts.
We are still backward
and our past makes us despair.
  Have mercy on us!

TUESDAY OF THE FOURTH WEEK

IMMERSED IN THE WATER
Ezekiel 47:1–9, 12: The author of the Book of Genesis speaks of a spring

rising from the earth to water the surface of the ground. Near it, surrounded by lush vegetation, was the tree of life. In Palestine a spring was frequently regarded as a symbol of God's life-giving power and a sanctuary was often built in the vicinity. This had happened in Jerusalem in the case of the springs of Siloam and Gihon.

When he thought of the new Jerusalem, the prophet Ezekiel saw water flowing from the threshold of the temple. That spring was the sign that God had taken possession of the new sanctuary and had returned from exile, where he had been in company with his people, after having left the old temple. The spring, then, meant that the new temple, made holy by God's presence, would be a source of grace.

A source of unprecedented and abundant grace—this is clear from the size of the stream flowing from it. It was such a wide and deep stream that it irrigated the desert and purified the water of the Dead Sea. On its banks were trees of life with evergreen leaves, bearing a new harvest of fruit each month.

Psalm 46 is one of the canticles of Zion. It sings the praises of the city chosen by God to contain the throne of his glory.

John 5:1–16: Like the water at Cana and that in Jacob's well, that in the pool of Bethesda had no effect—it did not heal the sick. Like the water of the pool, the law of Moses could not give life to the sinner. All that it could do was to show him that he had sinned and reaffirm the poverty of the human condition. Instead of saving the sick man, it only made him a prisoner of his own past life. He had been paralyzed for thirty-eight years.

Jesus had to come to this sanctuary of Asclepios, to the northeast of Jerusalem. He had to bear the burden of human misery. He was to hear the cry of suffering and the prayer of superstition. He was to take on himself the sin of the world. He was to speak the word, and as the Word of life was to tell the sick man: "Get up, pick up your sleeping mat and walk," and the man would obey.

But it was the sabbath and the Jews criticized Jesus. They criticized God for breaking his own Commandment, and they had to be told once again that the Son of Man was master of the sabbath.

■

They dragged themselves along, the crippled beggars, under the colonnade. The only sound was the long litany of their complaints and groaning. They waited at the edge of the pool in the hope that one day they would be able to enter the water when it began to boil. They were together the image of a humanity that survived in the expectation of a very risky salvation that was always disappointed.

The water was barren—it could neither give birth nor give rebirth. It was a long time since the sick man had been able to walk or run normally, a long time since he had been able to look at himself without feeling sick—so long that he could hardly remember. Man was created by God and placed by him in a beautiful and fertile garden. The stream watered it. The river of life made it bear fruit.

Jesus came by and asked: "Do you want to be well again?" The Son went down into the place of death. He took our infirmities onto himself. In the midst of our complaints, the promise could be heard. The Dead Sea was incapable of containing life, but it could yield a miraculous catch. The man who had been paralyzed for thirty-eight years, imprisoned by his unhappy past, was able to get up and walk. The earth was recreated. The trees were no longer bitten by frost and bore fresh fruit each month. When God gives living water, the old world ceases to be.

We are a new creation. God has made blood and water flow from the pierced side of his beloved Son, a river of life that purifies everything that it penetrates. Our life becomes green and flourishing when we are immersed in the Spirit. We have been baptized in the death and resurrection of Jesus, and we belong to the earth that he has set free. He has enabled us to cross the sea and has immersed us in the river of life. We belong to the new world. On the night of Easter, Christ will swallow up our barren works and we shall hear the cry of victory.

∎

Immerse us in your love, Lord.
Do not let us be paralyzed by our old man,
  who has been put to death by our baptism.
By your Spirit you have put abundant life into us.
May it bear fruit each day—
  fruit that will last to eternal life.

WEDNESDAY OF THE FOURTH WEEK

LIKE FATHER, LIKE SON

Isaiah 49:8–15: How could you ever say, Jerusalem: "Yahweh has abandoned me, the Lord has forgotten me"? Have you not known the immense tenderness of your God? Do not fear! Your exile is ending. You have been scattered among the nations, but you will soon be their covenant. You have been scattered, but you will come together again. Processions are already forming in the Land of the Two Rivers and beside the sea, and there are lines of your people in Upper Egypt, ready to depart.

Psalm 145 is a hymn of praise to the Lord who has done great things. God has revealed his loving kindness and his mercy in his actions.

John 5:17–30: Following the healing of the sick man at Bethesda, Jesus was at once accused of breaking the sabbath law. His defense is brief but concentrated: "My Father goes on working and so do I."

"My Father goes on working": this statement was possibly not so satisfactory as it seemed at first sight. When Jesus said that, was he not going counter to Scripture, according to which Yahweh ceased working on the seventh day? Even such a notable rabbi as Akiba had said, of course, that the Lord never ceased working, and Philo of Alexandria had tried to deal with the Greeks' insistence on an absolute and unchanging deity by explaining that, after the six days of earthly creation, God had devoted himself to divine matters. God gives life and judges on the sabbath as on other days.

"I also go on working": Jesus is claiming to carry out the functions that are God's alone. Like his Father, he makes the dead rise again and gives them life. Like his Father too, he gives life to those who listen to his word and he judges the others—even on the sabbath.

Is Jesus in competition with God? Is he breaking with the monotheism of the Jews? Not at all! It is precisely because he is in such complete communion with his Father that he is able to carry out divine functions. Each one of his actions is an act performed by the Father.

■

Like father, like son. Long before the discoveries made by psychologists and educators, the depths of family ties were well known. Every man was someone's son, and however much the adolescent might question his own model of parenthood and education, and however firmly he might, as an adult, want to reject his own past, he could not deny his origins. Like father, like son. They are tied by bonds that are stronger than those of blood. They have learned about life from each other.

"Whatever the Father does, the Son does too." A son always imitates the one who has given him life. He has learned to look at life through the eyes of the one who has initiated him into the secrets of his existence.

"The Son can do nothing by himself." From eternity he has learned to look at life as the Father looks at it. Better than anyone else, he knows the importance that the Father attaches to man's existence. The Son was there when God made life come into being from his Father's hands in the first days of creation. He was there too when God entered into a universal covenant with mankind in the days of Noah, and he learned then how to embrace all men in his outstretched arms. And when God asked Abraham to sacrifice his only son, he knew already that the Father would not refuse to hand over his only Son to renew the covenant.

Yet you can say: "The Lord has abandoned me, the Lord has forgotten me!" But have you looked long enough at God's only Son? Have you really understood that if you want to see God now you have to look at that man on his way to Jerusalem? God has not spoken any words other than those spoken by Jesus. Look at the Son, then, and you will know the Father. Look at the Son and you will learn from him what makes God live. "What is visible in the Father," Irenaeus wrote, "is the Son." You, then, should become a son of the Father and you can learn how to do that by letting yourself be initiated into the secrets of life by your elder Brother. "I tell you most solemnly, whoever listens to my words and believes in the one who sent me has eternal life."

Jesus is the first-born among many brethren (Rom 8:29). By his death, he broke down the walls making the family home a closed place. "The hour will come—in fact it is here already—when the dead will hear the voice of the Son of God and all who hear it will live."

And again: "The dead will leave their graves at the sound of his voice." The house will be opened by the breath of the Spirit, and the long line of those who feel exiled by their misery can go in. The voice of the Son is obedience: "Father, may your will be done." Jesus is born to the true state of sonship by giving his life to the only one who is able to give it back to him. The real Son is born on the cross. Jesus relies completely on the one who speaks the word that gives birth: "You are my Son; today I have become your Father" (Ps 2:7).

When you were baptized, Jesus opened the whole house. You heard the voice calling you, and, in Jesus, you replied: "May your will be done." Become, by grace, what you already are in truth. One day God will have the name inscribed in your flesh, for you bear the name of the only Son. One day he will recognize himself as he looks at you, and he will smile and say to you: "You are like me—come into my house!"

■

Blessed be your name, Lord.
You have come to our rescue
   and you have taken us out of our darkness.
Who can separate us from your love?
Who can accuse us on the day of judgment?
You are for us—who will be against us?
We bless you, Lord, who have spared us.
Your word is our source of life
   and blessing.
With it, we inherit eternal life
   and carry the name of your beloved Son.
With all those whose names are engraved in your hand,
   we praise you, God.

■

You love us, Lord, more than a mother loves her child
   and you bend over man, your creature.
Do not leave us on those days
   when we feel abandoned.
Tell us that we are dear to you
   and that you hold us in your hands.

*You are more than a mother or a father—
you are our source of life and love.*

■

*God, do not judge us
  because we are simply dust.
In your risen Son, let us experience
  your forgiveness
and in your grace give us
  eternal life.*

---

4. *The Community of the Beloved Disciple* (New York, 1979), p. 25.
5. *Genèse et structure d'un texte de Nouveau Testament* (Paris, 1981), pp. 44–46.

FROM THE THURSDAY OF THE FOURTH WEEK TO THE SATURDAY OF THE FIFTH WEEK OF LENT

The Trial of Jesus

The days preceding the great week leading up to Easter are marked by the rapid development of the crisis brought about by those who opposed Jesus. "He came to his own domain, but his own people did not accept him" (Jn 1:11). His trial began with the commencement of his ministry in Galilee. Some who met him saw him as a new prophet with the words of eternal life, but others regarded him simply as a blasphemer. For some he was a stumbling block, for others the keystone of a life based on his words. The trial of Jesus was ultimately a trial of God himself. Jesus was in fact criticized not so much for proclaiming himself God as for manifesting God in such a way.

We are invited in the liturgy to be present at the final sessions of the trial and at Jesus' defense of himself. Jesus reveals the mystery of his being, his relationship with the Father and the meaning of his ministry in those extraordinary pages of the Fourth Gospel. There is an increase in dramatic intensity up to the last word of his defense: "When you have lifted up the Son of Man, then you will know that *I am* he and that I do nothing of myself" (Jn 8:28). Before letting us participate in the final unfolding of the trial, then, the liturgy tries to answer the question that has been asked throughout the whole of Jesus' life: "Who am I?" Those who have opposed Jesus cannot surprise him because he has provoked that opposition. He has contradicted all the usual interpretations provided by the religious establishment. He has denounced the hypocrisy of the religious and political leaders. He attacked the idea of the temple being used for trade. Everything that he said and did was bound to arouse the hostility of those who counted in the religious, commercial and political establishment. During the last weeks of his life, Jesus was conscious of the knots tightening around him. As far as he could, he avoided open strife, but, when the hour came, he faced death. He was at the mercy of an unhappy trick, played on him by Judas.

Jesus knew that he was going to die violently, and he saw his death as taking place within the history of man's salvation. He was conscious of the presence of evil and of boundless cruelty as an aspect of that evil. He had to be "handed over." Being "handed over" became one of the great themes of his passion, and it was heard more and more insistently as his "hour" approached. It expressed very well what that hour meant, as seen by the one who was unable to avoid it. It meant that he had to succumb to the forces that were capable of anything and that he had no defense against them. Yes, evil was present, but it did not determine what was going to happen, nor did it triumph in the end. Jesus was convinced that his death formed a mysterious but essential part of God's plan. "No one takes my life from me," he declared. "I lay it down of my own free will" (Jn 10:18). His struggle was a real one; it became in the end an agony. His passion was certainly not just a bad dream; it was an unleashing of sin against an innocent man. But the result of the struggle was quite certain. Jesus was certain that he was the culmination of Scripture. He knew that his death was the highest point of God's work.

He was ready to go to the very end to bear witness to his conviction that his message was God's word. He recognized that one of the constant and essential elements in the history of man's salvation was the killing of the prophets. The people and their leaders had always treated those whose words went counter to their own understanding of the law of Moses in precisely that way. His death was even a kind of theft. His life had been taken from him by a form of legal murder, and the meaning that he gave to his death had been distorted. He had wanted it to be a proclamation of the good news, showing that God saves men independently of the works of the law, but it was seen as the wretched fate of a political agitator. He was obedient "even to accepting death, death on a cross" (Phil 2:8).

"When you have lifted up the Son of man, then you will know . . . " (Jn 8:28). His only defense against the accusation made against him was to go to the very end, since it was only by being totally abandoned that he was able to demonstrate what he really was—the Son who was entirely given over to life-giving love, the Son born of God.

■

The hour is approaching
when love will be victorious over death.
Keep your eyes firmly
on Jesus, the Son of Man.
Follow the trace of love
and be ready for the time
when love will ask you
to give everything
and to go to the very end
so that life will be victorious.

THURSDAY OF THE FOURTH WEEK

GOD ACCUSED
Exodus 32:7–14: Many of the nations in the Ancient Near East regarded the calf as a symbol of the deity. The god of the storm, for example, was often represented standing on a young bull, which was the image of power and fertility. It was seen, then, as supporting the deity, rather like the cherubs in the temple of Jerusalem. There was, however, obviously a danger that the image of the god and his pedestal would be confused in worship, and this in fact happened in Israel, when Jeroboam I introduced

the cult of golden calves at Dan and Bethel, with the aim of competing with Jerusalem.

Do the traditions found in Exodus 32—34 refer to this event? It has certainly been claimed that they do, but whether this is the case or not, they are undoubtedly a reflection about the breaking and the restoration of the covenant. Moses expresses his solidarity with the sinful people of Israel and, in so doing, acts as a true prophet. His intercession is based, not on the merits of the people, but on the honor of Yahweh himself and his faithfulness to his promises.

Psalm 106 is closely connected with the idea of national supplication and expresses in great detail the ways in which Israel has been unfaithful.

John 5:31–47: Jesus claims that he is the mediator of eternal life, saying that "whatever the Father does, the Son does too." But what proof can he provide? There is the evidence of John the Baptist, who had been favorably received for a time by many Jews. But the important evidence is provided not by a man, but by God. That evidence is given to men through Scripture and through the works of Jesus. Since the works of Jesus are the works of the Father, those who are able to recognize divine action are also able to recognize the real nature of Jesus' mission. What of Scripture? It proclaims the coming of the Messiah.

The Jews, however, did not accept the evidence either of Jesus' works or of Scripture. They did not have the love of God in them, so they were unable to welcome and recognize the truth. They were only seeking their own glory and they only listened to what flattered their self-esteem. Does this perhaps also apply to us?

■

"Father, I have glorified you on earth and finished the work that you gave me to do. Now it is time for you to glorify me" (Jn 17:4). The Light came into the world to illuminate anew the lives of men. People were able to see the true face of God in Jesus of Nazareth and to see God as a God of love. They were able to discover that only God could give life, since Jesus healed those who had already been marked by death. They were able to discover that only God could save them, since Jesus did not hesitate to say: "Your sins are forgiven."

How unfortunate Jesus was! He claimed that his works bore witness to him, but it was precisely those works that were rejected. Was it possible for God to eat at table with public sinners? Jesus preached a "different" God. How, then, could his works bear witness to the fact that he came "from God"?

How indeed can those who nowadays proclaim a "different" God call on God as a witness? Throughout the history of religion, the same accusation has always been made. God cannot have such a humble, ordinary face. Men can accept saints and heroes from God, but not a God of sinners and simple people. However Jesus said that his glory did not come from men: "My glory is conferred by the Father" (Jn 8:54).

"These same works of mine testify that the Father has sent me," he declared. When he was on the cross, he was an object of derision, but that was above all the work that proved the authenticity of his mission—a life totally handed over. The cross overturned the pedestals of the false gods. What were those false gods? They were the gods of the righteous, rich and satisfied men and the gods whose favors could be bought and manipulated. They were shoddy golden calves and images that had been badly shaped by their makers. They were only worth being thrown to the ground. The true God had the face of one who was mocked, unjustly condemned, rejected by human society and crucified.

"The Father who sent me bears witness to me himself." In the desert, men were tied to gods that conformed to their own desires. It was also in the desert that Moses lifted up another sign, a rod bearing a bronze serpent. It was a ridiculous and disturbing sign, but those who looked at it were saved. God too has raised up in the world the only sign in which he is recognized—a cross placed in the heart of the world—and those who look at it are saved.

■

God our Father,
 do not forget your work.
You have delivered us from sin.
 Destroy our idols—
 they enslave us.
Show us your real face—
 Jesus who died and was raised again.

FRIDAY OF THE FOURTH WEEK

TESTING GOD

Wisdom 2:1a, 12–22: In the Book of Wisdom, the fate of the righteous is contrasted with that of the ungodly, who trust in their own wisdom, reject all idea of transcendence and condemn themselves to death. The presence of righteous men is a living reproach, and they want to get rid of them as quickly as possible. If this passage is read in the light of the Fourth Gospel, two statements stand out: the good man "boasts of having God for his Father" and hopes for a divine intervention to escape from death.

Psalm 34: In this Psalm the good man thanks God for delivering him from his enemies.

John 7:1–2, 10, 25–30: "He was in the world . . . and the world did not know him. He came to his own domain and his own people did not accept him" (Jn 1:10–11). Chapters 7 and 8 of the Gospel form the central part of the so-called Book of Signs, and the dominant theme in them is the conflict between Jesus and the authorities in Israel. The threat of death is present throughout these two chapters. The symbolism is very pronounced and points in particular to the increasing blindness of the Jews. To begin with, Jesus hides in Galilee, to avoid being killed; then he goes up to Jerusalem, but does so secretly. Finally, he leaves the temple to escape from being stoned. Before leaving, however, he chooses his time and appears publicly in the temple during the Feast of Tabernacles. This appearance is the fulfillment of the prophecy of Malachi: "The Lord you are seeking will suddenly enter his temple" (Mal 3:1).

∎

Tests are very fashionable just now. Electric domestic appliances are tested, for example, to discover which perform best for the lowest cost. The technical possibilities of the latest discoveries are regularly tested. Students have to take intelligence tests and workers are tested for their adaptability. Candidates for a post are tested to their ultimate limit to measure their powers of resistance and endurance.

"Let us lie in wait for the virtuous man, since he annoys us and opposes our way of life. . . . He claims to have knowledge of God and

calls himself a son of the Lord. He is a reproof to our way of thinking
. . . and boasts of having God for his Father." For a long time, the
religious leaders of Israel drove Jesus to his ultimate limit. They
tested his powers of resistance and measured the effectiveness of his
words. They knew that he would not give way and that he would not
fall into any of their traps. But the results of the tests were clear and
could only be interpreted in one way. Jesus was dangerous, and it was
better for one man to die than the whole of the people. The chief
priests recognized that he did not fulfill all the expectations that
people had of him. They knew very well where he came from. "If this
righteous man is a son of God, then God will help him and deliver
him from his adversaries," they said. "Let us condemn him to a
shameful death, then, because he claims that someone will watch
over him." They anticipated the mocking statements made at the foot
of the cross: "He saved others and he cannot save himself. He is the
king of Israel; let him come down from the cross now and we will
believe in him" (Mt 27:42). That was the ultimate test, but Jesus did
not even scrape through. He had to die. Would God confirm the
decisions made by men? Even the disciples were not sure.

Testing God—if only he would give us some guarantees, we might
then, possibly, agree to commit ourselves. If only he would give us an
assurance that what he was urging us to do was worth investing in and
we would do what he wanted. Testing God—knowing where he came
from and where he was taking us, calculating how much he was
offering us and what we had to give ourselves, instead of just giving
ourselves freely, handing ourselves over. You think you know me and
you say you know where I come from. But you have already lost me.
No one can really understand the mystery of my being. The only test
that God will take from us is the risk of a word that gives itself and
the foolishness of a life that is committed. Love cannot be tested or
measured. We must simply accept that it exists.

It was the Feast of Tabernacles, held at harvest time. Jesus had
already submitted himself to the test. He was going to the wine-press
of the cross. Wine is only there to be poured out. But very soon love
would appear at a new wedding. The one who had been caught in a
trap set by men would be raised again by God to life.

■

God, our rock,
  denounce those who accuse us.
  They are: our unbelief, our fears,
  our certainties and our confusions.
Do not let us be caught
  in the trap of our fickleness.
Show us your love.
Continue the work you have begun in us.

SATURDAY OF THE FOURTH WEEK

IN DEFENSE OF THE STUMBLING BLOCK

Jeremiah 11:18–20: This pericope forms part of what has sometimes been called the "confessions of Jeremiah," in which the prophet recognizes God's freedom of choice when he calls men to speak in his name. The whole of Jeremiah's life bears witness to the fact that the word of God had broken into his life and made him proclaim God's law, even though he would often have preferred a quiet life.

He had fled to Anathoth, seeking refuge, but the people there wanted to kill him. V. 20 is at first sight difficult to accept, especially for sensitive readers, but it really only reflects the sufferings of the persecuted prophet who does not hide his thoughts from God. It certainly contains a reference to the *lex talionis*, but it is significant that Jeremiah does not exact punishment himself, but leaves vengeance to the Lord. Jesus, we know, goes further and prays for his enemies who persecute him.

Psalm 7 is the complaint of a persecuted individual, who asks God to deliver him from the ungodly men who are pursuing him.

John 7:40–53: On the last day of the Feast of Tabernacles, Jesus cries out in the temple: "If any man is thirsty, let him come to me. Let the man come and drink who believes in me. As Scripture says: From his breast shall flow fountains of living water." This quotation, probably from Zechariah 14, which was one of the passages traditionally read at the feast, certainly fits in with the ritual of the occasion. Water was brought from the spring of

Siloam to the temple and sprinkled on the altar of holocausts.

Jesus' words caused a division among those who heard them. Some were prepared to accept him as a prophet and as the Messiah, but others, notably the scribes, disagreed with them, insisting that the Christ could not be a Galilean. Jesus' words, then, acted like a sword. He forced men to make a decision. He did not come to judge the world. On the contrary, men were their own judges. Christ brought light into the world and men judged themselves according to whether they chose light or darkness. The Jewish leaders were crouching in the shadows throughout the whole of this time, waiting for the right time to act.

■

Some said: "He is the one," but others thought differently. "No," they said, "he doesn't fulfill the conditions." For some, Jesus was simply a stumbling block. For others, he was the cornerstone—the most important stone in the foundation of the building. Some people believed that the tree could not bear fruit and wanted it to be cut down to its roots. Others thought that the seed would grow into a huge tree in which every bird would build its nest. Jesus will always be the question asked of our faith: "Who am I for you?" or "Am I a stumbling block or am I the cornerstone of your faith?" We are always hesitating between astonishment and blasphemy. God is so very close to us—can he have such a human face?

But those for whom Jesus is a living question are lucky. They are confronted with a face, the existence of which they had not imagined. The people with whom we are forcibly confronted are often those with whom we then begin to share an intimate relationship. Someone resists us and from that time onward he really begins to exist for us. He can no longer be reduced to what I imagined him to be. In opposition or confrontation, he reveals himself to me. Faith is enriched, not by imaginary communions, but by struggles and difficult encounters. How fortunate Jacob was to be able to wrestle with God throughout the night! How lucky are those who find Jesus a stumbling block! Like Jacob, they will be marked by a wound that will not heal. They will be able to take up the stone over which they have stumbled and make it into the cornerstone of their lives.

■

Jesus caused divisions among those who heard him.
Some said: "He is the prophet."
Others declared: "The Messiah cannot come from Galilee."
  Lord, our hearts too are divided.
  Throw light on our path
  as we approach your light.
  Have mercy on us!

The leading priests were surprised and asked:
"Why have we left him in freedom?"
The guards replied:
"No man has ever spoken as he does."
  Lord, we put you on trial.
  Stir up our love
  so that we can once again be surprised
  by your tenderness.
  Have mercy on us!

Nicodemus asked: "Why should we condemn him?"
They mocked him, saying: "You have been led astray too."
  Lord, we are always seeking a compromise.
  Strengthen our faith
  so that we can become what we believe.
  Have mercy on us!

MONDAY OF THE FIFTH WEEK

JUDGMENT
Daniel 13:1–9, 15–17, 19–30, 33–62: She was very beautiful to look at and was called Susanna. She was married to a rich and faithful husband, but she was accused of adultery by two old men whose sensual appetites had not been controlled by their study of the law. According to that law, the woman was condemned to death, although she had been wrongly accused. As she was being led away, however, a very young man, Daniel, appeared. He was filled with the Spirit. The crime was reconsidered and Yahweh was seen to be the true and faithful God.

Psalm 23 is one of the most beautiful canticles in the whole Bible. The author proclaims his trust in God who will, he knows, deliver him from all evil. He prepares himself to offer God a sacrifice of thanksgiving.

John 8:1–11 (Years A and B); *8:12–20* (Year C): The story of the adulterous woman does not really belong to the Fourth Gospel. It is an independent tradition that was inserted later into the Gospel. The woman was caught in the act and, according to the law, she had to be put to death. Jesus lets the sand run silently through his fingers. He does not say that the woman's action was a good one, nor does he judge those who have brought her to him. He does, however, do what the law cannot do. He sets the woman free. He accepts her and directs her on a new way—the way of life. "Go and sin no more."

"I am the light of the world." The Jews could not accept these words of Jesus. What proof could he offer apart from his own words? A man's testimony was not enough to justify his own claim, but Jesus said that it was: "My testimony is valid." Was he not the only one who knew where he came from and where he was going? But the Jews would not accept either his testimony or his Father's, and later they would condemn the blind man to whom Jesus gave light.

■

A tree is judged by its fruit. A man's worth can be measured at the difficult moments of his life. His adversaries are closing in around him. Jesus is beginning to feel the vise tightening. His own judgment commences when he interrogates the woman who has sinned.

Look at the wretched woman standing in front of Jesus, waiting for him to ratify the sentence that has already been passed on her. She is no longer haughty and dares not raise her eyes from the ground. She has broken the law. The law can condemn her sin and can do nothing for the sinner. She is already dead. Those men standing around, undressing her with their eyes—they can only see an adulterous woman. She is reduced to the level of her sin and can no longer be allowed to live.

Look at Jesus. He denounces the judgment. He is clever enough to approach the Pharisees, not in the sphere in which they are making their attack, but in the sphere of their own behavior. "Woman, have they condemned you? Neither do I condemn you." Until he spoke no

one had spoken to her. People had only spoken about her and her sin. Now, however, someone speaks to her without naming her sin. He calls her "Woman." He does not excuse her sin. He does not behave as though she had not committed it. He simply speaks to her: "Woman."

His own trial has already begun. We cannot save the lives of others without giving up our own life. In accepting the accused woman, Jesus already places himself on the Mount of Olives. The judgment has already been pronounced. The one who sets others free will be put to death in the very act of opening the way to forgiveness and salvation.

Easter is approaching. It is the feast of judgment, since God's judgment is the victory of Easter. At Easter the past wakes up to new life and sin remains at the bottom of the tomb while we rise up to look at the future. Christ declares: "Neither do I condemn you." Do not stay there in your dust, with your eyes fixed on your own sin. God is calling you. On Golgotha judgment was already pronounced on your life forever. God has been reconciled with you, whatever your sin may have been.

■

People point their fingers at them.
They whisper about them.
They know the sins they have committed.
"Woman, neither do I condemn you."
  God, fill our hearts with mercy.

They are always lying in wait and righting wrongs,
full of contempt and perfect in fulfilling the law.
"If there is one of you who has not sinned,
let him be the first to throw a stone."
  God, denounce our hypocrisy.

Behold the man!
Nailed to the cross, hope seemed to have died.
Men had condemned hope to death
and God seemed to have forsaken it.
"Why look for the living among the dead?"
  God, reveal our future.

TUESDAY OF THE FIFTH WEEK

THE EXALTED SERVANT
Numbers 21:4b–9: The symbol of a healing god that the Jews called Nehushtan and that King Hezekiah had destroyed together with the other remains of pagan cultic practices was for a long time preserved in the temple of Jerusalem. This religious reform during Hezekiah's reign is described in 2 Kings 18. But where did this bronze serpent come from? The cult of healing gods was very widespread in the Near East and had existed since the earliest times. Aesculapius with his caduceus was, for example, worshiped by the ancient Greeks. The origins of Numbers 21 are therefore probably to be found in a cultic legend that was developed with the aim of providing a reason for the presence of the bronze serpent in the temple.

The author of Numbers 21 claims that Moses was the first to use it. He had, it would seem, made it on the instructions of Yahweh. It is therefore quite likely that the people's memory of the dangers encountered in Sinai is preserved in this story. But, whatever the case may be, changes were certainly made to the ancient tradition. The most important of these is that, whereas the bite of the "fiery serpents" in the desert was regarded as a punishment that the Hebrews had deserved because of their speaking against Yahweh and Moses, the bronze serpent was a sign of Israel's coming together again and therefore a source of their salvation by God.

Psalm 102 is fundamentally a cry for help.

John 8:21–30: Jesus knew how much the Jews hated him. He had so far succeeded in avoiding their attacks, because "his hour had not yet come." Now, however, he announces his departure for a destination where they will not be able to follow him. They have obstinately refused to recognize him as the one sent by the Father, and that has set the seal on their own destruction: "You will die in your sins."

They think that Jesus is going to commit suicide, but he insists that his death will reveal his true identity and manifest his divine state. The words "When you have lifted up the Son of Man" refer to a play on words that was widely known both in Jewish and in Hellenistic circles. They also refer to being raised socially as well as to being put to death. In raising Jesus up on the cross, the Jews were also promoting his heavenly exaltation. The words "I am" are also important (v. 28). They contain a reference to the revelation on Mount Sinai, and the meaning of their mystery is revealed in Jesus' exaltation.

■

"When you have lifted up the Son of Man, then you will know that I am he and that I do nothing of myself: what the Father has taught me is what I preach." Jesus' trial is coming to an end, and the evangelist's conclusion is that "as he was saying this, many came to believe in him." God has given his sign. Jesus has nothing more to say. He has revealed everything and the hour is approaching when he will sum everything up in a final encounter in which men will be able to recognize God's gift and his grace.

Moses interceded for the people and God told him: "Make a serpent and put it on a standard. If anyone is bitten and looks at it, he shall live." Now God is about to intervene again for his people by raising up a cross which will save those who look at it. That is the only sign that can proclaim the grace and salvation of God. We have contemplated the glory of God, but what we saw when Jesus was transfigured we have now to discover, throughout the days leading up to Easter, in the contradictions, humiliations and sufferings of Jesus in the last stage of his life on earth. All the documents have been placed in order in the file. Each of us has to decide for himself now about Jesus. We know that the serpent may be a sign of death, but it is also a sign of life.

"When you have lifted up the Son of Man, then you will know that I am he." The only sign is a cross and a face disfigured by blows and suffering. Can that reflect the glory of God? It was, after all, not simply because he wanted to identify himself with man's condition that Jesus became a slave, exposed himself to men's hatred and scorn, suffered and died. In Gethsemane, before his judges and on the cross, he was above all the "image of the unseen God" (Col 3:15).

His trial is coming to an end and we are bound to see in that tortured man—although we cannot explain how or why—that God is, in the mysterious depths of his life, like someone who kneels down to serve his disciples, that he is like a man in agony and that he is like that man who died in complete loneliness.

The hour is approaching. All that remains for Jesus to do is to gather up his life in one supreme act. When the cross has been raised up to heaven, God will save those who have not turned away from it.

■

God our Father, raise up in our lives
  the sign of your tenderness.
By the cross erected on Calvary
  make our deserts green again.
By the wood that brought death
  make us live.

WEDNESDAY OF THE FIFTH WEEK

THE SON OF ABRAHAM

Daniel 3:14–20, 91–92, 95: Written during the persecution of the Seleucid ruler Antiochus IV Epiphanes, the Book of Daniel aims to emphasize the faithfulness of the Jewish people to the true God. It does this partly by showing how insecure the empires of this world are and partly by proclaiming an eternal Kingdom entrusted to the "Son of Man," that is, to God-fearing Jews.

The book itself is enigmatic and could only be read with understanding by those who were initiated into its secrets. The history of the people is, for example, presented as taking place at the time of another persecutor, the Babylonian king Nebuchadnezzar. Daniel's three companions refuse to worship idols—one is reminded here of the altar dedicated to Zeus in the temple—and prefer to die. The king's anger represents the increasing intensity of the persecution, which reaches its peak as the martyrs resist.

John 8:31–42: "If you make my word your home . . . you will learn the truth, and the truth will make you free." According to the author of the Fourth Gospel, truth is an intimate knowledge of the reality of God, the ultimate reality. It cannot be reduced to a merely intellectual understanding. It calls for more than that—union with the one who is the truth, Jesus Christ.

Knowledge of what is authentically real sets man free and, because of his deep communion with the Father, only the Son is able to make enslaved man free. The Jews, however, reject this widening of perspectives and keep to the freedom that they think they have because they belong to Abraham's race. But, instead of imitating the patriarch's faith, they put Jesus to death, showing clearly that they were not Abraham's sons, but sons of lies.

■

A routine question at the end of any trial is put to the accused man: "Have you anything to add in your own defense?" Everything has already been said, but he has that final right to speak. For four days the liturgy presents us with Jesus' final speech in his own defense. The Gospel has been deeply concerned with Jesus' question: "Who am I for you?" Now Jesus wants to make sure that there will be no mistake about the way in which he proposes to answer that question. He accuses his hearers with the words: "If you were Abraham's children, you would do as Abraham did."

Abraham! His very name calls to mind a risky journey without paths and a faith based on an existence that finds its own way. A tree is known by its fruit, and love discovers itself in loving. The Spirit blows wherever he pleases, and the one who gives himself up to his breath can never know where he is going.

Abraham is the freedom of a heart that responds to that appeal. We should watch him as he climbs up the mountain to make his sacrifice. For us, religion is a matter of rights and obligations. For him, it was not. He went off trusting in the faithfulness of the God who would himself provide for his promise.

Abraham was also the father of faith. Although his body was already marked by death, he had a son. He experienced what he had hardly dared to hope for—a new life. Faith cannot bear fruit—it is quite uncreative—as long as we try to restrict it to laws and habits. Love can only thrive in open spaces and in desert country with unmarked paths, but we try to confine it to soulless temples.

Faith is children who sing of God's grace when the tyrant tries to silence them by throwing them into the fiery furnace. It is the hope that goes on singing when death seems to be victorious. Let us admit it—Christians who claim to have faith are often more preoccupied with sin than with grace. They have often preferred the pessimism of the world to a joyous assurance of a new future.

"The slave's place in the house is not assured. But the son's place is assured." Jesus is the legitimate child, the only true son of Abraham, because he is the only true believer. Today he accuses us: "If you were Abraham's children, you would do as Abraham did."

■

God of the promise, we praise you.
Your Son, the only righteous man,
has taken us into your home.
In him we recognize the word
that leads us to you.
We thank you for the child of the promise,
   the Son of Abraham,
because, in him, you have given yourself
   a people as numerous as the sands on the seashore
   and the stars of heaven.
He is the eldest of many brothers,
   and through him we are a race of believers.
That is why, together with all who follow your Christ,
we set off on the way
   where the shadow of the cross is already outlined
and, as we wait to sing the hymn of victory,
we stand before you as your beloved sons.

THURSDAY OF THE FIFTH WEEK

A COVENANT OF LIFE
Genesis 17:3–9: Abram, "the father is raised up," became Abraham, "the father of a multitude." According to the priestly tradition, this very artificial change of name was connected with the offer of the covenant. That covenant resulted not only in the giving of land, but also in the

establishment of a new relationship with God. Yahweh was, from that time onward, to be the God of Abraham and his descendants. There were to be no limits to the validity of God's promise, and it was also to include all the people of the earth. It is surely of great significance that the history of the patriarch and his descendants began with a blessing that mankind was right to accept.

Psalm 103 celebrates the great deeds of Yahweh, beginning with his convenant with the father of all believers.

John 8:51–59: The tone of Chapters 7 and 8 of the Gospel of John is polemical. The descendants of Abraham pick up stones to throw at Jesus, and he, after having come in secret to Jerusalem, now leaves the forecourt of the temple and slips away into the country.

Before he goes, however, he sounds a very disturbing note: "I tell you most solemnly, before Abraham was, *I am.*" He does not claim to be greater than Abraham, but he does situate himself in a different order of being. The Son is eternal (he dwells forever in the house; "his place is assured"—v. 35) and "Abraham rejoiced to think that he would see his day." According to a rabbinical exegesis of Genesis 24:1 ("Abraham was an old man well on in years") this may be an allusion to a prophetic vision of the future.

■

"Here now is my covenant with you: you shall become the father of a multitude of nations." The covenant is linked with fertility. In Abraham, all the nations of the earth were to be blessed. This link between faith and fertility is something that we find difficult to understand. We usually associate faith with such concepts as light and truth, as opposed to darkness and ignorance. At the same time, it is important to recognize that our faith is not affirmed in a confrontation with ignorance or error, but rather when we are faced with death. The sign of the covenant given to Abraham was not a light that eliminated all hesitations, but rather a son who was born when he was an old man. Abraham was confronted with death, experienced in its most elemental form. He had no child and heir and he had no longer any element of life in his old body, which was already marked by death. Yet he relied on the word of God and believed, despite all experience to the contrary, that he would be able to transmit life although he had not been fruitful for so long.

He was to be a blessing for all people. Faith is a struggle for life. It is a confrontation with death in its most everyday and injurious form. At such times, we say: "Life is useless. What is the use of trying? There is nothing I can do."

Jesus is the true descendant of Abraham because, in the struggle between death and life, his faith discloses unbelievable hope to everyone. He opens a breach in the walls of distress that imprison us and life flows in. "Your father Abraham rejoiced to think that he would see my day." Jesus applied the name of Creator to himself and in so doing simply identified himself with life. He brought a new element into the age-old struggle between death and life. He was to be a blessing for all people, because, in him, life was victorious and all men would be able to hope in life.

■

God of Abraham and Jesus Christ,
  God of the promise,
  make our hearts fertile.
Let your Spirit renew our lives
  until the day when your Son's victory
  is revealed to all men.

Because he still hoped,
  our father Abraham did not die.
Whoever places his trust in Christ
  will go on living.
God of the living,
  you are blessed in your risen Son.
In him, our future
  is shining like a light
  in which the world without end
  is illuminated.

FRIDAY OF THE FIFTH WEEK

SONSHIP

Jeremiah 20:10–13: "Sing to the Lord, for he has delivered the needy from the hands of evil men." This is the last "confession" of the prophet, who feels bound to recognize the great power of God's word. Although he may be treated badly, he has to speak. But he also knows that Yahweh will never forsake the faithful man. He therefore entrusts his cause to God.

Psalm 18 is a song, composite in its construction, of trust in God.

John 10:31–42: It was the Feast of Dedication. More explicitly than ever, the leading Jews were calling on Jesus to describe the nature of his mission: "If you are the Christ, tell us plainly." The context in which this statement is placed shows that the author of the Fourth Gospel believed that Jesus' trial lasted throughout his active life. In the Synoptic Gospels, this kind of demand only occurs during the trial in the presence of the Sanhedrin.

Jesus' reply is simply: "The Father and I are one." He says quite clearly, then, that he is the Son of God, and the Jews are conscious of the difference between his claim to be the Messiah and the title "Son of God" that is given to the Israelites so often in Scripture. They at once accuse him of blasphemy.

He leaves Jerusalem and goes beyond the Jordan, to the place where John had been baptizing. On the eve of the most important stage in his ministry, he appeals to the Baptist.

■

"We are not stoning you for doing a good work, but for blasphemy; you are only a man and you claim to be God." This is the charge that they bring against him, but the accused man's only reply is his actions. His only testimony is his life. The only way in which the truth about him can be known in the action that is brought against him is by looking at his life.

Jesus never provided a long account of his incarnation—he lived it. Later on, the Church proclaimed that he was divine. This profession of faith was made when Christians had prayed, reflected and listened together for long enough to be able to name the mystery revealed in the life of Christ. But the names which made the wealth of their encounter explicit at the same time impoverished it. We are not saved by confessing a title given to Jesus. We are saved because of our personal relationship in faith with him. The title is only there to help us to enter into that relationship.

That is what Jesus himself says. "At least believe in the work I do—it speaks of me." All his discourses in the long run say only one thing, and that is what the disciples themselves experienced both before and after Easter—that God does not forsake the righteous man. The only way of coming to the good news of salvation is through the beloved Son of the Father. When we confess that Jesus is that Son, we are saying that his person is the guarantee that God has given to the world. Christ is therefore in a unique and total sense "of God." He is the Son because he was everything for the Father—his love, his will, his life, his being, his joy, his Kingdom, his glory and his name.

But how could this sonship be so essential if it only concerned Jesus? It would be no more than a title of glory. No, our confession of faith goes further than this. We confess not only that Jesus is "of God," but also that he is the "eldest of many brothers." Through Jesus and in him, we are born of God. We have become "naturalized" and deified—the natural sons of God. Jesus' sonship was expressed supremely when he spoke from the cross, opened wide his arms and embraced all men with the words: "It is accomplished." On that day he became the Son and we were given birth by God and entered into a new life.

■

God our Father,
your name has entered our history
and we believe that Jesus' works
   will reveal your true face.
We bless you.
When he breaks the bread,
   we know that you are giving yourself
   without counting the cost.

When he is stretched out on the cross,
  we learn that you take our dying on yourself.
When you raise him again,
  we are amazed at our own victory.
We thank you
  for the life and death of your Son
  now and forever and ever.

SATURDAY OF THE FIFTH WEEK

A COVENANT MADE IN BLOOD

Ezekiel 37:21–28: The prophet makes a symbolic gesture—he takes two pieces of wood and brings them close to each other so that they form a single piece. The first piece has the name Judah written on it and the second Ephraim. This spells out a message of hope—that one day those who are exiled in Babylonia will find their country united again (vv. 15–20).

Yahweh will reign over Israel and will conclude a covenant of peace with his people. The temple will be there in the center of the country and a shepherd like David will lead those who believe in the Lord.

The canticle of Jeremiah 31 forms part of what has very suitably been called "The Book of Consolation." In it, the prophet proclaims the restoration of Israel in language that speaks of the end of the country's religious divisions.

John 11:45–57: The new covenant was to be concluded and Israel was to be reunited. Was that to be done in the blood of Christ? Jesus was, according to the Gospel of John, the shepherd proclaimed by the prophet Ezekiel (Ez 34). He knew his sheep, saved them from the wolf, led them back to the fold when they were scattered, and finally laid down his life for them.

The leaders of the Jews feared for the future of their institutions, and Jesus died to give life to men. He bore supreme witness, and the veil of the temple was torn in two from top to bottom.

■

Everything had already been put at stake. "You don't seem to have grasped the situation at all; you fail to see that it is better for one man to die for the people." The chief priests had given their orders, and anyone who knew where Jesus was had to denounce him so that he could be arrested.

"I am going to take the sons of Israel from . . . where they have gone. . . . They will no longer defile themselves with . . . all their sins. I shall rescue them . . . . I shall cleanse them; they shall be my people and I will be their God." God so loved the world that he gave his own Son. We have taken ourselves into exile and do not know what we have done. In the garden of Eden we left the place where God put us, and he looked for us, but could not find us. God searched throughout the world to find his beloved son—man who had left him. Now at last he has found him: *Ecce homo!* Behold the man!

God had no intention of placing us back in the paradise where we began. He never acts as though we had been righteous. He did not want to take us to an artificially pure country or to repatriate us to a country that had an illusory innocence. On the contrary, God himself became expatriated in order to re-establish communion with us. "I will settle my sanctuary among them forever. I shall make my home among them. I will be their God and they shall be my people and the nations will learn that I am the Lord, the sanctifier of Israel, when my sanctuary is with them forever."

In order to find man again and renew with him the covenant that had been broken again and again, God came to us. We did not make ourselves righteous. We were made righteous by God himself. In an eternal gesture of giving grace, God forgave us and proclaimed our salvation. We were not taken back to a sinless country, but God transfigured our earth and our very fault became his dwelling place. As we sing on Easter night: "Happy fault!"

Ecce homo! Behold the man! God finds man again and restores the covenant. But salvation is not achieved by waving a magic wand, and God's renewal of his marriage with mankind is not a romantic happy ending after a period of unfaithfulness. The cost of renewing the covenant is a man condemned and already dead. Salvation could never be simply wiping out a stain. It had to be offered as a sacrifice by God—his blood "poured out for many." The covenant had to be sealed in blood. "There will be only one shepherd—the good shepherd who lays down his life for his sheep." Jesus died to "gather together in unity the scattered children of God."

"My sanctuary will be with them forever." The sign of the covenant is a cross raised up and a cup passed from one person to another so that everyone may live from the same blood shed for many.

∎

Who is like you, Lord?
You always want to forgive us.
You have concluded a covenant with us
    sealed in the life offered by your Son.
Make us your dwelling place among men,
    so that everyone will know
    that you are our God.

FROM THE MONDAY TO THE WEDNESDAY OF HOLY WEEK

Farewell to God
Before dying, Jesus wanted to celebrate the passover meal with his disciples. He knew that his hour had come and all that he said was a reflection of that certain knowledge. Everything had been accomplished, and Mary was able to spread the perfumed ointment on the body of the condemned man. Jesus knew that his end was near because of Judas' behavior. It was time for the Kingdom to be founded. The disciple was about to challenge the Master and call on him to manifest himself.

He remained in complete control of everything he said and did, but he was conscious of his approaching death and strove to give meaning to it. During the passover meal, he handed over his body and blood in the form of bread and wine. In the knowledge that he was going to be offered up to death so that the Kingdom of God might be established, he anticipated the time when he would be put on trial by men. His sharing of the bread and wine was a prophetic act, and it was effective in the lives of those who received it in faith, as it is effective now in the renewal of the Last Supper. "This is my body." Jesus' body is that piece of bread that is shared. His body is given only as a promise of his death and as a sign of his words that he kept to the end: "A man can have no greater love than to lay down his life for his friends"(Jn15:13).

Ever since the Last Supper, Christians have reflected about the importance of that encounter, at the same table, with the one who hands over and is handed over, in which the meaning of the events that took place in Jesus' experience is to be found. His words and actions are prophetic. They are a proclamation of what is bound to happen. On the next day, when Jesus is on the cross, the words spoken during the Last Supper will be fulfilled, and from then onward, that is, from the afternoon of the first Good Friday, they will continue to be effective. When two or three are gathered together in Christ's name to share the bread while they wait for the Lord's coming, they will pass together with him from death to life.

∎

The hour when the Son of Man
   will invite his Church
   to share with him the cup
   of bitterness and hope
   is approaching.
Let us, then, follow Christ.
And if the memory of our faults
makes us lose heart,
   let us remember that the Son of God
   so loved sinners at the hour of his passion
   that he handed over his life for them.

MONDAY OF HOLY WEEK

THE WHEAT GRAIN IN THE GROUND
Isaiah 42:1–7: During Holy Week we are invited to read again four passages of Second Isaiah. They are very impressive, but full of difficulties.

Who is the "servant" to whom these songs refer? Is it Israel or is it an individual? Does the author want us to think of the people as a whole or of a small group within the nation? Is it one person or several? Israel may well have been called the "servant," but the word can also be applied to the Persian King Cyrus or even to the prophet himself.

It would not be wrong to assume that Cyrus is the servant of the first poem at least. Yahweh has filled him with his "breath" in order to restore Israel's rights since the nation's conquest by Nebuchadnezzar. The Babylonian king had in fact only been carrying out the punishment that Yahweh had wanted his unfaithful people to suffer when he ordered them to go into exile. Then, when the Persian king Cyrus proclaimed the end of that exile in 538 B.C., he was acting as Yahweh's servant by setting the prisoners free. Nebuchadnezzar had treated the Israelites savagely, whereas Cyrus had an impact even on the most distant nations and was a father to Israel. He did not "break the crushed reed" or "quench the wavering flame." His rising star included the promises of the rainbow of the covenant (Gn 9), and it was clearly the intention of the Creator of heaven and earth that he should gather together the many nations and make a light shine on the exiles.

The songs of the servant of Yahweh include one great promise—that the people will be set free. This is perhaps why each generation of believers have applied it to themselves and have interpreted the songs as pointing to the coming of the Messiah. The Church has often regarded the servant as the image of Christ who, through his death and resurrection, made the light of a new morning shine on the world.

Psalm 27 is a song of trust in the Lord. The psalmist is sure that he will see "the goodness of Yahweh in the land of the living."

John 12:1–11: If the wheat grain falls to the ground and dies, it will yield a rich harvest. Jesus called Lazarus to life and in so doing came closer to his own death. Six days before the Jewish feast of Passover, he went to Bethany again and took part in a dinner in his own honor. During the course of this meal, Mary anointed his feet with a very expensive perfume. Her action caused general annoyance, since the money that had been spent on the perfume could have been used for the poor. Jesus, however, who had been impressed by the significance of the woman's action, silenced the critics. The Jews' penal law in any case did not allow those who had been condemned to death to be embalmed. Jesus also realized that many of those who were closest to him would be carried along with the wave of feeling and forsake him, so that he would suffer and die alone, without a friend to comfort him. This made Mary's action even more meaningful.

The evangelist brings together the episode of the anointing and the words of Jesus about the grain of wheat that dies. Jesus was anointed as a dead body is covered with oil. He had already been marked out as the servant of God by the water of baptism. Now Mary's anointing marks him out for death.

■

The time has come for Jesus to be buried. Six days before Passover, he returns to Bethany. He stays for the last time with his friends there. The final crisis is already taking shape. Mary has been keeping the perfume for the day when the Lord would be buried and now she comes to anoint his feet with it.

Jesus is already marked out for death, as a lamb is marked for the slaughter house. Judgment has already been passed, and now it is only a question of time. Jesus has been condemned, but he has a few days' respite. There will be no appeal—he is already dead. "Leave her alone," he says—let her anoint me. He is on his way to the tomb and does not call out. His voice is not heard in the public place. He is silent in the presence of those who accuse him. It is the time of the seed buried in the ground. The hour of the wheat grain is an hour of silence.

It is the hour of burial—the hour of Bethany, where Lazarus, whom Jesus raised from the dead, still lives. Already marked by imminent death, Jesus relies on the man who will deliver him from the tomb. Lazarus, who came out alive from the place of the dead, bears witness to the fact that the Lord of life will not remain a prisoner in a sealed tomb. It is the hour of hope—the earth will open and the seed will rise to new life. The lamb that has been sacrificed will be the paschal Lamb who takes away the sin of the world. "I have endowed him with my spirit that he may bring true justice to the nations." The one whom men have already condemned will proclaim the forgiveness of the Father of mercy. It is the hour of burial, but the one who has already been embalmed will be anointed with the Spirit. The way to Calvary is already illuminated by the light of Easter.

Christians, you have already been marked by your baptism. God has pronounced his judgment on you and has called you in his justice. The present hour is often enough an hour of condemnation for us, but we can follow Jesus on his way to Jerusalem and say: Through our baptism we have already entered a world set free from slavery. We have been consecrated by the Spirit, and although our work is not good, we are already engaged in building up a world that is marked by the resurrection. The hour of Bethany is the hour in which we are already aware of the perfume of Easter.

∎

Lord our God,
 your Son did not break the crushed reed,
 but took our wretchedness on himself
 and lifted us up to you.
Do not quench the flickering flame,
 but revive in us the fire of your Spirit.
We would like to breathe already
 the breath of eternal life.

TUESDAY OF HOLY WEEK

THE SERVANT GOES

Isaiah 49:1–6: Let all the nations of the world listen, because the Lord God has remembered the name of Israel. He has told the people: "You are my servant, Israel, and it is for you that I shall make my splendor manifest." The people, discouraged, thought that they had exhausted themselves in vain, but Yahweh held them hidden in his hand in order to send them out at a suitable time armed with his word. And that word was as fearful as an arrow fired from a bow. To the great astonishment of the cities and the islands, the Lord intended to set his people free and bring together all those who had been scattered in the four quarters of the earth. In that way, Israel would be able to bear witness to the salvation of their God in the presence of all the nations.

Psalm 71: The psalmist calls on the Lord here to rescue him from the hands of evil men.

John 13:21–33, 36–38: During the Lord's Supper, Judas is revealed as a traitor. He goes out into the night. The choice is made—Judas prefers darkness to light because his works are evil. After he has gone, only those who have welcomed Jesus remain at table. They will be given the opportunity to become "children of God."

Jesus' passion has already begun. He has already offered himself freely and has asked the Father to complete his work of love through his death (Jn 12:28). The Father will in turn glorify his Son. Jesus goes, but his disciples, like the Jews, cannot follow him now. He is going on a journey of voluntary death, and they are not yet ready for that. Before the cock crows, Peter will have denied him.

■

"Scripture must be fulfilled." The end is near. Jesus knows that he is going to his death, and he attempts to give meaning to what is about to happen. His life will be taken from him, but that is because he had always given it freely from the very beginning. He breaks the bread, an age-old action, but performed now in a meal celebrating man's emancipation from slavery. "This is my flesh, delivered for you." Jesus has decided to go to the very end, and in this action he delivers himself entirely into the hands of men.

For three days the liturgy invites us to enter into the mystery of Easter by presenting us with three passages from the prophet Isaiah. These prophetic words provide us with an image of the servant whose mission was to restore the covenant between God and man. Indeed, that servant was the covenant. This is clear from the first of the three songs. He was chosen by God and lived in humility, serving men. The second song of the servant shows him as predestined for that mission. By his words he will not only gather together the scattered people of Israel, but will also be a light for the nations. In this way the liturgy shows us both aspects of the drama that is unfolding. Even when it speaks of treachery and denial, it is also revealing the hidden face of the events that are taking place. The one who goes, forgotten by everyone and abandoned even by his friends, is also the one whom the prophet announced.

"Scripture must be fulfilled." Jesus carried out the message of the prophets, making it a reality in his life. He encountered great opposition to his prophetic acts. The scribes accused him of blasphemy when he forgave the paralyzed man's sins, and from that time onward he lived and worked in an environment of ever increasing tension. Many of his words and actions went against the law of the Jews, and he knew that he risked being put to death. But was not death inherent in the prophetic ministry? Jesus certainly succeeded in giving meaning to everything that had happened and was going to happen. He presented himself as the Bridegroom who would one day be taken away from his friends. He made it clear that he would have to drink the cup of bitterness, and he called himself the son of the owner of the vineyard who was seized and killed by those who wanted his inheritance. With astonishing freedom, Jesus gave new meaning to Scripture, mingling his own destiny with that of the servant of Yahweh. He was certain that he was, as it were, at the summit of Scripture, and this ensured that his imminent death would be at the summit of God's work. The way of the cross was also the way of life, and the man who was to be annihilated by darkness was also the "light of the nations."

■

Lord our God,
  the hour has come
  when your Son must drink the cup.
Night is approaching
  and with it the darkness of our treachery.
For your beloved Son
  let the day of your glory appear,
  and let us pass with him
  over to the new covenant.

WEDNESDAY OF HOLY WEEK

THE HOUR IS NEAR
Isaiah 50:4–9a: The Lord, who has given his spirit to his servant and

prophet, now entrusts him with his plans so that he can strengthen Israel. But the people's liberation is slow in coming, and Second Isaiah is not believed and even persecuted. Unlike some of his predecessors, however, such as Jeremiah, he does not shrink from the thankless ministry that has been entrusted to him. He does not hide his face from blows and spittle, but turns his back on those who strike him and his cheek to those who tear at his beard. His strength is derived from his certain knowledge of God's help. He does not fear the judge's sentence, and he knows that Yahweh will make the truth of his oracles appear by hastening the day of liberation.

Psalm 69 is an individual lament. The Church interprets it in the light of the events of the passion.

Matthew 26:14–25: Jesus spent the last days of his life in the country close to the desert, in hiding. The Jewish authorities, having decided to have him put to death, had given orders that anyone who knew of his whereabouts should inform them (Jn 11:57). Judas was prepared to play the part of informer. He came to an agreement with the priests and waited for a suitable occasion to hand Jesus over. He acted during the period of Passover, a time when Jerusalem would be so full of pilgrims that such an event would probably escape notice. Matthew adds the words "for thirty pieces of silver." This was the price of a slave, the contemptible wage that Israel had once paid to get rid of God (Zec 11:12).

During the meal, Jesus disclosed that the traitor was among the guests at table. He was deeply grieved by his friend's treachery: "Alas for that man by whom the Son of man is betrayed!" The righteous man was to be delivered into the hands of ungodly men, who would do to him whatever they wanted. It was the hour of the prince of darkness—but God would not let his friend see corruption (Ps 16:10).

■

Night was already descending on the city and from time to time the Twelve, who had just gathered around the table in the upper room with Jesus, were conscious of the noise of the pilgrims outside. There was a festival mood everywhere, a pervading spirit of liberation, composed of memories brought to life by the renewal of the Passover. Judas remained silent, because he was not yet fully aware of having sold for the price of a slave that one who was to set his people free from slavery. "What you are going to do, do quickly" (Jn 13:28).

Jesus did not turn away. He offered his back to those who struck him and did not protect his face from those who insulted him and spat at him. The meal had begun, and everyone present sensed that the hour was at hand.

The sign of the inauguration of the new world was not, however, to be a plot to overthrow the established order. New wine was not to be put into old wineskins. God did not intend to set up his Kingdom with power. His sign was the mockery and dishonor of a gallows. He wanted to set his people free by being nailed to a cross. The sign of his new world was blood poured out and bearing witness to a life handed over unhesitatingly. The sign of the last days was bread broken—leaven for a world united in a hitherto unknown communion. The sign of man's salvation was a teacher kneeling down in front of his disciples washing their feet. Love and the covenant together formed an act of faith in which everyone is lost in giving himself to his fellow men.

The new wine is poured out, and it smells of God's new order. Unhappy Judas, who does not understand, thinking that it is possible to mend an old garment with new material. The cup of the new covenant is already being passed from one person to the next. The new world has been born. It is based on the love of the servant. The city is shrouded in darkness and an armed band is gathering in the forecourt of the temple. "The Master says: My time is near."

■

We praise you for your glory, God our Father,
and with all your Church we proclaim
   that Jesus Christ, your Son, is Lord.
He came from you, full of grace and truth,
but he did not try to exert his right
   to be treated as your equal.
He assumed the condition of a servant
and became like men in all things.
   He abased himself and became obedient,
   going so far as to accept death on a cross.
That is why you defended him
and raised him high above everyone,
giving him the name

that transcends all names—
so that every being should kneel down
and every tongue should bless
the one whom you have sent.

CELEBRATING EASTER

A NEW SONG
In the morning, as the sun is rising
   to herald the new day,
   we bless you, God our Creator,
   for making life spring up in the pit of darkness.

In the spring, when the sun sings
   to make our earth flourish,
   we bless you, Father of Jesus Christ,
   for making the stones of our tombs burst open.

And when evening falls
   over our endless ways,
   we bless you, our hidden God,
   for your Son Jesus, who has left us for you.

Like the grain of wheat hidden in the ground
   until springtime returns,
   our life is hidden in Christ
   until he comes again.

And like bread broken and shared in the evening
   at the end of a way that will be resumed on the next day,
   we know in faith that he who gives us his body
   has been raised from the dead.

Why should we mourn because he has died?

He is going on before us,
   and day will dawn and proclaim hope
   and our earth will soon yield its fruit.

Father of Jesus Christ,
   with all those who believe without ever having seen,
   with all those who look without tiring
   and with all the poor and humble in heart,

we believe
   that Jesus lives, that he is a source of life,
   that his body is the bread that gathers us together in you,
   that his blood is the wine of a secret feast.

Through the Spirit of your Son,
   we ask you:
   let your children continue to believe,

let us bear witness to the hidden mystery
   that you revealed one day in the silence of the morning,
   when you took your first-born Son by the hand
   so that he would be the hope of all
   who die and are reborn in him.

Give thanks to the God of life, alleluia, alleluia!
In the morning the stone is rolled away from the tomb, alleluia, alleluia!
Christ has come out of the tomb, alleluia, alleluia!

On the morning of the first day of the week, alleluia, alleluia!
Jesus comes in the midst of his Church, alleluia, alleluia!
His hands and his side show life, alleluia, alleluia!

He gives us peace and the Holy Spirit, alleluia, alleluia!
He sends us out to proclaim peace, alleluia, alleluia!
Blessed are those who believe without having seen, alleluia!

Death is conquered by life, alleluia, alleluia!
Your life is hidden in Christ, alleluia, alleluia!
Lift up your hearts on high, alleluia, alleluia!

He who was dead is living forever, alleluia, alleluia!
He has risen in glory from the tomb, alleluia, alleluia!
Today is a day of infinite peace, alleluia, alleluia!

Tell all those who are afraid, alleluia, alleluia!
He is going before you on the way, alleluia, alleluia!
He is preparing a table for you, alleluia, alleluia!

Bless God when you share your bread, alleluia, alleluia!
Thank God when you lift up your cup, alleluia, alleluia!
This is the body and blood of the beloved Son, alleluia, alleluia!

May death pass away and grace come, alleluia, alleluia!
May peace rise up in our times, alleluia, alleluia!
Give thanks to the God of life, alleluia, alleluia!

Blessed are you, Lord our God, alleluia, alleluia!
May heaven and earth praise you, alleluia, alleluia!
Hosanna for a feast without end, alleluia, alleluia!

We give you thanks, hidden God, our Father,
  for Jesus Christ, your Son, your Word and your Face.
He is the way that leads to you
  and all truth dwells in him.
No one can know your name
  if he does not dwell in him.

We proclaim him.
  Through your Son, life is made manifest.
  In him, the hope of an infinite peace
  is reborn for all men.
In the communion of heaven and earth,
  we bless you, living God.

THE WEEKDAY LECTIONARY FOR EASTERTIDE

The fifty days of Easter form one single feast. Athanasius called this time one "great Sunday" celebrated in joy and exultation. The first week, the octave of Easter, nonetheless occupies a special position in the liturgy of this period. This is clear from the fact that, as in the case of Holy Week, no other celebration is permitted to take place during it. Why should each of these days, which are still bathed in the light of the paschal candle, not, then, be marked by special solemnity, with the constantly repeated alleluia forming a simple but very impressive hymn of praise?

Beginning with the second week of Eastertide, the Gospel of Saint John is read every day. This is not, however, a strictly continuous reading. It only becomes more or less continuous from the Thursday of the fourth week onward. Some of these readings are worth noting and choosing in particular, especially if it is not possible to follow the readings every day: the conversation with Nicodemus (Monday, Tuesday and Wednesday of the second week), the account of the miracle of the loaves and the discourse on the bread of life (from the second Friday to the third Saturday and, among these, especially the second Friday, the third Tuesday, the third Friday and the third Saturday) and the discourse following the Last Supper (from the fourth Thursday onward and especially the fourth Friday and Saturday, the fifth Tuesday, Wednesday and Friday, the sixth Wednesday, Thursday and Friday and finally from Tuesday to Thursday of the seventh week, when the high-priestly prayer of Jesus is read).

There is also an almost continuous reading of the Acts of the Apostles during Eastertide. It is not at all easy to make a selection from the episodes presented in this narrative, and one suggestion that might be worth following, if it is not possible to hear or read this first reading of the liturgy every day, is to read the passages that have been omitted on those days when the liturgy is celebrated. Surely it would be wrong not to take advantage of this opportunity to read each year the account of the early Church's apostolic activity from beginning to end?

There has no longer been an octave of Pentecost since the reform of the liturgy. This is, of course, also because Pentecost is regarded as the closing feast of the fifty days of Easter. The week preceding Pentecost, however, is strongly marked, more perhaps in the prayers than in the choice of readings, by an expectation of the Spirit. We have made a number of suggestions for prayer based on this expectation, so that these last days anticipating the coming of the Holy Spirit can be celebrated as fervently as possible.

The weekday liturgy from mid-Lent onward, then, is inspired above all by readings from and meditations on the Gospel of John. Our commentary aims principally at fundamental meditation in which prominence is given to themes that are essential in the life of faith. These include the sacraments of baptism and the Eucharist, the presence and absence of Christ, the Spirit and the Church.

Finally, we have given preference during the octave of Easter to a meditation on the resurrection of Christ.

THE ACTS OF THE APOSTLES

The Acts of the Apostles has been read in the liturgy of the Eucharist during paschal time since the fourth century at the latest. In addition to inspiring and guiding the lives of the first Christians, Acts has also encouraged those who have at every period of the Church's history believed in the ideal of the apostolic life as reflected in the early Christian community.

The book consists of two parts that are easy to distinguish. The first part (Chapters 1 to 15:35) is composed of a number of elements in juxtaposition. These are Semitic in flavor and consciously archaic in thought. The second part (Chapters 15:36 to 28) is better organized and consists of memories carefully preserved by the churches from the time when they were founded and of important aspects of their history. The author also includes personal memories in this second part.

The author was a historian who believed. He was therefore not content simply to report events. He interpreted them in the light of his faith. He saw the history of mankind as a history of salvation—a history of the different stages in the covenant between God and men. The first stage, that of the promise, was the Old Testament. Jesus' incarnation marked the beginning of the time of fulfillment. The resurrection was a pause in the fulfillment of God's promise, which, because it applies to all nations and people, cannot be completed until God has restored all things to Christ. The Church therefore opens a time and a space in which the history of salvation continues, but in which, from the first day of its history, the Word is proclaimed to all people (Acts 2:9–11). In that context, it is hardly surprising that openness to the pagans (Chapter 15) is the main theme of the book and that it is with Paul's arrival in Rome that this is achieved.

The history of man's salvation is the work of the Spirit. Luke had already emphasized that in his Gospel. Jesus, who was conceived by the Holy Spirit, was the only one who could act with the power of the Spirit. The Acts of the Apostles describes the dynamism of the Church and thus bears witness to the power of God's Spirit.

A reading of Acts, then, especially during Eastertide, can provide us with a real theology of the Church. We should be less concerned with wonder and astonishment about the miracles described or with following closely in the footsteps of the first Apostles and more alert to the work of the Holy Spirit everywhere in the events described. He is the leading actor in the Church.

He who raised Jesus from the dead and gave life to his body continues to animate the Church through the words and acts of the Apostles. It is not possible to read Acts without feeling urged to work faithfully for a Church that is always young.

THE OCTAVE OF EASTER

THE OTHER PROCESS
Jesus of Nazareth was dead. A man who was unique and without parallel had been crucified. Was his cause made ineffective because of his death? It should not be forgotten that there were two processes at work here. On the one hand, there was the human process and, on the other, the process initiated by God. God himself had taken sides. Wishing to vouchsafe for the authenticity of Jesus' life, God had, as it were, signed the pages written by it: "The one you crucified, whom God raised from the dead" (Acts 4:10). Christian faith is here presented as a solemn judgment—the judgment of God.

Something had happened between Easter and the birth of the Church. Something had changed during those fifty days. The disciples, who had been deeply disturbed and who had scattered in fear, had become ardent defenders of Christ's cause. It was simply not possible for them to remain silent. They had an experience that revealed to them the meaning of Christ's death on the cross: God's Christ had to suffer (see Acts 3:18). Christ's death was not a defeat, but a necessity.

Jesus' resurrection is a mystery. It did not form part of the visible world of the senses. It was God's action and is only accessible to us through faith or the signs of faith. The empty tomb, the post-resurrection appearances and all the other signs and events are traces of that mystery left in our human history, but they have to be interpreted if their profound meaning is to be known. It is not just on the basis of an empty tomb that the man who had died should have been proclaimed the Son of God and Lord.

There is a need for interpretation. This interpretation has sometimes been made deductively, from the events themselves: God, in other words, raised

Jesus from the dead. But what use is this, if it is based on nothing other than logic? In other cases, the risen Christ has been proclaimed and a message is derived from the events. Sometimes the facts are interpreted by referring them back to human existence and asking what they mean for us today. All this has led to the development of a paschal theology and a quest to discover the saving significance of Christ's death and resurrection.

The central element of the Christian confession of Easter is the affirmation of Christ's resurrection. When we say that Jesus has risen from the dead, we are affirming an eschatological event, that is, an event that is related to the "end of time." What we are saying, in other words, is that Jesus' resurrection placed him in his function as the Savior and Judge of human history.

God's actions are always signs. Faith is always concerned with the meaning of the events in Jesus' life, just as we can always and only understand the reality of Jesus Christ through a way of speaking or an interpretation. Our recognition of Jesus as Lord comes to us from a group of men who experienced a new relationship with him. That relationship was only possible because something had happened. It was, then, an experience combining an event and its interpretation: "We have seen and we bear witness, since Scripture had to be fulfilled."

Christ's resurrection is of the order of faith. As an act of God, it inaugurates a time of promise. Like faith itself, it can only be expressed symbolically. When we say that Jesus was raised from the dead, we have to resort to a very simple image and speak of a man lying down asleep waking up and rising. The two Greek verbs translated into English as "raise" or "rise up" mean primarily only that: to be awakened and to stand up. Christ, then, was put on his feet again by the power of God. But this basic image is obviously not sufficient, and the New Testament authors added others with new symbolic content, such as glory and exaltation. Resurrection, then, is a communication of power and authority. Christ was, from the time of his resurrection onward, "Lord."

But there is still more to be said about Jesus' resurrection. It was an event which was first and foremost concerned with Jesus' own personal destiny, but which was at the same time a mystery of salvation, in other words, an event containing within itself the essence of the salvation of the whole of mankind. The power that God brought into play to raise his Son from the dead will be applied by him to those who form one body with Christ.

Our life does not lead simply to death. Jesus is our pledge and our source of eternal birth. Christ has achieved for us a victory of life that does not point toward an illusory future but is above all a victory today. The Passover that we celebrate with Christ enables us to pass even now into that true life that is communion with God. Since Easter morning we have been living in the order of the resurrection. "In that everyday existence which we receive from your grace, eternal life has already begun" (Preface for the Sixth Sunday of Ordinary Time).

Throughout this week, the Octave of Easter, the liturgy proclaims the same message with many variations: "The old world has passed away and a new world is already born."

MONDAY IN THE OCTAVE OF EASTER

DRAMATIC TURN OF EVENTS
Acts 2:14, 22b–32: "Men of Judea and all you who live in Jerusalem, make no mistake about this. Jesus the Nazarene . . . was crucified by men outside the law, but God raised him to life . . . and all of us are witnesses to that." The same sacrificial rites and the same prayers may continue in Jerusalem, but nothing will ever be the same again. A community of people living from the Holy Spirit has come into existence. They will proclaim words of grace and reconciliation. They will also perform actions which will before long cause great divisions among the Jewish population with regard to the Mosaic law.

The word of God is seen in this passage to be at work already. The Church is examining the teaching of the prophets in the light of recent events. David had spoken of a righteous man who would not know the corruption of the tomb. Who was that man? Of whom was David speaking? Many Jews thought he was speaking about himself. But how was it, in that case, that David's tomb was still with us, Peter asks. Surely he was speaking of someone else—one of his descendants who would succeed him on the throne.

Psalm 16 is a Psalm of trust in God, who is faithful and will raise up the righteous man. The first Christians interpreted this Psalm in the light of Christ's resurrection.

Matthew 28:8–15: During Jesus' time, most of the people living in Galilee were pagans, and the land and the trade there were to a great extent in the hands of foreigners. As in ancient times, then, the province was threatened. Then it had been in danger of being invaded by the Syrians (Is 8:23), whereas now it was menaced by pagan blackness and night.

The prophet Isaiah had promised, however, that a light would rise over the country of dark shadow (9:1) and that a Messiah would come. It was in fact in Galilee that Jesus had begun to preach and his first disciples had come from the villages around the lake there. After his resurrection, he met his "brothers" again in Galilee before sending them out into the whole world.

At the same time, since his resurrection, a rumor had spread among the Jews that Jesus had not really been raised from the dead, but that his disciples had stolen his dead body. Matthew's community was in constant conflict with the synagogue and felt bound to reply. That is why the Gospel contains the explanation of the story as the work of the priests, who had bribed soldiers to ensure that it was believed.

▪

On Psalm 16

Would a man leave his friend alone in death?
Will the night of the tomb continue forever?
And how is it possible for the man who has believed
in the living God to end in corruption?

Blessed be God for the morning of Easter,
when life is victorious and overflowing with joy!
Blessed are you, God, my refuge and my happiness!

▪

Jesus had been condemned to death with considerable skill. The Jews had gotten rid of a blasphemer by presenting him to the Romans as the mastermind behind a hypothetical popular uprising. After his death, however, it was rumored that his tomb had been found empty. Certain people even claimed that God had passed judgment in the "Jesus affair."

"No, we are not drunk, as you imagine." We affirm today that this man, who was handed over to carry out God's plan, has risen again. "Jesus the Nazarene . . . God raised him to life . . . and all of us are witnesses to that"—witnesses until the end of the history of mankind. When we bear witness now to Christ's resurrection, we are not simply affirming that God has turned the situation in favor of Jesus alone by not letting his friend end in corruption. We go further than this, claiming that this new turn of events inaugurated an entirely new era. Death was, as a result of this change, no longer able to hold man in its grasp and the history of the world had turned toward life.

A new world has indeed begun. To ensure that we shall live, God has thrown all his credit onto the scales. Man, disfigured by blows and spittle, has emerged from the tomb, transfigured and radiating the beauty that God had given him in the beginning. "The one you crucified—God has raised him from the dead." God raised that man up so that all men at all times may be reborn. This means that he gave his approval to all that Jesus said and did, adding his signature, as it were, to the document of Jesus' life. In bringing Jesus back from death, God was bearing witness to the fact that Jesus' way was his own way—the way, the truth and the life.

"No, we are not drunk," because when we confess our faith in the resurrection of Jesus, we say that we believe in everything that made up his life. If we were to affirm simply that the tomb was found empty, we could be criticized for having stolen the body and for having retained nothing but a corpse. For us, however, the empty tomb is a challenge to look elsewhere for the one who was not found there. The open tomb will in fact always act as a stimulus, because it was a living man who rose again to give new life to others. The body of the Lord is not a dead body, but a life handed over, a man spanning the earth to set captives free and open the eyes of the blind. "We are not drunk." Our faith is not a wild excitement, but a deep commitment. The "Jesus affair" is really only just beginning.

■

God has raised him up.
Lord, waken us up to the mystery of life.
May love triumph over violence

and justice over hatred.
May a new world be born.

God has raised him up.
May we have the courage to overcome
   the forces of evil that destroy man—
   despair, loneliness and injustice.

God raised him up.
The Church is born.
May all those who are seeking meaning in their lives
find that their longing is the first-fruit of eternal joy.

God our Father,
   your Spirit transforms our earth today.
Give us enough breath
   to pass over into the new world
   where tomorrow's earth will be born.

When our hearts are full of joy
   all the words in the world mean very little.
We can only utter one word in thanksgiving,
   Lord, God of the living.
So let us pronounce it gladly: Alleluia!

Blessed are you for the victory of your Christ.
Blessed are you for your Eucharist, the seed of eternity.
May our praise of you never cease.

■

Death has died and peace has been offered up.
God our Father,
   let us share the body of your beloved Son
   in the joy of a rediscovered unity
and in it taste something of eternal joy.

TUESDAY IN THE OCTAVE OF EASTER

"THEY HAVE TAKEN HIM AWAY"
Acts 2:36–41: The first sermons and the first conversions! "God has made this Jesus whom you crucified both Lord and Christ." When they addressed the members of the synagogue, the Apostles always set about it in the same way. They began by recalling the great events in Jewish history and the message of the prophets. Then they presented the good news of Jesus Christ as the fulfillment of the old covenant. Finally, they called for conversion and faith on the part of their listeners. The converts were baptized without delay in the name of Jesus Christ. In this way, baptism was directly linked with the name, in other words, with the very person of the risen Jesus.

Psalm 33 is a hymn in honor of God's great works.

John 20:11–18: "Do not cling to me, because I have not yet ascended to the Father." When Jesus yielded up the Spirit on the cross, he died of love. He had glorified his Father and the Father had glorified him (see Jn 17:1), and from then onward he belonged to the world of the Spirit. Only believers, those who accepted rebirth "from above" and "through the Spirit" (see 3:3–5), could really know him.

Outside the tomb, Mary wept. Then the two names were whispered: "Mary" and "Rabbouni"—and only the heart heard them. Calling a child who has just been born by its name is to take hold of it in the very act of its birth. Calling Mary by her name meant, then, that Mary was being reborn. She dries her tears, since they belong to the past, and "turns again."

It is only then that she knows Jesus. To begin with, she had thought he was the gardener. But she had not been so very far from the truth. After all, who was that gardener, if he was not the new Adam who had just been given charge of the new garden—paradise regained?

■

On Psalm 33
The Word of God is upright.
It is a faithful word of love,
filling heaven and earth.

Alleluia in the whole universe.
Happy are the people who praise God.
Happy is the man whose joy is in the Lord.
Alleluia in a new song,
Alleluia in all upright hearts.

■

She ran to the tomb. Of course she wanted to complete the burial rites, but, even more than this, she wanted to find the one who had been lost forever. She wanted to relive the presence, artificially, of the one she had loved—to be there and thus give herself the impression that he was still there. She needed to feel his sweet presence and to revive her memory of his words—words that she would in any case never forget. So she went to the tomb. She knew that the affair was closed, just as the tomb would be closed by a stone, but she had to cling to the past for a little longer.

"They have taken my Lord away." Not only had they put her Lord to death, but they had even taken away the last trace of him she had loved so much. They even wanted his lifeless body to be removed. Was it really necessary to blot out everything that had happened?

We ran to the tomb. We wanted to venerate what was left to us of God, even if it was no more than lifeless relics. There were words to be repeated, even though the letter is bound to kill the spirit, principles to defend, even though the fundamental message—bringing good news to the poor—is obscured by them, and titles to be announced, even though they take the place of a real encounter. We ran to the tomb, in other words, to look for something to replace God. At the risk of enclosing nothing but a lifeless body, we wanted to touch it, see it and keep it contained.

"They have taken my Lord away." We looked for him in a tomb and wanted to keep him in a reliquary. The tomb is empty and will be empty forever. God is elsewhere. We do not know "where they have put him."

"Why are you weeping?" Mary thought it was the gardener who was speaking to her in this way—the one who sows the seed, who patiently watches the slow growth of the plant and who understands life because he knows the secrets of death. "Why are you weeping?"

Who is it who is questioning her in this way? The gardener who prunes the vine so that the sap will rise with the coming of springtime and the new wine will flow in the autumn.

"Mary!" She trembles when she hears the voice she knows and loves so well. "Rabbouni!" Her heart speaks the words that her reason still refuses to utter. The Spirit reveals the only place where God lives—he has always dwelt and will dwell forever in the loving heart. It is there that he can be sought and found.

"Mary"—"Rabbouni." Love is the only way of faith. The unforgettable appearance of this Easter morning—the Lord himself—depended on this appeal and the whole of faith was contained in the response. Mary wanted to touch a dead body, and the living Christ said: "Do not cling to me." Love always goes on ahead.

Why, then, do we repeat to each other the words first spoken by those who witnessed Christ's resurrection? It is to arouse in ourselves an understanding of their real meaning for us. "Do not cling to me." He is the Word, and all that he has since that time and forever are our fleeting words. In him, however, those words become a vow promising a love that he makes eternal.

We try to keep to his way of looking at our life because we want to be reborn through his grace. "Do not cling to me." He is the way, and he has since then and forever followed all our ways, so that, in him, they all lead to the Kingdom of God.

We call him Lord and God. This is because we want to be in communion with him. He is the life, and he takes not only our ultimate death, but also all our daily deaths into himself. Through him, those little deaths are filled with the seeds of a life that has no end.

Mary wept at the tomb and we were mourning with her. We too were looking for God in the land of the dead. Yes, they have taken him away. But from now onward his body is ourselves. He has chosen to dwell in the loving heart, and he tells us: "Go and find my brothers."

■

What would the bread be if it had not been broken?
What would the wine be if it was not shared?

*Lord, loosen our hands when they try to keep you captive
and let us know the joy of encountering you.*

∎

*I went to the rock in the garden,
my heart and soul plunged in gloom.
I went to keep vigil with the one I love.*

*I stayed by his tomb—
no other place could give rest
or repose to my spirit.*

*The cave was empty, his body had gone.
The tomb was open, I did not ask.
But who could keep silent?*

*Who is calling me?
One word, and I know it is he.
I will repeat his name to my brothers.*

WEDNESDAY IN THE OCTAVE OF EASTER

COMMUNION
Acts 3:1–10: It was three o'clock in the afternoon, near the "Beautiful Gate." Peter and John were going up to the temple to pray. A cripple called out to them, asking for help. They replied: "In the name of Jesus Christ the Nazarene, walk!" That is all they have to give him—a name.

But enormous importance was attached in the ancient world to knowing a name, because it defined the person's being and function (see, for example, Gen 2:20). Knowing a person's name was equivalent to possessing his being, and the name that the Apostles revealed to the lame man outside the temple was prestigious. It was the name of the Lord's anointed one, whom the prophet Isaiah had praised with the words: "The Lord has anointed me. He has sent me to bring good news to the poor and to bind up hearts that are broken" (Is 61:1).

Psalm 105 narrates the wonderful acts of God in Israel's history.

Luke 24:13-35: It was the evening of the first day of the week. Two men were walking along a road. Their life had ceased on the Friday before, when Jesus was in agony on the cross. Since then, they had repeated the ancient curse to one another: "The one who has been hanged is accursed of God" (Dt 21:23). Who, then, had been right? Was it the Jewish authorities who had decided to put the agitator to death, or was it Jesus, who claimed the title of Messiah for himself? The two men went on their way, sunk in gloom.

They were soon joined by a Passover pilgrim. Their unknown companion began to speak to them, quoting Scripture and explaining the life and death of the one who had been crucified. The two disciples' hearts burned within them, especially when the stranger took bread, blessed it, broke it and gave it to them, performing the actions of the Last Supper—actions that were already being performed in the young Church in memory of the Master. They experienced the joy of Easter again in those actions: "Yes, it is true. The Lord has risen and has appeared to Simon." That happened on the first day of the new week.

■

They were walking along the road in the dust and heat, the two of them, crushed by the unhappy experience of two days ago. They did not understand. The Master had been arrested and put to death. The crowd had rejected him and everyone could see him there, outside the Holy City, hanging like a criminal on the shameful gallows. The great adventure had come to an end. The feast had become a time of grief and tears and the laughter had ceased. The sacrificial Lamb had become a sheep led to the slaughterhouse. The disciples had scattered and the flock, without its shepherd, had become dispersed.

On the road, the two men talked about why they had committed themselves to Jesus and why they had had such high hopes. They also discussed Jesus' failure and his unbelievable death. Then a man without a name and without a face came up to them, and he listened to their story of disappointed hopes and reawakened fears. They had many anxieties, clearly, and were troubled because it seemed to them that death was to have the last word.

Then he began to speak, presenting the whole of Scripture to them.

He began with Moses, Egypt, the exodus, the long period of Israel's slavery, the liberation and the covenant concluded in the desert. Then he went on to talk about the prophets, the exile and the return. Their hope could not be disappointed. Life would rise again from the ashes. The wheat grain had to die so that it could bear fruit.

They invited him to stay in the inn with them. His words had warmed their hearts. The dawn could not disappear, surely, when the first rays of light appeared in the darkness. "Stay with us." The table was set. The journey was over. The bread was broken and shared. The loaf of friendship was there in front of them, the sign of the Friend. "They recognized him."

It will never be the same for us as it was before. In the depth of solitude, when it seems inevitable that despair will triumph, all that we can do is to go on walking, in the expectation that, when evening comes, he will have to stay with us.

All that we can do is to keep his words with us. They reveal him to us and disclose his secret. We may always have been familiar with the old story of the kings and prophets, but only he can make clear to us what God's great plan is. His words open up hidden paths in our hearts which we thought had been buried under the impenetrable remains of our uncertainties and questions and hidden beneath a thick layer of mediocrity and disappointment. His words disclose elements that we thought had been completely forgotten. God is faithful and keeps his promises. We can always make a new beginning. We have, after all, been marked by the Holy Spirit, who arouses in us the sound of voices that we have silenced: "You are my beloved children." "I will make sources of living water spring up in your deserts." Our hearts are already being seized by love.

He has come in to stay with us. He has broken the bread, as friends do when we share a daily meal together. And we shall never be able to forget the taste of that bread. The one whom we were seeking is with us. The one whom we recognize in the familiar action of blessing, breaking and sharing is alive. Our eyes are opened and we have to get up. He has already left us, but he is calling us to go forward.

■

Lord,
let us see your face.
Let us know you and hear your voice.
Take us to the table where bread is broken.
How are we to know that you are the God of life
if you do not take our lives in hand?

∎

We thank you, God our Father
and Father of all mankind.

We bless you and seek you,
our God, whom men would not seek
if they had not already mysteriously
sensed your presence.
We continue on our way
in order to seize hold of you
and we listen to you
in order to discover you.
Our lives are inspired by your Spirit
and our hearts are warmed by his love.

You are blessed by the great crowd of people
on pilgrimage through the night
and looking out for your dawn.
We praise you, God our hope,
with those who are poor in their poverty.

∎

Stay with us, Lord Jesus,
on the road we are following.
Warm our hearts to receive your words;
open our eyes to discover
that life is stronger than death.
For you transfigure all things
today and forever.

THURSDAY IN THE OCTAVE OF EASTER

PEACE

Acts 3:11–26: A struggle—a life and death struggle. Pilate thought that Jesus should be released, but his suggestion was rejected by the Jews who wanted a murderer to be pardoned and the Holy and Just One to be handed over. They brought about the death of the Prince of Life and God raised him from the dead. Jesus became a servant and went to the furthest limit, giving himself. Because of this, God exalted him and "gave him the name which is above all other names" (Phil 2:9).

"It is the name of Jesus which, through our faith in it, has brought back the strength of this man." The healing of the lame man had bewildered the crowd, and Peter had to interpret the meaning of the event the people had witnessed and make it clear to them that God was the author of it.

Jesus became a servant and was rejected by everyone. That is the true way of conversion. Only those who follow that way, the Apostle says, will be sent a "time of refreshment." One final period of respite is granted to Israel—Jesus Christ is put in reserve until the end of time, when he will come again to take possession of the eternal Kingdom promised by God through his prophets.

Psalm 8 is a hymn to the God who gave man his name. "What is man, Lord, that you should spare a thought for him?"

Luke 24:35–48: It is the evening of the first day of the week. "Peace be with you." Jesus gives peace to the unbelieving disciples. Peace—an ever present dream in the hearts of men—enemies clasping each other's hands, arms laid down. The prophets had so often promised that peace for the "time of resting," and now it is here in the midst of the stunned Apostles. The Kingdom of God and all that it contains is here in an endless feast.

Jesus is in the midst of his own. There were numerous stories of appearances of specters or demons in both the Jewish and the Greek traditions, but Jesus was not a phantom. He was not dead, but alive!

He shows them his hands and feet where the nails had been and eats a piece of fish. Then he goes on to instruct them, explaining how his death and resurrection are the fulfillment of Scripture. The Church will also continue to repeat those prophecies and Psalms that throw light on the life of the Lord, but before that the Spirit will come and renew all things. It will soon be the time of the Church's mission.

■

The doors were closed and bolted. They were very frightened. But a few weeks later they were to be in the public places and the assemblies proclaiming their faith to the crowds. Now, however, they were paralyzed, almost dead with fear. The coldness of the tomb had chilled the place where they had sought refuge since that Friday when their hope had been sealed off with the stone.

They had locked themselves in. Brooding about their mishap, they had almost destroyed themselves. They had become weak and depressed. They had lost hope. Life was ebbing away. Man is not made to shut himself up, vegetate and die.

What, then, had happened on that evening? What breath of new life had liberated that handful of men from their funereal sadness? One word: Peace! "Peace be with you." One word and life began again and hope was renewed.

"Peace I bequeath to you," Jesus had said, "a peace the world cannot give. This is my gift to you" (Jn 14:27). That evening Jesus was in the midst of them like an explosion that blew off all the bolts on their hearts and minds.

Fear tears at Christian hope. There is fear of the world—fear to take a risk. That is in itself a prostitution of faith. Then there is fear of what is new—we prefer to keep within the confines of doctrine and want to forget the vital force of the Gospel. There is also fear of denouncing what debases man and of disputing what diminishes him. We forget that God gave himself a single image, but that is preferable. We also fear the disturbing words and actions of those who speak and act in the name of the Gospel and attribute them to clumsiness. Our fear is often hidden behind a veil of prudence or diplomacy.

"Peace!" The first Christians were born on that evening, when the doors were opened to admit the Word of God. Peace was coming back—a peace that told them to go further, to be open and to let in the fresh air from outside.

The peace that he brought could not then and cannot now be associated with a fear that blocks the flow of words and prevents breathing, a fear that shuts one in. The peace of a joyous lack of care has the boldness of experience and can be carried by the breath of the Spirit.

"Peace be with you." One word and life began again. Faith cannot be born in fear. It opens out in the peace of a heart that knows that it is loved and that it can love and that calls for no proof of this. Faith is like life itself—it dies when it only experiences pain and it is poisoned when it dare no longer dream.

"Peace!" One word makes all bowed heads straighten up. Life is possible because the dream of hope was not crushed by a stone closing the tomb. Love is possible because God is faithful to his promise.

One word blows off all the bolts on our hearts and minds and faith is set free.

∎

God of peace,
 you awaken the faith of your Church.
Fill us with your Spirit.
 May he reveal to us the presence of your Son
 and call on your Church
 to proclaim Peace restored
 and Love renewed.

∎

Our doors are closed, Lord—
 open them.
You came to share with us
 the bread of hope.
Break down the walls of our fear.

Send us to our brothers
 to proclaim peace and joy to them.
You make us witnesses to your good news
 until you come again.

Lord Jesus Christ,
   you make peace shine
   like the morning star
   for those who believe in you.
Do not remember our failures,
   but give us your Spirit.
We will join hands for your feast
   and build up your Church,
      where our hope and our future dwells.

FRIDAY IN THE OCTAVE OF EASTER

BY THE NAME OF THE ONE WHO WAS CRUCIFIED

Acts 4:1–12: So it was not enough just to crucify Jesus. His disciples also have to be called to account. Peter and John talk to the people and continue to tell them that Jesus was raised from the dead. Many of their listeners are converted and the community of believers grows. This is something that the high priests, who simply shrug their shoulders when they hear about Christ's resurrection, cannot bear. They resolve to nip the movement in the bud and cause a division in the sect. For the Church, it is clearly a case of bearing witness.

"By whose name have you done this?" Peter at once replies: "By the name of Jesus . . . for of all the names in the world given to men, this is the only one by which we can be saved." The cripple had been saved by the name of Jesus. Was Jesus' name not the stone rejected by those who were persecuting the young Church, but chosen by God to be the keystone around which the new Israel would be built?

Psalm 118 is an individual act of thanksgiving. V. 22 seems to have been interpreted by the Jews as a proclamation of the building up of the eschatological community, but the Church soon applied it to Christ, the founder of the new people of God. There is a play on words in Aramaic which makes it possible for the "builders" to be understood in an anti-Jewish sense as the "scribes."

John 21:1–14: "Do not be afraid, Simon. From now on it is men you will catch" (Lk 5:10). In obedience to Jesus, they had thrown the net out and had brought in one hundred and fifty-three fish. Jesus had glorified his Father and now the Father was glorifying him (see Jn 17:1–5). He had risen from the dead and was fulfilling the promise that he had made to a group of pagans: "When I am lifted up from the earth, I shall draw all men to myself" (Jn 12:32). Now it was the time of the Church's mission. Peter was the leader of that mission. Had he not jumped into the water when he recognized the Lord? Had he not run to the empty tomb on Easter morning? The catch was enormous, but the net did not break with the weight of fish. Against all hope, then, the Apostles were going to bring people from all parts of the known world into the unity of the one Church. Without Jesus, however, they would be able to do nothing. During the night, before he came, they had caught nothing.

Coming ashore, they found a charcoal fire over which Jesus had placed fish. There was also bread, which Jesus gave them. No one asked him now "Who are you?" because they all knew it was the Lord. They recognized the bread of life, the bread from heaven, the one who gives eternal life in the bread broken and shared.

■

A fresh start! Jesus had been arrested and crucified and it all seemed to have been in vain. But today his disciples are preaching. Jesus had been accused of healing with the power of the devil, and today Peter and the others are summoned to appear before the elders and scribes. "By whose name have you done these healings? "Jesus' trial is not at an end yet. It is clear that Golgotha was only one incident in the great lawsuit and that the disciples were behaving and were being treated like their Master. Throughout history, Jesus' disciples have lived and will continue to live in their own flesh the fate of their Master. The trial goes on. From age to age, the cross has been and will always be a stumbling block.

Jesus was on trial. The Messiah had to be crucified—because of his life, because he changed everything, society, religion and man's idea of God, and because he spread a dangerous contagion among men, that of love and freedom. He had to hand over his own life so that Life would live.

The Church was and still is on trial. The disciple is not greater than

the Master. The Church is on trial when it upsets the idols made by men's hands and denounces everything that reduces man to slavery—the tyranny of money and the passion for power. The Church is on trial when it shakes the social and religious order by revealing false gods and pointing to the dignity of man. The Lord's disciples show their passionate determination when they set fire to traditions that wither men's spirit and the powers that destroy his soul. "By what power have you done this?"

"The stone rejected by you the builders has proved to be the keystone." Apart from that stone there is no salvation. Jesus' trial did not end with a condemnation—it ended in victory, because God was on the side of the condemned man. And God has also linked Jesus' fate with that of his disciples. "It is by the name of Jesus the Nazarene, the one you crucified . . . that this man is able to stand up, perfectly healthy, here in your presence today."

If you feel that you are on trial because you are criticized for your Christian hope, for the friendly links you have established and for working for a better world, remember the law of the cross. That law is that the seed had to fall to the ground and die (see Jn 12:24) so that the Easter flower will blossom. God always counterattacks when his own are put on trial and accused. You should not forget that on Easter morning the one who was accused became the counsel for our defense and death itself had to retreat when life attacked. "They recognized them as associates of Jesus, but when they saw the man who had been cured standing by their side, they could find no answer."

∎

Lord, make us live
  by the power of your name.
Denounce those who accuse us.
  Deliver us from the bonds
  that prevent us from using your Word.
By the resurrection of your Son
  set us free from the power of death.

∎

"Come and have breakfast."
>   Some bread on our table
>   is a sign to us to go to you.
> Let us, Lord, trust in your word.
>   You pronounce your name over us
>   and at once we belong to you
>   forever and ever.

■

"Follow me,
and I will make you fishers of men."
>   You will work for peace,
>   harvest the bread of life,
>   gather grapes for a feast without end
>   and prepare the way for the future.
> We bless you, Lord.
>   You need us, our hands,
>   our minds, our hearts
>   and our poverty.
> Whoever we are,
>   you call on us to follow you.
> Let us be so moved by you
>   that we will become true disciples
>   and leave everything joyfully
>   in order to be with you.

■

On the other shore, in the morning mist,
>   he is there—fascinating us
>   and holding out his hand to us.

Looking at us, Lord, you have pierced our hearts
>   and have drawn us to you.
> Lead us further and further
>   by your love.

SATURDAY IN THE OCTAVE OF EASTER

BEARING WITNESS

Acts 4:13–21: "You must judge whether in God's eyes it is right to listen to you and not to God." The elders and scribes criticized the Apostles for speaking about Jesus, but how could they remain silent? Jesus had seized hold of them, as he was later to seize hold of Paul of Tarsus. They had given him their faith. They had placed their lives in his hands and they had been set on fire by his Spirit. It was not simply a contract that existed between the risen Christ and his witnesses, but a passionate relationship. Peter, John and the others could not be silent about what they had seen and heard, because it had to do with man's salvation. What they had seen and heard they had to proclaim to all men, so that the whole of mankind might be in communion with them—their communion was, after all, a communion with the Father and with Jesus Christ (see 1 Jn 1:3).

Psalm 118: see Friday in the Octave of Easter.

Mark 16:9–15: There is general agreement among exegetes today that this concluding section does not form part of the original Gospel of Mark, because its vocabulary and style are different from those of the rest of the text. It is a summary of the accounts of the post-resurrection appearances of Christ mentioned in the other Gospels, with the addition of certain allusions to events reported in the Acts. Its authenticity was disputed as early as the second century.

■

On Psalm 118

Give thanks to the Lord,
you who have been set free from death.
Give thanks, for his love is everlasting.

The stone rejected by the builders
has become the keystone—
Christ has risen from the dead.

Bless God and join the feast.
Let your song be for God.
Death has been overcome by life.

∎

"We cannot promise to stop proclaiming what we have seen and heard." Throughout history, men and women have continued to stand up in the trial of life and bear witness: "I believe in the resurrection of Jesus Christ."

"Christ has risen!" For a whole week now we have been singing this theme with many variations. But let there be no mistake—we are not bearing witness to an event in the past which may be very important but is no more than a pious memory. We do not in any sense believe in an event that can be proved by historical investigation. No, what we believe in is this: Jesus no longer experiences the limitations imposed by the human condition and is now experiencing the condition of resurrection. We believe in and bear witness to the fact that he is experiencing this now for us and for all people. He was a man among others and like us he saw that his universe was limited by his own possible contacts and interchanges with others. Now, however, he is risen and has broken through the barriers imposed by his own person. He encounters all people at all times in the secret places of their own hearts and at the inexpressible source of their own lives. No person and no thing is now remote from him. Every human undertaking is known intimately to him and his Spirit dwells secretly in it, with the result that our work to make the world more human secretly makes his body grow. When we proclaim his resurrection, we bear witness to the fact that everything that we do is dependent on the activity of his Spirit and that everything is worth the attempt, because he makes everything live and grow.

"We cannot promise to stop proclaiming what we have seen and heard." Today, in handing on the confession of faith made by those who experienced the victory of life over death, as Christians have always done throughout history, we are declaring our own faith in the risen Christ. At a time when death is every day threatening our lives and we become every day more conscious of how difficult it is to love, we continue, in our faith in his resurrection, to live and to love with an obstinacy that is quite supernatural.

∎

We have seen with our own eyes

the salvation that you have prepared for us:
  your Son, risen and alive,
  clothed in your glory.

We ask you, then,
to let the light of his face shine on us.
May our world be awakened to the life
  promised for eternity.

FROM THE MONDAY TO THE THURSDAY
OF THE SECOND WEEK OF EASTER

New Life

Christian faith is in no sense an indoctrination. Each Christian is called to live the universal truth manifested by Easter personally and to experience it in his own existence. The resurrection is the pivot of our faith because it is the turning point of our life. Life was moving toward destruction; now it is moving toward fulfillment.

Believing in the resurrection is bearing witness to the fact that someone—and, what is more, someone in our own history—is "full of life" forever. Believing that Christ is alive is proclaiming the meaning of life for every person. But believing in the resurrection goes even further than this. It is experiencing in the secret recesses of our heart that we are, in Christ, victorious over the power of death, even though it may continue to keep us a prisoner. That victory is, moreover, not only ours, but also the world's, because our hope is not simply for our own inner satisfaction; it is for the world. We are filled with wonder and discover that we have been awakened to life without end. That wonder is for the whole world. It is good news for all people. And we are the consciousness of what has been given to the world, although it may not know about it. In us, the world can learn that death is against nature.

We cannot eliminate the tragedy of man's existence without cost to ourselves. Believers and non-believers alike are confronted with the absurdity of life, suffering, emptiness and death. But we who have faith are humbly convinced that new blood is already flowing in us. We bear witness to the fact that, since Easter morning, we have been born to a new life. "The old world has passed away and a new world is already born."

Believing in the resurrection is becoming enthusiastic for life. Believing in Jesus is discovering the love of life that Jesus manifested in his words and deeds. It is believing in the world and doing all we can to ensure that the world reaches its end. Believing in the resurrection is discovering the power of life that God lets us experience. Our life, we know, is not moving toward destruction. Live and enjoy life—that is what God is telling us. We believe in life because we have discovered in Jesus' resurrection that the dark secret of the world is the beating of a loving heart: "God loved the world so much that he gave his only Son" (Jn 3:16).

We confess this and bear witness to it together. It is very significant that the first experiences of the risen Christ took place in the Church, when the disciples were gathered together. There are individual experiences of the risen Lord reported in the New Testament, but those individuals are always referred to the community: "She went and told the disciples" (Jn 20:18), "They went back and told the others" (Mk 16:13), and so on. Faith cannot remain hidden in the intimate recesses of the individual consciousness—it has to belong to a whole people. We believe together and we share our experience with others of the secret of life.

MONDAY OF THE SECOND WEEK

REBIRTH

Acts 4:23–31: "With gratitude in your hearts sing Psalms and hymns and inspired songs to God" (Col 3:16). When Peter and John were released by the Sanhedrin, Christians at once gave thanks to God and at the same time felt impelled to talk about their experience.

Psalm 2 provides the point of departure for their meditation. In this Psalm, a king repeats certain sacred words describing him as a son of God. He is thus able to confront all those who dispute his legal right to kingship—

something that commonly happened whenever a new ruler came to the throne. Interpreted in the Christian perspective, this Psalm proved very suitable as a means of making the meaning of Jesus' destiny clear, and the early Christians saw Christ in the role of the anointed king and the leaders of Israel and the Roman procurator, who condemned him to death, in the role of the earthly rulers. In addition to this, they also saw Peter and John as continuing in their own flesh the sufferings of Christ when they too were dragged in front of the Sanhedrin after the miracle at the Beautiful Gate. It was in being put to the test in this way that the early Christian community learned how closely it conformed to the passion of its Lord. The thanksgiving of the believers ends, in this passage of the Acts of the Apostles, with a pouring out of the Spirit that is reminiscent of Pentecost and emphasizes the permanent presence of the Spirit in the Church.

John 3:1–8: "Those who were not born out of human stock or urge of the flesh or will of man, but of God himself" (Jn 1:13). Nicodemus had seen the signs, especially the water of purification changed into wine and the cleansing of the temple, but however favorable he may have been toward Jesus, he was still a representative of the old order that was being swept aside. If he really wanted to understand the full meaning of the signs of the Kingdom, he had to be reborn from above.

What, then, is that rebirth, that regeneration in water and the Spirit, that Jesus speaks of? Judaism does not seem to have had any real teaching at that time about regeneration. That is quite strange, because the prophet Isaiah had proclaimed "new heavens and a new earth" (Is 65:17). Jeremiah had spoken of a "different heart" (Jer 32:39), and Ezekiel had replaced the idea of purification by that of a "new heart and a new spirit" (Ez 36:26). The restoration of man to the original glory of Adam appeared therefore as a repetition of the original act of creation. This theme had also been fully developed in Qumran, and John the Baptist expected a Messiah who would purify Israel.

The members of the dualist circles, like those of the Baptist, in fact postulated two orders of existence—the world of the "flesh" and that of the "spirit." The "flesh"—this term did not at that time have the pejorative meaning that it so often has today—referred to existence here on earth with its potential for good and evil, whereas the "spirit" called to mind God's power as the basic condition for a religious life. "Being born again of the spirit," then, pointed to man's need to move from one order into the other.

■

Advertisers are not silly or peculiar, and they know a great deal about our hidden concerns. They persuade us to stay young and to keep the shape that we had when we were twenty, because they know that we really want that. The old myth of paradise is not dead, and we are still fascinated by the myth of Doctor Faustus. We long for eternal youth.

How is it possible for us to be reborn? We try to penetrate deeper and deeper into the world's secrets and to master the processes of our existence. We want to control our lives by perfect knowledge and skill, but for all our ability we cannot quench our thirst or extinguish the fire that so often burns us. What is the purpose of living if it only leads to death? We long to know why we are alive, and we come at night to consult Jesus.

"What is born of the flesh is flesh." Our lives are moving toward death. Many of us become exhausted in an attempt to love, and however many bonds we establish that may be stronger than death, our victories are too doubtful for us to continue to live for very long in an illusion. Others try to build a more human world, sometimes devoting the whole of their lives to it in a noble and heroic effort, but they cannot conceal the fragility of all human relationships from themselves. All that we can really establish are temporary truces. "What is born of the flesh is flesh." Life eludes our grasp at the moment when we believe we have hold of it, just as water slips between the fingers of those who receive it in their cupped hands. "Do not be surprised when I say: You must be born from above." The secret of life is concealed in a garden in which man's destiny has been turned upside down because a tomb was found empty, unable to keep new life captive. It is not possible to put new wine into old bottles or the skin will burst. The Spirit cannot be kept in chains. The stone always has to be shattered.

The Spirit must be born. It is, after all, the Spirit that transfigures our human love in all its weakness and enables it to proclaim at least some aspect of the new world. Being born of the Spirit! When we receive Communion, we are consecrated by Life and become the place where encounters that form the fabric of the new world are initiated. Being born again of the Spirit is being reborn of the Wind! No one knows where it is going. No one can ever know where the new

life of God is born, but we can through faith say that the resurrection of Jesus Christ is at work in this age. When we turn toward God and humbly call on him in faith, the place where we are begins to tremble—like the tomb on Easter morning.

■

God of eternal youth,
  time passes but you remain the same
  and nothing can tarnish
  the love that flows from you.
But all things pass away
  and man bears the seeds
  of his own death in him.
How are we to know you, the living God,
  if you do not let us be reborn each day?

We bless you for your Holy Spirit,
  for his freedom and his generous breath.
May he be in our lives
  the source of renewal every day,
  a renewal in which we shall experience
  the eternal youth of eternal life.

■

We have been plunged into the death
  and resurrection of your Son Jesus.
Through baptism
  we have been made one body with him.

We ask you, God our Father,
  to let your Spirit fulfill in us every day
  what has begun with your grace.
May we live our lives in this world
  hoping for your Kingdom
  and committing ourselves totally
  to your service.

■

Who can ever understand what we are?

Who will ever penetrate the secret of our lives?
We bless you, living God,
  because the meaning of our being
  is hidden in you
  with your risen Son, Jesus.
Keep us, we implore you,
  in a state of wonder,
  so that we shall be, for you,
  as free as the wind
  and like the wind
  do good, but elude the grasp.

TUESDAY OF THE SECOND WEEK

TOGETHER

Acts 4:32–27: "Everything they owned was held in common." The Christian ideal of community life is summarized in that one short sentence. What an enormous power it was for the early Church! How firmly the apostolic activity of the first Christians was supported by the love of the brethren! It was, after all, not only material goods that were owned in common; faith was also shared, all concerns were mutual, and there was the joy of being together.

Christians were left free to share their goods in Jerusalem. Some put all or part of their possessions at the disposal of the community. Ananias and Sapphira were condemned not because they kept their property to themselves, but because they let it be known that they had offered the whole of it when nothing had in fact been asked of them (Acts 5:1–11).

Psalm 93 celebrates the enthronement of Yahweh in Jerusalem within the framework of the Feast of Tabernacles.

John 3:7–15: "You must be born from above." This disturbs Nicodemus, who cannot understand this new way of speaking. The reason is that he does not grasp the language of the heart or the way that love speaks to vast horizons. Jesus does not, however, deny the mysterious nature of the words that he utters and to explain them he makes use of a simile, that of the wind. The wind, which is, in Hebrew, the same word as "spirit," is also mysterious. Its effects can be observed, but it cannot be seen. It is the same with those who have been born of the Spirit. They can be seen. They are the people who have received the words of Jesus. But what cannot be known is when and how they have been born of the Spirit. Certainly the process of rebirth is not at all like that of physical birth (see Jn 1:13).

The discourse gradually moves to a higher level. The work of Christ is considered and the cross of Christ appears outlined beneath the surface of

the discourse. Regeneration is possible. We can be reborn, but only as the consequence of a twofold process on the part of Christ. The Son of Man, who has knowledge of "heavenly things," had first to "come down from heaven." God had, in other words, to become incarnate. Then he had to be "lifted up," like Moses' serpent in the desert. Anyone looking at that bronze serpent was, according to the Book of Numbers (21:9), healed. This means that whoever turned to God was saved. In the same way, "everyone who believes" in Christ will "have eternal life in him."

■

A crowd of people celebrating a festival or preparing for a demonstration may well have certain claims to make or react collectively, but they do not necessarily experience community life. When people are called to form a single community, they have above all to learn how to live together.

"The whole group of believers was united, heart and soul." Because of its very nature and the way in which it came into being, Christian life is communal. We could never claim to live together if we did not have a common origin. This statement is certainly true of the whole community of human beings, but Christians experience its validity in a very special way as people living in community. Our births have all been inscribed in the same book of life. Our community is not based on some unity of thought, nor is it rooted in any need to carry out together the same program. We are a community because of blood and living breath. We are one people because we all share the same Spirit.

Christians belong to one race. They believe in common. Their faith is not concealed within the intimacy of personal, individual

consciousness. It is above all the breath of a gathering called together and united by a Word.

There is no need for us to suppress the fact that we are, as a people, marked by tensions and painful divisions. We have often tried in the past and indeed still try to hide these wounds from ourselves in an attempt to avoid open conflict, but this kind of self-deceit is incompatible with the truth of our origin. It is precisely because we want to live together that we agree to endure dissension. This is certainly risky, but it contains a promise that we try to include within human history and a sign that bears witness to man's hope of ultimate reconciliation and his attempt to find it.

We could never claim to live together if we did not have a common origin. We can also only continue to live together because the love of the one who wants to bring us together dwells in us.[5]

■

"The whole group of believers was united, heart and soul."
To our regret, Lord, we are full of contradictions
   and we destroy each other.
But you—
   you are stronger than all our divisions.
Give us a new heart.

"The whole group of believers was united, heart and soul."
To our regret, Lord, we live in fear of each other.
But you—
   you are stronger than all our fears.
Give us a new heart.

"The whole group of believers was united, heart and soul."
To our regret, Lord, our hearts are dead.
But you—
   you are stronger than our distress.
Give us a new heart.

WEDNESDAY OF THE SECOND WEEK

A NEW HEART
Acts 5:17–26: All the Apostles have by now been arrested. Before long, Stephen will be put to death for being faithful to Christ, and Peter and then Paul will be imprisoned. There is no respite for the Church of Jerusalem. Those who oppose Christians are still the same. They are the Sadducees, men of influence in worship, financially powerful and closed to all new ideas, but in a majority in the Sanhedrin.

Were they able for those reasons to silence the word of God? It should have been possible for them to do that. They had, after all, been responsible for having Jesus put to death. They had, however, not been able to prevent the stone from rolling aside on Easter morning. And now, today, the prison gates are powerless against the Holy Spirit.

Psalm 34 is a prayer of thanksgiving, proclaiming the faith and trust of the man who knows that God is always close to the heart of suffering.

John 3:16–21: "Everyone who believes" in Jesus has "eternal life in him." Christ's incarnation and his exaltation have the same source: God's love of the world. "God sent his Son into the world not to condemn the world, but so that through him the world might be saved." The Son gave his life and at the same time also brought light—a light which "tries minds and hearts" (Ps 7:9). The conflict between light and darkness takes place on the battlefield of the human heart. The sinner "hates the light" because his works are evil. He knows that his sin will be revealed in that light. The righteous man, however, comes to the light, knowing that his works are good. He thanks God for the light, in the conviction that God is the source of all goodness.

The coming of the Son of Man, then, throws light on men's actions. Jesus came to save men, and that salvation means that man must decide about the person and the message of Jesus. He has to be regenerated by the Spirit, and that presupposes that he is prepared to pass through death to resurrection.

■

"God loved the world so much that he gave his only son." How is it really possible to believe that the dark secret of the world is to be found in the beating of a loving heart?

"God loved the world so much"—that is the only thing that we have to confess in order to remain faithful to our origins. We no longer need to look for God in the realm of what can be used. Since Golgotha, since the time of Jesus, he cannot be reduced to "playing a part." He does not guarantee the social or moral order of the world. He is not an engineer supervising the whole plan of the world and controlling the universal scenario. The only statement that the Gospel allows us to make is almost incredible: "God loves the world." Since Jesus' suffering and death, when we think of God, we think of love. We know that God loves us because of Jesus crucified and cast aside in the center of the world. The God of the philosophers would have us believe: "There is risk and there is necessity—seek and find." The God of the wise men would say: "Wait and you will find Truth." The God of the moralists would tell us: "Thou shalt . . . You must . . . That is your duty." The God of the ideologists would ask us: "What have you constructed? What is your struggle?" But the God of Jesus Christ, because he loves us, simply says: "Do you want to?"

A defenseless question that disarms us: "Do you want to?" But it is our only image of God. How, then, is it really possible to believe that the secret of the world is to be found in the beating of a loving heart? One is reminded here of that strange, almost unbelievable event that has been interpreted as applying to each one of us in our daily struggle. A man was able to go on living when the heart of another man was transplanted into his body. When the patient died, the heart surgeons told us that his whole organism, from his brain down to the smallest cells in his body, fought with astonishing cunning for at least a year to reject the alien heart that had, in the meantime, become the most essential part of his own life. "God loved the world so much that he gave his only Son." A heart transplanted into our world—and becoming indispensable for our survival. "Do you want to?"

There is, however, a difference between these two cases. Unlike the heart in the patient's body, this heart is transplanted anew each morning into the world and God will never abandon the operation as long as the transplant has not taken.[6]

We glorify you, God our Father,
  and with the whole of your Church
  proclaim that Jesus has risen
  and lives in the light.

He came from you, full of grace and truth,
  not to condemn the world, but to save it.
To reveal your love,
  he became like men in all things
  and wants to lead them in his victory.
In him we see your light
  and know the secret of our life—
  you love us without restraint
  and remove the accusation that has been made against us.
That is why we are sure of your tenderness
  and are already able to praise you
  with those who are living forever and ever
  in your light.

THURSDAY OF THE SECOND WEEK

BEARING WITNESS
Acts 5:27–33: "You seem determined to fix the guilt of this man's death on us. You want to hold us responsible for the death of Jesus," Jonathan the high priest declares. But he has a very short memory. He has apparently already forgotten that his family plotted against Jesus and that his brother-in-law Caiaphas conducted what was no more than a parody of a trial.

The Apostles are brought face to face with their judges, the representatives of legitimate authority. Whom, then, should they obey? Should they bow to those in power or should they follow God? Should they obey the men who condemned Jesus and treated him as a scoundrel, or God who raised him from the dead and exalted him as Prince and Savior? Peter and his companions have no doubts at all. When he raised Jesus from the dead, God guaranteed his preaching, and the witness borne by the Apostles had the guarantee of the Holy Spirit.

Psalm 34: see Tuesday of the Second Week.

John 3:31–36: "I tell you most solemnly, unless a man is born through water and the Spirit, he cannot enter the Kingdom of God" (Jn 3:5). Both Jesus and John the Baptist administered water baptism, and this led to a vigorous debate between John's and Jesus' disciples (see Jn 3:22ff), mainly because Jesus soon began to influence those who had welcomed him after his own baptism. The evangelist refers to the existence of this conflict and uses it to contrast the water baptism of John with Jesus' baptism, which is borne up by the presence and power of the Spirit. Jesus, he claims, is the bridegroom, whereas John is simply the bridegroom's friend, and Jesus has to "grow greater" as John "grows smaller." John baptized with water, but Jesus will baptize in the Holy Spirit. Jesus is quite unique. He is the one "who comes from heaven" and "bears witness to the things he has seen and heard."

Jesus received the Spirit "without reserve" when he was baptized. The Father told him that he loved him and put everything into his hands. Jesus is therefore at one and the same time the one who possesses the Spirit and the one who baptizes in the Spirit. He is thus the mediator of eternal life.

■

On Psalm 34

Poor man—in your darkness
raise your eyes and look at Jesus.
Listen to what he has to say to you.
Hear from him about your rebirth.
If you turn your face toward him
it will become untroubled and shining.
Poor man, you will lack nothing.
Never cease to bless the Lord.

■

"We are witnesses to all this, we and the Holy Spirit whom God has given to those who obey him" (Acts 3:32). In every age, men and women appear and bear witness to God's work and to their experience of the new life that they have come to know through the Holy Spirit. Judgment has, after all, been pronounced: "Anyone who believes in the Son has eternal life." Our faith is not a moral law, however remarkable that might be. It is first and foremost our way of confessing in our lives what has happened to us in Jesus Christ. We do not have to conquer a Kingdom that has been given to us subject to certain conditions. On the contrary, in faith we are plunged deep into the reality of that Kingdom. "Anyone who believes has eternal life."

Who, then, already has that life in abundance? It is the person who can live every day in the humble recognition that his life has meaning and direction. It is the person who believes that Jesus is the Christ. Jesus—a man among men, a child from Nazareth and a prophet in Judaea, a man who came into the world in order to die there. Jesus—a history of a life like so many others, but also a word that calls for faith; a death that was as sad as every other death, but at the same time an absence that speaks of the eternal presence. "Anyone who believes in the Son has eternal life" because God has expressed the hidden meaning of life in his Son Jesus, a man for others.

Anyone who believes that Jesus is the Christ is born of God. Faith is a birth because it overcomes death. We bear witness to what God offers to men and women through grace. It is not simply a question of affirming that Jesus is the Christ, however; it is also necessary to accept being a son of God in him.

I believe in Jesus Christ in order to be born of God with him. I believe that he has lived in me and shared my experience since he has become my way. I believe that my death is transfigured in his because his words have radically changed the meaning and direction of my way. With him, everything is directed toward love. We who believe are all witnesses to the only victory that is neither transitory nor futile, because it is the victory of love. The one who loves can look at the cross, which saves because it gives his life a meaning and an aim. He knows from whom he has been born and death has already been overcome in his case.

Judgment has already been pronounced, and it is the only testimony that we have—that we have already been born of God. Our lives are simply the gradual incarnation of our existence.

God our Father,
   let us be born in your Son.
He is the way
   and no one comes to you without believing in him.
He is the truth
   and no one knows you without walking with him.
He is the life

and no one can be reborn without being immersed in him.

5. This meditation is inspired by P. Jaccquemont, J.-P. Jossua and B. Quelquejeu, *Une foi exposée*, pp. 128–130, of which we provide a summary here.
6. This meditation has been taken from B. Bro, *Dieu seul est humain* (Paris).

FROM THE FRIDAY OF THE SECOND WEEK OF EASTER
TO THE SATURDAY OF THE THIRD WEEK

Bread Broken for a New World

"I am the bread of life. . . . Anyone who eats my flesh and drinks my blood . . ." Jesus' discourse following the story of the feeding of the five thousand (Jn 6) undoubtedly refers to the Last Supper and the Eucharist, despite the fact that exegetes have pointed to major and minor differences.

"He gave them the wheat (= bread) of heaven": these words from Psalm 78:24 are at the heart of the Johannine discourse. Reading that discourse, we are at once taken into the desert and our thoughts go back quite spontaneously to the exodus and God's gift of manna. Jesus had multiplied the loaves for the crowd gathered at the lakeside and the meaning of the sign had been misunderstood by many. The discussion had therefore to be raised to a higher level.

Jesus was not simply a worker of miracles. He gave bread to men, but they had "to do the works that God wants" (Jn 6:28). Faith is the place where

God and man meet. But who is Jesus exactly? Is he a prophet? Is he the king? These are easy interpretations, and as such they are dangerous. We have to go laboriously through the stages of faith. Jesus reveals himself to his disciples at night in a strong wind when the water is rough and calls on them to commit themselves. What is more, this event takes place "shortly before the feast of Passover" (Jn 6:4), and we are reminded of the great feast, the Easter when the Son of Man is to be revealed as king through the gift that he will make of himself by dying.

Death and life! "Your fathers ate the manna in the desert and they are dead" (Jn 6:49). Why multiply the loaves at all if the bread was not able to give eternal life? How is it that we still have within our reach a man who gives us the food of immortality? Yet we certainly have him. But the conditions for our meeting with him are faith and the sacrament.

Faith first. Jesus is the bread of life. Whoever lives in him lives in God (see Jn 6:56; 1 Jn 4:15). It is a question of living in him, not simply of associating with him when we feel the need to. Living in him is doing what the first disciples did—believing in Jesus and following in his footsteps. Life is always movement. It is an exodus or a crossing. We can never remain where we are, but always have to go further. We have to cross from death to reach the shore of life. There is always a risk. Jesus is, after all, only the "son of Joseph" (Jn 6:42). How could he know the way?

But appearances are transfigured by faith. Jesus claims to be the Son of the Father and greater than Moses himself. Not only does he give bread that is better than manna—he is the "living bread which has come down from heaven" (6:51), the gift of the Father. What proof can Jesus provide for this? The whole tragedy of the Fourth Gospel is, unfortunately, that no proof can be given, apart perhaps from Jesus' words: "No one can come to me unless he is drawn by the Father who sent me" (6:44). Faith, then, is sent back to its true place—the heart. Remaining or dwelling is entering another kind of life in which we are able to find what has so far been hidden—the mystery. Jesus gives us signs, of course, and here we have the striking one of the multiplication of the loaves. But what is this or any other sign if there is no tacit understanding with the one who has to interpret it? The discourse on the bread of life is first and foremost evidence of the exceptional and original part played by faith.

Faith, then, is the pre-condition for the food of eternal life. But faith is expressed in the sacrament. We have to "eat"—in the most radical way imaginable—"the flesh of the Son of Man" and "drink his blood" (6:53). The words spoken at the Last Supper are echoed clearly in Jesus' words in this discourse: "The bread that I shall give is my flesh, for the life of the world" (6:51). But what is that sacrament instituted at Christ's Last Supper?

What we have here in the sacrament is certainly not just a free distribution of a "food of immortality." It is not enough simply to hold out our hand or our tongue to be saved. Jesus has given his flesh and blood—the whole of himself. Eating him is, like faith itself, following him as far as that. It is becoming one with his body, the body that he handed over to die, and the blood that he shed. Coming to the resurrection is accepting the same way as he did, the way of the Passover. The Jews found it almost impossible to accept the need to eat his flesh: "How can this man give us his flesh to eat?" they asked (6:52). This is not because they were unwilling to do such an astonishing thing, but rather because they were aware that his invitation to eat his flesh placed him at the center of everything. What right had he to claim to be the way and the life? He had even less right to say that as one who was soon to be crucified. The same reason led many of his own disciples to complain against him and say: "This is intolerable language. How could anyone accept it?" (6:60). Yes, it is true. The language of the sacrament is intolerable—or, rather, it is, as the Gospel says, "rough," as rough as the way of the cross. But there is no one else who can save man and "raise him up" (6:40). So with Peter, we say: "Lord, to whom shall we go?" (6:68).

In the tradition of the Gospel, the story of the feeding of the five thousand is included within a group of texts which lead up to Peter's and the Church's recognition of Christ. Peter says: "We believe and we know that you are the Holy One of God" (6:68). But faith will never simply be a safe investment. It is not secure in this sense even in the sacrament. We cannot eat the flesh of the Son of Man without taking our place with him at the Last Supper and the passion. If we refuse to do that, life could not flow from death. Christ's resurrection was only possible when he had transcended the test of Calvary. That is why the Eucharist is a sacrifice. The bread broken for a new world goes far beyond all our human attempts to share the bread more fairly. It is the sacrament of death that enables life to flourish. In the Gospel, the account of the multiplication of the loaves is not just a call to be generous. Generosity is always disappointing if it is not grafted onto faith in Jesus, the bread of life for those who are ready to follow him to the end.

BREAKING BREAD AND GIVING THANKS

We share the bread,
  the body of your Son,
  who died for love of his own.
We raise the cup of salvation,
  his risen life,
  the hope of a love
  that is always new.

Father, we bless you
  for so much loving kindness
  given freely to your people.
What can we offer you
  to show how much we thank you?
  Only a humble promise
  to share without reflecting
  what we have received from you.

We stand before you, our Father,
  begging bread and thirsty for life.
Give us today our daily bread.
  Open our hands that are closed to sharing.
All that we have is a little bread
  and the poverty of our lives.
We ask you to break open our pitifully meager offering
  and make it a fertile spring in our desert.

May your Spirit
  keep your Church faithful
  to the mission it has received from you
  to go to all those who are hungry in the world.

May all your children be generous
  in serving the poorest people,
and may those who have nothing
  find that they are rich in you
  and strong in the love of their brothers.

Then, with one heart,

    we shall be able to praise you
as your Spirit inspires us to
    when we take our place at the table
    at which your Son multiplies for all men
    the bread that gladdens their hearts.

■

Everywhere in the world,
    both far away and close at hand,
    people are asking:
    "Who will show us the way to life?"
Lord, let us share their cry of hunger.

The desert has invaded our lives
    and everything is withering.
    Everyone is intent on preserving his own possessions.
Lord, lead us along new ways.

We ask you, Lord,
    give those who eat their fill every day
    the grace to feel uneasy when confronted
    with the misery of this world thirsting for justice.

Let those who receive your Eucharist regularly
    encounter you every time as a new word.
    You give yourself only to be shared.

We pray too for those who are far from your Church.
    Let them find in the witness we bear
    food that satisfies their hunger.

We ask you, Lord, that no one should abandon faith
    without having ventured
    on unexpected and demanding ways.

■

Whoever believes in you, Lord,
    will never be thirsty—
    he will himself be a source of life.
We believe that, in you, death is overcome
    for anyone who hands over his life with yours.

We thank you for this, God,
   who are blessed forever and ever.

■

God, you love life
   and are at the heart of every true wish.
When we want to live better lives
   our hunger drives us toward you.
Give us today once again
   the bread of life, the source of eternity.
Give us the body and blood of your Son,
   for he alone is the food
   that can direct this world without flinching
   toward a future that will never cease.

FRIDAY OF THE SECOND WEEK

FOR HUNGER
Acts 5:34–42: Gamaliel, a liberal-minded Pharisee, took Paul's side in the Sanhedrin. When the Apostles were arrested, he suggested that things should be allowed to continue as they were. If the Christian movement came from God, he argued, men could do nothing to oppose it. If, on the other hand, it came from men, it would simply disappear of its own accord. There were, after all, countless examples in the recent history of Israel of movements that had been no more than a flash in the pan. Gamaliel gave two examples: that of Theudas, who had claimed that his supporters had crossed the River Jordan dry-footed and had eventually been killed, and that of Judas the Galilean, a leader of the Zealot movement at the time of Gamaliel himself and fiercely opposed to the Roman occupation.

What the eminent Jewish teacher had underestimated, however, was the revolutionary character of the apostolic preaching. The Apostles had no political aims and they did not call on people to withdraw into the austerity of the desert, but they spoke to men's hearts and claimed that they could provide an answer to the questions raised in their hearts. Their preaching was inspired by the Holy Spirit and expressed the love that God had in superabundance in his heart for mankind. It was in fact becoming apparent that a little leaven was enough to make the dough rise.

Psalm 27 expresses the trust felt by those who have faith in the Lord and the joy of the Apostles who are glad to have been regarded as worthy to suffer for the name of the Lord.

John 6:1–15: It was "shortly before the Jewish feast of Passover," when the tender covenant that Yahweh had established in setting his people free from slavery in Egypt was celebrated. Moses and his followers had left the sea behind them and had penetrated into the desert. Very soon, however, they had been put to the test by hunger, and this had dampened their enthusiasm. They had complained against God and Moses had been at his wits' end (Num 11:13). Even so, Yahweh had sent them manna.

By the lakeside in Galilee, Philip was also uncertain, so Jesus "took the loaves, gave thanks and gave them out to all who were sitting ready."

There was quite enough bread for the five thousand people and twelve baskets were filled with the pieces that were left. It was the time of plenty—the time of the Messiah who was soon to give his own body to be eaten.

The people were not mistaken. In Jesus they greeted the prophet of the end of time—possibly Elisha, who had, at an early period of Israel's history, fed a hundred people with twenty barley loaves (2 Kgs 4:42–44). At the same time, however, they were mistaken. Misinterpreting his mission, they wanted to proclaim him king so that he would lead them in their revolt.

So Jesus "escaped to the hills by himself," and his disciples got into a boat to go to the other side of the lake. There was a state of crisis existing between Jesus and the people he encountered. That tension was to penetrate into the intimate circle of disciples. He may have been the Messiah, but not in the sense they hoped. The bread that he gave was not a "food that cannot last" (Jn 6:27), like manna. Even the loaves that he had multiplied were no more than a sign, and the pieces left over had to be gathered up "so that nothing gets wasted." The bread that Jesus was to give at the approaching feast of Passover was his life for the salvation of the world. That bread would last, because it was the bread of life.

■

Bread—the most ordinary thing in the world, the food we all share. Bread—that is what men work for. It is, in a sense, the whole of their life.

Jesus wanted to unite himself with man at the heart of his existence and to do this he chose bread. He made himself bread, in this way establishing a mysterious bond between God and bread. God entered men's lives under the sign of bread in Bethlehem, the "house of bread." God was able to live forever in men's lives when Jesus took bread at the end of his life on the eve of his crucifixion. A mysterious bond links God with bread, because God wants to be of the same substance as we are. "Where can we buy some bread for these people to eat?" Jesus asked Philip. The people are in the desert. They try every kind of food, and when they have nothing at all, they ask: "Give us today our daily bread." God therefore took bread, the simplest thing of all, the shared life of all men. To become of the same substance as ourselves, he made himself flesh of our flesh, our everyday bread.

"It was shortly before the Jewish feast of Passover." If he was to multiply the loaves for the people there and for all people, Jesus had also to pay the price. For God, the sign of the bread is inseparable from the sign of the cross. On Maundy Thursday, Jesus is to celebrate in advance what he is to fulfill in his passion. There is only broken bread, bread handed over. Jesus "made the people sit down." Soon he will be stretched out on the wood of the cross. Bread is made to be eaten. "The bread that I shall give is my flesh, for the life of the world" (Jn 6:51). For God, the price of bread can no longer be calculated now, since, to become bread, he handed over his Son. God has paid a price of such a kind that he will never be able to forget the taste of bread.

"Five barley loaves and two fishes; but what is that among so many?" What is a word of salvation in the presence of so many questions asked by men? What is the life and death of one man in the presence of the lives and deaths of millions upon millions of people? "Give us today our daily bread." What difference could the existence of Jesus of Nazareth make to the hunger of so many men? There is only shared bread. It is true that bread is not multiplied today for so many countless people dying of hunger, but that is not because God is not present for mankind. It is because man is not present for his fellow men and indeed because he is not present for himself.

There is only bread to satisfy hunger. But, to our great misfortune, we have kept our bread to ourselves and piled up stocks of it. In the desert we thought that we were stuffed full of it—faith became an all too easy reply to all our questions and to our hunger. Bread is there for hunger, fierce hunger. The people thought that Jesus was a prophet, the greatest prophet, but he "escaped to the hills by himself." He was something different and his path led elsewhere. There is only bread that will save us in the kind that takes us further on the way where we suffer hunger. When he multiplied the loaves, Jesus wanted to make God hungry.

∎

We bless you, Lord,
 who have tasted our lives
 and who have shared our flesh
 in your Son Jesus.
We ask you:
 inspire us with the power of your love
 and let your Spirit be the leaven of eternity in us.
May we, through your grace,
 become the body of Christ
 for all ages.

∎

You satisfy our hunger with broken bread,
 the life of your Son, handed over for the world.
Fill us with desire and hope, Lord,
 that this Eucharist may be bread for our journey
 and keep us as we go up to eternal life.

SATURDAY OF THE SECOND WEEK

IN THE STORMY COURSE OF HISTORY
Acts 6:1–7: Although it was persecuted, the Church of Jerusalem continued to grow. It was a community that was full of life and the Spirit was at work in it. The word of God was proclaimed and the number of Christians increased. Even priests came to join the community.

At the same time, however, there were also conflicts. Although Luke was primarily concerned with communion—to such an extent that he refers again and again to the ideal of the community—he did not try to conceal the fact that confrontations are inherent in the development of any group.

The first serious conflict was between the Christians of Palestinian origin and the Hellenists. It was a very ordinary conflict and the Twelve settled it by appealing to the members of the community to take an initiative and choose "seven men of good reputation, filled with the Spirit and with wisdom," to take care of the shared meals and the administration of the Church's property. It is clear from this that the expansion of the Christian community created new needs and the Apostles tried to deal with these by creating new ministries.

A very ordinary conflict, yes, but one that had arisen as a result of quite serious tensions in the Church. Christians of Hellenist origin, such as Stephen and Philip, were increasingly playing a leading part in the life of the Church. They were more broad-minded than their Hebrew brothers, and the Church was very soon going to be more open to receive pagans.

Psalm 33 calls on the people of God to give thanks on the harp and the lyre and with songs sung in praise of the Lord.

John 6:16–21: Jesus had refused to endorse the popular ideas about the Messiah and had "escaped to the hills by himself." The disciples had also gone away, taking a boat to Capernaum on the other side of the lake. No doubt they talked about what they had experienced. Night was falling and they were in every sense completely in the dark.

The sea was getting rough, and Jews, who were people from the plains and the mountains, were always afraid of the sea. For them, it was a place where monsters lurked and the forces of evil were hidden. Yet Yahweh had conquered the sea, separating the waters of heaven from the lower waters, which had fled in panic from the claps of thunder. They had, in the words of Psalm 104:8, "cascaded over the mountains, into the valleys, down to the reservoir the Lord had made for them."

But now the frightened fishermen see Jesus walking on the waters and coming toward their boat. Like Yahweh, he is in control of the waves. Today the disciples look at him in fascination. Tomorrow, after his resurrection from the dead, they will give him the title of Lord—a title reserved for the one God, the King of creation. Jesus is the Messiah, the one sent by God. He can give the bread of life.

■

The Church has always been tempted throughout its whole history to cling to traditions and to fail to be open to the Spirit, who is always unexpected. It has always tended to abandon the word of God and to prefer to serve meals. In maintaining traditions and preserving habits, it has forgotten its first task and the very reason why it exists—the proclamation of the Gospel. The great temptation of Christians throughout the centuries has been to care for those for whom they have always been concerned and to forget those whom they do not know, the strangers and the younger brothers. If the first Christians had given way to that temptation, then clearly they would have rejected the non-Jewish Christians and, a little later, the pagan Christians.

But there is only one tradition that the Church has to follow in season and out of season and that is its task to proclaim the Gospel. It is difficult to understand how the word "tradition" could ever have been changed in meaning to such a degree that it was turned completely around and given completely the opposite significance from what it had originally. From meaning "hand on" it has come to mean "keep"; from meaning "transmit in sharing" it has come to mean "preserve"; from meaning "convey" it has come to mean "maintain."

Human history is seldom a calm lake and almost always a rough sea. We are driven in many different directions by various currents. At different periods of its history, the Church has always been and probably always will be tempted to steer a safe but very unadventurous course toward the past. But it is on the stormy waters

of the lake that the Church encounters the Lord. The disciples had to row strenuously before they saw his radiant form. The Church can never remain in safe waters. The Lord himself has made sure that its fate is inseparable from the dark forces of human history. The Church has to live in the stormy struggles of life. It has to be tossed about by every wind and by all kinds of dark forces. Men and women have to tire themselves out and risk going around in circles before they can know that their laborious search has from the beginning been led by the Spirit. It is only by venturing to speak that they can experience the happiness of meeting. Faith does not mean that we shall escape fear or anxiety, but it does give us the certainty that God will appear and respond to our fears.

■

God our Father,
we are tossed about
　between faithfulness and imagination,
　fear and risk.
Go ahead of us, we ask you, Lord,
　and steer our boats.
　Take us to the port
　where you live forever.

MONDAY OF THE THIRD WEEK

GOD IN FLIGHT

Acts 6:8–15: The Church was growing and would soon receive pagans. Paul was soon to be aroused by the Spirit and become the Apostle of the Gentiles. But even before then, there was Stephen, a man who was full of religious fervor and enthusiasm. He was probably the first of many to break with his Jewish past.

As a Hellenist, Stephen preferred to preach in synagogues reserved for Jews with a Greek cultural background. He spoke plainly and clearly. In that respect he was like his Master. Like Jesus too, he regarded the temple worship and the Mosaic law as null and void. He refused to cling almost superstitiously to the temple in the material sense and followed Jesus' example in declaring that the law was for man, not man for the law. This disturbed the Jews deeply, and it was not long before Stephen was arrested. False witnesses were found to testify against him, as they had testified against Jesus.

Psalm 119: The structure of this Psalm is alphabetical. It is fundamentally a hymn in honor of God's word. The theme in these particular verses is the righteous man's keeping of the law of God despite the deliberations of the great men of the world against him.

John 6:22–29: The crowd follows Jesus, but what are these people really looking for? They are looking for the man who gave them food. They are hoping to get something at once. They are superstitious, and they are also anxious about the immediate future. They feel uneasy and do not really know what they want. The story of the Samaritan woman is repeated here. The attitude of the Jews is very different from the way in which Jesus sees his mission. The people are looking for a king who would give his hungry subjects bread, but Jesus is the one sent by God.

It is, however, only by faith that Jesus can be recognized as the Messiah. When the people ask him "What must we do if we are to do the works that God wants?" he says at once: "This is working for God: you must believe in the one he has sent." It is, then, the hour of faith, but it is also a time when men may refuse to believe.

∎

They were looking, like the people of France on the eve of the Revolution, for a king who would provide them with bread. But, unlike Louis XVI, this man had already fed the crowd. They could believe in him and felt they should anoint him king.

The crowd, like all crowds, wanted a God who could be used. A God who serves our own little interests, a tradesman-God who distributes his goods when we ask insistently enough—that is the kind of God we all want and can believe in.

But, if we are honest, we are bound to reject the image of God that is no more than an extension of ourselves. If that is our image, then

those who buried him were right. In that case, those who are courageous and honorable enough to remain alone, without God, are perhaps following the truth. If God were simply a despotic ruler who insisted that we should patiently wait and never express our true longings, we ought to denounce him and put him on trial. If he were no more than a God of the gaps, filling in the deficiencies in our own lives, or a kind of superman or merely a prolongation of our own desires, then we would not be wrong to put him to death.

They were looking for a king who would provide them with bread. Perhaps we begin our search for God at the wrong place. Are we looking for a God whom we expect to find in our disappointed hopes, our complaints and even our groanings, a God who is our own size and who will satisfy our little needs? "You are not looking for me because you have seen the signs, but because you had all the bread you wanted to eat."

Dietrich Bonhoeffer declared in his *Letters and Papers from Prison* that he wanted to speak of God not at the limits, but at the center, not in weakness, but in strength, and not in the context of death and sin, but in the life and goodness of man. There are, after all, many signs—Jesus heals, makes the paralyzed walk, cleanses lepers and forgives those who can no longer bear the burden of their sinfulness. God is not to be found in man's weakness, but in his nobility. The people wanted to make Jesus a God and king who would provide them with bread and he sought flight. The God of faith is always to be found in silence and adoration, when his face can be seen in the traces of his presence. Only God can speak authentically of God, and only Christ can truly interpret the Father's will. "This is working for God: you must believe in the one he has sent." Jesus, then, left and invited others to follow him. No one can put his hand on God.

■

Open our hearts, Lord,
enlighten our minds
and make us love,
so that we may receive your Kingdom
   like children receiving bread
   from the hands of their father;
so that, in silence,

*the secret of your presence
and the riches of your name
may be revealed to us.*

TUESDAY OF THE THIRD WEEK

MANNA

Acts 7:51—8:1a: Stephen's speech is the longest in the whole of the Acts of the Apostles, but only the conclusion is included in the Church's liturgy. However those last words are very significant. Stephen denounces the hypocrisy of those who accuse him and who have not kept the law given to Moses on Mount Sinai any more than their ancestors did. Israel's history is a holy one—from the time that he first called Abraham until the building of the temple, God has been incarnate in the life of his people, but Israel has unfortunately always wanted to keep Yahweh within the limits of his laws and rites. In this way, the people have fundamentally misunderstood the new covenant based on the blood of Jesus.

Just as they got rid of Jesus himself, so too do the Jews get rid of Stephen. The theme has not changed—it is still one of accusal. The last words uttered by Stephen recall those spoken by Jesus at his death. Stephen is a true disciple to the end, following Jesus even in dying. Jesus is killed again today and Simon of Cyrene carries the cross again today.

Psalm 31 is a long individual lament, containing both appeals to be rescued and expressions of trust in God. It shows, as it progresses, the serenity of the martyr as he entrusts his cause to God.

John 6:30–35: John 6 is not homogeneous in its structure, and the way in which the liturgy divides it up does not help us to understand the first part of the discourse in particular. It is useful to remember that literary critics of the texts are generally agreed that the discourse consists of three sections (6:26–51b; 51c–59; 60–71), each with a different origin and subject matter, but all formed within the same Johannine tradition. The main aim of the first of these units, which is a sapiential homily, seems to be to show that the bread given by Christ is superior to the manna given by Moses. Jesus disputes the traditional Jewish interpretation of the food in the desert.

In the synagogue, manna had come increasingly to be understood in an allegorical sense. It was seen as spiritual food and had become a symbol of the Mosaic law or of wisdom, both of which were able to give life. For Jesus, however, manna was not the true bread of life. On the one hand, those who had eaten it in the desert were dead (Jn 6:49); on the other, it was the Father, not Moses, who gave true bread (6:32). Jesus was above all the new norm of life—the Wisdom of God. Those who listened to his teaching would therefore be fed on the true bread of life and would live forever.

■

In the early hours of the morning, just as the dew was beginning to evaporate, the Hebrews saw something like small, fine grains on the ground, shining like hoar-frost. They asked each other: "What is it?" To sustain them on their way to the promised land, God had given them manna.

"What sign will you give us to show that we should believe in you?" They question one another: "Who is he, then?" For those who have no ready-made answers, who do not allow evil suspicions to trouble them or who simply welcome his presence, Jesus is simply a question. Where does his authority come from? Does his gathering the people together on the mountain and distributing bread to them mark the end of time? God had, after all, promised to call the people to a great feast.

"Who is it?" Jesus declares: "I am the living bread which has come down from heaven" (Jn 6:51). He is speaking of himself—of his own person. He invites us to follow him, along a road that leads through the desert of death. But that desert is also the place where the manna lies scattered and life is welcomed. Deep down in ourselves, a hunger for life which lifts us up has perhaps seen that here is our true food. That manna is, after all, love, friendship, justice, brotherhood and reconciliation. But the bread that satisfies our hunger is not our ordinary daily bread. It has come down from heaven. Yes, Jesus will always be a question. His presence with us will nourish us by creating an appetite, and that will continue until the end of time.

"Sir, give us that bread always" (6:34). We call on God without really knowing what it is we truly want. Our words echo those of the Samaritan woman. It is in the depths of our questioning that our hope sinks down and we venture to reply because of that hope.

At the table, the bread will be shared among us and we ask: "What is it?" At the same time, we also ask: "Give us that bread." Our astonishment becomes admiration and a humble request.

■

We are hungry, Lord.
  We do not want false manna,
  illusions, lies or empty happiness.
Tell us again that you forgive us
and give us the bread of life.
The water drains out of our cracked tanks—
  why are our lives being destroyed?
Be our salvation.
Give us your bread of life.

WEDNESDAY OF THE THIRD WEEK

GROWTH

Acts 8:1b–8: Stephen's martyrdom was at once followed by the bitter persecution of the Church in Jerusalem, the members of which began in this way to share in the mystery of the death and resurrection of their Lord. But the grain of wheat that had fallen to the ground and died was yielding a harvest. The word of God was forced to leave the Jewish capital, but was heard elsewhere. Philip, another Hellenist, went to Samaria. Peter went to Caesarea and Antioch. At the same time, Saul of Tarsus took Stephen's clothes and was ready to carry out orders from the temple against the Christians of Damascus.

The people of Samaria welcomed Philip and his message and were as happy to receive it as their compatriot had been when Jesus had proclaimed the need to "worship in spirit and truth" (Jn 4:24). For them too, the messianic age had come. They believed in the good news proclaimed by Philip and were baptized. The Spirit confirmed God's work by signs and miracles. Very soon after this, the Apostles were to come to Samaria and ratify the first setting up of another community by the Church of Jerusalem (Acts 8:14–17).

Psalm 66: Vv. 1–12 together form a hymn which concludes with a reference to the crossing of the Sea of Reeds, when Yahweh intervened to save his people. This hymn may have been used in worship as a thanksgiving for Israel's victory over its enemies.

John 6:35–40: "Whoever comes to me I shall not turn him away." There is a clear allusion here to the first chapters of the history of man's salvation. Driven out of paradise after sinning, Adam no longer had access to the tree of life. He was destined for death. It would seem, however, that the synagogue had never believed that man's situation was beyond repair, although that view, it was also claimed, was supported by the Genesis story. In some of the targums, it is said that the law is the "tree of life for all who study it." In the sapiential literature, on the other hand, wisdom clearly takes the place of the law.

Jesus' discourse on the bread of life is a powerful reminder of the saving will of the Father. At the same time, it also shows us Jesus as true Wisdom. Thanks to him, the curse that had been upon mankind since original sin was lifted. No one who is nourished by his teaching will be turned away. Those who are fed in this way receive from Jesus the knowledge of good and evil.

∎

In the beginning, man wanted to taste the fruit of the tree of life in order to become like God, with the result that what had been a source of life became a poison. Instead of receiving his food by grace, man wanted to make his own happiness for himself. He was therefore driven out of paradise because he wanted to live on his own earth and make it himself.

"Whoever comes to me I shall not turn away." As we listen to Jesus' words, we rediscover the country where we originated. Jesus calls on us to accept grace and forgiveness and we are brought back into the garden to taste the fruit of the tree.

Jesus draws everyone to himself. His cross is planted in the heart of

the world and is a new tree of life in which everyone can be reborn. "The will of him who sent me is that I should lose nothing of all that he has given me."

There is no question of "all rights" being "reserved" for salvation, and the Holy Spirit has no registered trademark. Grace is not confined to a game preserve or any kind of paradise for privileged people. The tree of the cross was planted outside the walls of the city on a hill, because many people passed that way, since "the place was not far from the city," and the name that saves was written in Hebrew, Latin and Greek, so that everyone would know "in his own language about the marvels of God" (see Jn 19:20; Acts 2:11).

Salvation is universal, because there are no righteous men. Everyone is sick and everyone is called to be healed. So that the tree might yield abundant fruit the seed had to be sown in the ground at Golgotha. The Word of grace can only germinate if it is sown in tears and blood. Life can only be victorious after it has been kept captive in the tomb.

The Church of Jerusalem was to be persecuted with great violence, and the members of the community were to be scattered and to spread the good news everywhere in the known world. Unless the grain of wheat dies, it cannot yield a harvest. In the Christian order, there is only one law of growth—that of life handed over, of risks taken in hope and of new beginnings based on the assurance that the Spirit is faithful.

The only reason why the tree exists is to shelter men who are looking for life. It can only grow if men and women are faithful to the law of growth that applies in the Kingdom of God, that is, if they hand over their lives freely and unconditionally to love, without reservation and in the freedom of the Spirit.

■

God our Father,
 do not let us keep your word
 in the fetters of our habits,
 certainties and sectarian attitudes.
Let what you have sown in us bear fruit—
 the freedom of the Spirit,

*the enthusiasm of renewal
and the happiness of having been saved.*

THURSDAY OF THE THIRD WEEK

BREAD HANDED OVER
Acts 8:26–40: Two roads lead out of Jerusalem: one goes to Emmaus and the other to Gaza. Along the first of these roads two Passover pilgrims are walking, their eyes cast down and their hearts full of grief. They are deeply disappointed by Jesus' arrest and death. Along the second road a God-fearing eunuch is riding in a carriage. Because he is a foreigner and also because he is a eunuch, he is not allowed to take part in Jewish worship. There are many similarities between the story of encounter on the road to Emmaus (Lk 24:13–35) and that of the meeting between Philip and the Ethiopian on the road to Gaza. Just as Jesus explains to his traveling companions "the passages throughout the Scriptures that were about himself" (Lk 24:27), so too does Philip explain to the eunuch the passage in Isaiah about the suffering servant. For this foreigner, then, Philip is a witness, proclaiming the good news of Jesus Christ. He is another Christ and, what is more, a risen Christ, just as Stephen, who died as a true disciple of Christ, also bore witness.

Jesus shared the Eucharist with the two disciples whom he had enlightened. Philip administers baptism to the eunuch. After that, he goes on his way, meditating on the words of the psalm: "Ambassadors will come from Egypt; Ethiopia will stretch out her hands to God" (Ps 68:31).

Psalm 66: Vv. 1–12 are a hymn, whereas vv. 13–20 are an act of thanksgiving. In this context, after the conversion of the Ethiopian, an event that points to the fulfillment of the prophetic oracles on the universal nature of God's salvation, these verses are particularly appropriate.

John 6:44–51: In the readings selected for the lectionary, John 6 is read as a whole, but without the verses on the complaining of the Jews. This is very regrettable, because, apart from the fact that they form an essential part of the whole discourse, these verses (41–43) also reinforce the impression of the exodus and draw attention to the fact that the synagogue was strongly opposed to Jesus' messianic claims. This is clear, for example, from the fact that Jesus' statement "The bread that I shall give is my flesh for the life of the *world*" is a reference to the universal nature of his plan, in contrast to the Jews' rejection of his teaching.

Vv. 44–51 emphasize the interplay between the Father and the Son in the work of redemption. It is God himself who teaches, fulfilling the words of Jeremiah, who had spoken about the end of time and the fact that Yahweh would at that time write his law in the hearts of his people, so that each person would have intimate, individual knowledge of him (Jer 31:33). It is also interesting to note in this passage in John 6 that the Father not only gives true bread, but also draws mankind to offer it to his Son. On the other hand, however, it is the Son who reveals the Father to mankind.

■

"I am the living bread . . . . Anyone who eats this bread will live forever." To live is surely everything. It is simply essential for all people. We really know very little about life, and what we do know we know imperfectly. We live continuously at a reduced level, satisfying our little desires and our paltry needs and boasting of our absurd achievements.

But Jesus said: "I am the living bread." Only God really knows about life. He understands Life itself—his beloved Son who came from his own hands on the first morning of the universe. No one has ever seen God—only the one who came from him knows him. When we consider how passionately and how deeply Jesus loved life, we are able to understand a little of God's passion for life. But we have embalmed God and made him into an idol to adore. We are surprised when we find ourselves submerged in the overflowing and totally unexpected vitality of our God.

"I am the living bread." God's overflowing life became flesh and blood. "Anyone who eats this bread will live forever; and the bread that I shall give is my flesh for the life of the world." But we have immobilized his flesh and blood and made them into idols to adore.

"I am the living bread . . . . Anyone who eats this bread will live forever." But we have to eat that bread as believers, since eating Jesus Christ means becoming one with him—becoming his flesh and

blood. The believer who learns from Christ the full dimension of life will live. "I am the living bread," Jesus said. One evening, he offered that bread, giving thanks, and it was an announcement of his passion that was imminent. He gave his body and blood, the whole of himself, for the multitude. "Anyone who eats this bread will live." All who hear his words are also committed to give their lives without restraint.

"I am the living bread." Jesus expressed in these words God's passion for life and his own passion and at the same time invited us to become his flesh.

■

You, Jesus Christ, are life that never weakens
   and you have taken the weakness of our flesh to the end.

You are filled with God
   and you became nothing to become our bread.

Make those who share in your flesh
   live from your Spirit,
and may death not dry up at its source
   the life that you have promised
   forever and ever.

FRIDAY OF THE THIRD WEEK

FLESH AND BLOOD

Acts 9:1–20: Saul had approved of the killing of Stephen, but the first Christian martyr had prayed for those who persecuted him. The Church had already opened its doors to Samaritans and Ethiopians and the time had now come for the name of the Lord to be brought, before pagans (9:15). That was to be Paul's task.

Jesus appeared to the man who was persecuting him on the road to Damascus, and Saul received the light and saw clearly. God revealed his

Son in him. In what seemed to be a flash of lightning, Paul recognized the limits of the Mosaic law that he had been defending so strenuously. It was, he knew, not by circumcision or by obedience to the Commandments that man was saved, but by God's grace and the cross of Christ. The Church opened its arms wide to receive the convert. A disciple who lived in Damascus went to where Saul had been taken and laid hands on him. It was as if "scales fell away from Saul's eyes." The Spirit burned him with a fire that would never be extinguished.

Psalm 117 is a short but typical hymn of praise, containing an invitation to praise God and stating why he should be praised.

John 6:52–59: The theme of the discourse and its terminology change in vv. 51–59. It is no longer a question of faith, but of the need to "eat the flesh" and "drink the blood" of the Son of Man in order to obtain eternal life. It is worth noting that the reality of the eucharistic food and drink is supported by the vocabulary of these verses. (The use of the word *trogein*, to chew the flesh, has frequently been stressed by exegetes.) These words are also not addressed, like the preceding ones, to the Jews. They are intended for members of the Christian community who had been calling the content and value of the sacraments into question. The "eucharistic" discourse is therefore a response to the need for orthodoxy.

The two discourses, however, form a single whole. The editor's work has resulted in a number of remarkable parallels between the two parts. The Old Testament quotation from Psalm 78:24 in John 6:31 ("He gave them the wheat of heaven = bread from heaven") is replaced in John 6:51, and the reply of the Jews in both cases are examples of this parallelism. The same applies to the similarity between Christ's two statements: "Whoever sees the Son and believes in him shall have eternal life" (6:40) and "Anyone who eats my flesh and drinks my blood has eternal life" (6:54). The bread of life is both Jesus as wisdom and the eucharistic flesh of Christ.

Two statements in this second discourse are well worth noting. In v. 56, there is a typically Johannine emphasis on the fact that we are united here and now with Christ when we eat his flesh and drink his blood. V. 53 speaks of eating the "flesh of the Son of man," thus affirming the reality of the eucharistic flesh and blood, while at the same time stressing, as does the chapter as a whole, that the flesh is not that of the earthly Jesus, but of the person of the glorified Lord.

■

The Jews are deeply scandalized by what they hear. "How can this man give us his flesh to eat?" they ask one another. We, on the other hand, are so used to these words that they hardly surprise us at all.

Yet their very realism is quite disconcerting. Bread—flesh—given as food, and blood poured out to quench thirst. Eating—the original text even has the word "chew." All this is a long way from spiritual nourishment that should not be touched by human teeth under pain of sacrilege. But we are no longer scandalized, because we have deprived the Eucharist of its fleshly attribute and have spiritualized it, making the host a spotless wafer that is quite remote from our coarse everyday bread.

Our celebration of the Eucharist should really be a public scandal. It should evoke the question: "How can they do that sort of thing?" People ought to ask one another that kind of question when they see us take the coarse bread of daily life, the lives of all men and women, heavy with the weight of their misery and hope, and when they hear us say the humble words of the Lord over it: "This is my body." That, after all, is the scandal. God has taken the life of the world on himself, and if we have made the "symbol" of the bread into a symbol of that symbol, it is because we have dehumanized God. "How can they do that sort of thing?" The only witness that we have to bear is this: to proclaim the disconcerting news that God has moved house and now lives in the world of men.

Eating is merging, incorporating, becoming one body. "I would like to eat you," the mother says as she hugs her baby. Taking the body and blood of Christ is entering into communion with love and destiny. Taking his body and blood is knowing that the Spirit is living in the body and blood of mankind today, in men and women who are suffering, looking and giving birth to the world in sorrow, in men and women who are happy and who sing and dance, and in rich and poor people and sinners and saints.

The Jews were right to be scandalized. From that time onward, whenever men and women have gathered together in the name of the Lord to share the bread and give thanks, they bring about the surprising news of God taking living flesh, the flesh of the life of mankind.

We bless you, Lord, the lover of life.

*The bread broken between our hands
   is already the flesh of a new world
   in which all men will be brothers.*

*The cup of our thanksgiving
   is already the blood shed
   for the salvation of the world.*

*Blessed are you, Lord,
   because our Eucharist looks forward
   to the table that you have set
   for us in your Kingdom forever.*

SATURDAY OF THE THIRD WEEK

FREEDOM

Acts 9:31–42: A period of transition before the reception of the pagans into the Church, this is also a period of transition during which the Church continues to grow. Peter, who guarantees communion, is constantly on the move.

"Get up!" The Judaeo-Christian believers interpreted their experience of Christ's resurrection in this way: We believe that Jesus was dead and was then raised from the dead. Christ stood at the entrance to the tomb, at the dawn of the promise on the morning of a new world. Peter therefore tells the man who has been confined to his bed for eight years: "Aeneas, Jesus Christ cures you. Get up and fold up your sleeping mat." He says very much the same to Tabitha, the Christian woman living in Jaffa, "Tabitha, stand up," and then he says it to the pagan Cornelius who comes to ask for baptism. This is the beginning of a new era for the Church of God.

Psalm 116 is a Psalm of individual thanksgiving. The liturgy contains that part of it that expresses the believer's wish to thank God in song.

John 6:60–69: "No one can come to me unless the Father allows him." It is a time of decision and the disciples are not exempt. "The flesh has nothing to offer"—it leads to death. The flesh is the temple of Herod, the water of Jacob or the bread of Moses. Only the Spirit can give life. The Spirit is the new law and the word of God handed on by Christ.

V. 60 presents us with a real difficulty. What can the disciples be thinking of when they say that Jesus' words are "intolerable"? What is that intolerable language? Most exegetes have referred it to Jesus' heavenly origin (see v. 38: "Because I have come down from heaven," which is repeated in v. 58). Interpreted in that sense, the meaning of v. 62 ("What if you should see the Son of man ascend to where he was before?") also becomes clearer, and the connection between the disciples' indignation can be seen to correspond to the complaints of the Jews in vv. 41–42.

The passage as a whole is a response to a crisis in the Johannine communities. Some believers refused to accept the divinity of Christ. On the one hand, there was the tradition which affirmed the faith of the Twelve and stressed Peter's confession of faith. On the other hand, there was a heresy, with some believers refusing to follow the Master and, so it would seem, not forming part of the community whose unity was symbolized in the Eucharist.

■

What people were saying about Jesus was: "What he is saying is quite intolerable. It doesn't make sense." However this time it was not his opponents but his own followers who were saying this. So far they had listened to him sympathetically and sometimes even enthusiastically. Now, however, they were beginning to leave him, one group after another. They could no longer understand him. They had lost heart.

What, then, was Jesus' reaction? He might have made different demands on them. He could even have made concessions. The failure might have led him to a number of decisions. But he was a prophet and his reaction was radical. "Does this upset you?" And he might have added: "The words that I have spoken are truth," but he in fact said: "The words that I have spoken are spirit and they are life—but there are some of you who do not believe." And, instead of encouraging the Twelve to rejoin him by means of a facile discourse,

he provokes them to make a decision: "What about you—do you want to go away too?"

We all know the kind of advertisement that tells us: "Trust in us—let us look after your interests—we are at your service." The trust such advertisers are looking for is a blank check and a real form of slavery on our part. But we pay a different price for our encounter with Jesus Christ. Our freedom is exactly matched by his commitment to us.

That is clear from this encounter between Jesus and his followers as recorded at the end of John 6: "Make your choice," he tells them. "Do you want to go away too?" That question confronts them with the need to become men. Get up! Like a plant growing without a stake. "If you want to, follow me." How could Jesus have proclaimed God's passion for life if he did not awaken men to freedom? We are all too familiar with the so-called "spontaneous" demonstrations staged by totalitarian governments and accompanied by fear of what people may say for us to be able to overlook the fact that every infringement of our freedom is also a violation of our human dignity. Jesus' disciples could not be simply a crowd of people whose souls had been destroyed, nor could they be no more than a heterogeneous and speechless mass. His "Do you want to?" is disarming, because its strength and power of conviction is to be found in its weakness. It is a statement that exists only as a risk taken in handing oneself over to the other person for him to do what he likes, and it is therefore both disarming and vulnerable.

"Do you want to go away?" Have you, fellow Christians, asked yourselves that question? Shall I stay or shall I go away? You cannot ever give a reply that will be valid for all time. After all, we have not really begun to experience faith if we have not felt somewhere in our hearts that fear and hesitation: "Lord, to whom shall we go?"

■

For the freedom that your Spirit
  brings about in our hearts,
  we bless you, Lord.

For the word of your Son
  that calls on us to go further,
  we bless you, Lord.

*For the share that you give us
  in his body and blood,
  in his life and death,
  we bless you, Lord.*

*To whom shall we go?
You have the message of eternal life
  forever and ever.*

FOURTH WEEK OF EASTER

THE LAW OF THE RESURRECTION

The resurrection is the world inside out. Looking at the world the right side out, we have to ask ourselves again and again whether our perspectives do not have to be changed continuously. Christ goes ahead of us on our way, leading us toward the end of our history—the place where God is. No one can come to the Father without going through the gate of the Kingdom built on his word. Christ's followers have always to learn how to change direction in their lives. The resurrection is not only the hymn of our victory, it is also the new law of our existence.

Our task is, after all, simply to imitate the Shepherd who leads us. St. Paul summarized the dynamic content of the resurrection in these words to his communities: "Now you are all sons of light and sons of the day" (1 Thes 5:5; cf. Eph 5:7–8).

The moral lesson taught by the resurrection is above all that it bears witness to our salvation. You belong to Christ, and no one can take from him those whom the Father has given to him. The Light has come into the world so that those who believe in it will not dwell in darkness. The new law is illumination and grace.

That law also comes to us from the one who did not claim for himself a rank that made him equal to God. There is only one Christian, and that is Christ. Only he who is Love itself experienced the need to love to the very end. Only he who marked the road that led up from Golgotha to the garden of Easter with his own blood and in complete trust can claim to be the Way.

"You will be like gods," the serpent whispered in the garden of Eden, and man, foolishly misled, believed the lie and was dragged down to the dust. But the believer who tries in patience and prayer to make his life similar to that of the word of God and who tries to imitate the features of the divine face will hear the words: "I have been with you for so long and you have always been like God." It is there that the world is turned inside out and the new law is to be found.

∎

Holy Father, we give you thanks
  through Jesus, your beloved Son, our Easter Lamb.
He came to give peace to men,
  the fullness of joy, peace and love.
He gave his blood to renew your covenant
  and to make the spring flow
  that will spread out into eternal life.
In him we know you,
  and by him we are led to you
  so that we may dwell in your presence.
Therefore, God our life,
  renewed in the Spirit,
  and together with all our brothers
  who have been sacrificed in his blood,
  we bless you.

MONDAY OF THE FOURTH WEEK

THE GATE OF THE KINGDOM
Acts 11:1–18: "The wind blows wherever it pleases; but you cannot tell where it comes from or where it is going" (Jn 3:8). The Spirit blows on the Church and changes the frontiers of Judaism. The Samaritans have already been reconciled, but the step that is going to be taken now is even more important. The pagans are already at the doors of the Church and seizing hold of the Kingdom. A new Pentecost is already dawning. At

Caesarea the pagans have proclaimed their faith in the name of Jesus and have asked for baptism. Urged on by the Spirit, Peter prophesies: "God has given these people the identical thing he gave to us when we believed in the Lord Jesus Christ, and who am I to stand in God's way?" What a happy situation for the people of God when their leaders do not imprison the power of the Spirit.

There are, of course, many problems to be solved. It takes time. Jews and pagans are not sitting together at the same table, sharing the same meal and the same Eucharist. But the Jewish law forbade Jews to eat with pagans, insisting that it was a source of impurity. Because of this, some of the Judaeo-Christians protest to Peter about this new practice. Their protest is unsuccessful; nothing can extinguish the fire of the Spirit. For God, man's heart, not food, is the only frontier between purity and impurity, and in the long run that also comes to apply to the Church.

Psalms 42 and 43 are individual laments, expressing in a vivid way the desire of the pagans to drink at the source of life.

John 10:1–10 (11–18 in Year A): "Blind? If you were, you would not be guilty, but since you say, 'We see,' your guilt remains" (Jn 9:41). The Pharisees have excommunicated the blind man cured by Jesus. Did they prefer darkness to light? Whatever the case may be, one thing is certain—they claim to hold the key to salvation and acquire a stock of merits by their scrupulous observance of the details of the law. The scribes are particularly odious, imposing burdens on the poor of Israel that are too heavy for them. They behave like those bad leaders, the "shepherds" of Israel, about whom the prophet Ezekiel had such harsh things to say (Ez 34). Here Jesus calls them "thieves and brigands" and sees clearly that they rule over the people without understanding their deepest needs and desires.

But Jesus is not like them—he knows his sheep. He has assumed their flesh and has made himself one of them. So, when he speaks to them, he speaks to their hearts and they know his voice. The Son of Man does not crush us, but raises us up and, in a loving and intimate conversation, shows us that love is indeed possible. Jesus is the gate that opens to the infinity of God, which is an infinity of goodness, mercy and freedom.

■

Once again Jesus is engaged in polemics with those who so often

oppose him, the Pharisees. They imprison people within the confines of their doctrines and rules. Jesus calls them thieves, brigands and wolves and says that they "steal, kill and destroy." At the time of the early Church, such Pharisees wanted to draw the limits of the temple on prayer and the frontiers of Judaism on man's salvation. At all times, pharisaical leaders have always wanted to restrict believers to a sheepfold so that they can watch over them, protect and keep them.

Jesus, however, says: "I am the gate." He rejects the idea of confinement and looks for openness to the world of God and the world of man. The gate is open to the green countryside and the wind. Jesus opens the way to infinite adventure with God. "I am the gate," he says and promises to break down the restrictive and protective walls of narrowness and fear. God is outside the walls. He was crucified outside the walls, at the gates of the city. "Anyone who enters through me will be safe." He will enter and be saved in the country where the Spirit of God, the wind of freedom, blows.

Jesus is the gate, a narrow gate through which the camel and the rich man can pass and a very demanding gate that leads to the steep way of the cross. He is also a gate of light, like the wide entrance to a tomb that is open to the mystery of Easter.

The gate is also the place through which we pass and encounter each other. "I am the gate," Jesus tells us. Anyone who enters through him joins a community with close bonds of knowledge, love and sharing that are stronger than those formed by restrictions and rules.

"I am the gate." Jesus is a gate that is open to a universe that has until now been forbidden to us. Two angels were placed by God to guard the paradise that had been lost to man by sin. Now God himself is the gate and the way through it. "I have come so that men may have life and have it to the full."

∎

Open our locked gates, Lord;
   break down our certainties
   and denounce our habits.
Let the breath of your Spirit invade us,
   be the breach in our defensive wall
   and lead us out of our dead-ends.
Be the gate opening on to freedom and life.

TUESDAY OF THE FOURTH WEEK

BELONGING

Acts 11:19–26: Caesarea was still in Palestine, but the Christian community had become scattered after the persecution of the Church of Jerusalem, the Hellenists, for example, going back to the countries they had originally come from. Some of them began to preach to the Greeks in Antioch, a very important administrative center of an overseas province of the Roman Empire, Syria, which included Jerusalem, but a very corrupt town.

This was a revolution, affecting the whole future of the Church. Until then, a few pagans had been accepted as members of the Christian community, but they were exceptional. Now, however, they were, as missionaries, Greeks with the Greeks, and "the hand of the Lord was with them." A new Church was born in the great pagan city of Antioch that was quite independent of Judaism. When the name "Christians" was given to these disciples for the first time, this was no mistake on the part of public opinion.

In Jerusalem too, people were aware that the wind had changed direction. The Apostles sent Barnabas to investigate the situation. He assessed it very positively and then went to Tarsus to look for Paul.

Psalm 87: Even though it lacks certain characteristics common to such Psalms, this Psalm is very similar to the canticles of Zion. It praises Jerusalem, the city chosen by Yahweh which was the mother Church of Christians, the community of those who believed first and who bore witness to Christ beyond their own frontiers and led people to God.

John 10:22–30: Ezekiel had prophesied that the unworthy leaders of the people of Israel would be replaced by one shepherd chosen by Yahweh, a Messiah in the line of David (Ez 34:23–24). Was Jesus applying the prophet's oracle to himself when he called himself the good shepherd? He ought to say so quite openly: I am the Messiah! A request of this kind is found in the Synoptic Gospels only in the context of Jesus' trial (Mk 14:61). In John's Gospel, however, the whole of Jesus' life is presented as a long trial, in which the darkness of men is confronted by the light of God.

But it is a fake trial, because those who accuse Jesus judge him and do not judge him impartially. "The Father and I are one," Jesus says, and for many who hear it, this is blasphemy. Simeon had certainly spoken the truth when he proclaimed that Jesus was "destined for the fall and the rising of many in Israel" (Lk 2:34).

■

The Feast of the Dedication of the temple was being celebrated in Jerusalem. The people present remembered the restoration of the altar of sacrifices that had been desecrated by the pagans and the splendor of Solomon's sanctuary. The many people taking part in the pilgrimage were given over to rejoicing. They were reliving the exodus, the crossing of the desert, the long journey to the promised land and the nights spent in tents. They remembered the time when God himself lived in a tent until the temple was built as his dwelling place.

"He lived among us" (Jn 1:14)—the Word lived in a tent among us. The signs disappear and their place is taken by reality. The real dwelling place of God among men is a son of man, the Son of God. This is surely a sign of contradiction. "If you are the Christ, tell us plainly." The Son came "so that those without sight may see and those with sight turn blind" (Jn 9:39). Those Pharisees who tried to wrench the sheep who already knew Christ from his hands were surely blind. The feast was a place of fierce controversy.

"The Lord is my shepherd." Only God is really able to lead his people, and he has put everything into the hands of his Son. Men will soon try to destroy the true temple of God, but the Lamb will rise again "to lead the flock to springs of living water" (Rev 7:17). Only the shepherd, who has become a lamb himself, in order to be one with his flock, can claim to be the real leader. Only the one who gives his life, handing it over completely and going to the very end, can take us to the source of life.

That is the only sign that God will give—the Lamb being led to the slaughterhouse. Despised and rejected by the people, he will go without defending himself. Like the scapegoat, chased into the desert burdened symbolically with the weight of the people's sin, he will be driven out of the city with a cross on his back. Those entrusted to the true shepherd by the Father "will never be lost," and "when I am lifted up from the earth, I shall draw all men to myself" (Jn 12:32). The only sign will be a shepherd abandoned by his flock just as he is gathering them together at a moment of extreme destitution. That same shepherd will also abandon everything himself and go off in search of one sheep, so that it will not be lost. There are blood ties between the flock and its shepherd, who cannot leave those whom he has called without denying himself. "This is my blood—do this in memory of me." Because he went to the very end of his life, he was able to open the way to pastures of salvation and to lead us to the place where God dwells. "Where I am, my servant will be also."

■

Father,
when the hour came
and men wanted to wrench from your hands
those whom you had given to him,
your Son handed himself over as a victim
   so that they would never be lost.
We ask you, Lord,
that we who share in the body and blood
   of the one who is our paschal Lamb
may be brought together by the Spirit
   into one flock,
   until the day when we shall be yours
   forever.

WEDNESDAY OF THE FOURTH WEEK

LIGHT
Acts 12:24—13:5: The Spirit was blowing in the Church of Antioch—a real tempest. When he fetched Saul from Tarsus, Barnabas took a great risk on the future. He then brought him to Antioch, where they both spent a whole year in the community there, teaching and preaching and building up a new Jerusalem that was free of the pressure exerted by the temple and the

law of Moses. There were teachers and prophets in the community, and Communion services were held regularly. When the Christians of Jerusalem, who were certainly not rich men, began to suffer from famine, their brethren in Syria at once came to the rescue of the mother Church. Like their fellow believers in Jerusalem, they too were faithful to prayer and the breaking of bread, and the words spoken by Jesus himself at the Last Supper gradually came to acquire a definitive form. It was, for example, during a eucharistic service that a prophet stood up and declared in the name of the Holy Spirit: "I want Barnabas and Saul set apart for the work to which I have called them." The Christians of Antioch fasted and prayed and then laid hands on the two who had been chosen. The work they were to do was to be that of the whole community.

Psalm 67 is not easy to classify. Vv. 1 and 2 are clearly a prayer and can be included among the Psalms of supplication, but the verses that follow seem to form part of a hymn.

John 12:44–50: The Sanhedrin has decided that Jesus must die. One of the women among his followers has already anointed him for burial (12:1–8), and "now the hour has come for the Son of Man to be glorified" (12:23). His death is now inevitable, and the whole of mankind is called to be present on the hill outside Jerusalem. The grain of wheat must die in order to yield a harvest.

Jesus is ready to bear supreme witness, but his sacrifice at the same time proclaims judgment on the world. He is the light of the world. He was not sent to judge, but to save. Yet those who prefer the darkness to the light are condemned and the light is in the world for only a little time. The "book of signs" is a history of man's refusal of life and light—the life and light of God himself.

∎

"I, the light, have come into the world, so that whoever believes in me need not stay in the dark anymore." That, then, is the judgment to which we are exposed: that the light has come into the world so that everyone who believes may have life. Men often avoid the light, of course, and prefer darkness, because the light reveals their own lack of justice and their mediocrity. But if we have the courage to expose ourselves to the light of the word of grace, even if it penetrates into the darkest corners of our being, we shall find that it will drive out the

shadows that condemn us and fill our entire existence with warmth and goodness. What Jesus is telling us is simply this: that anyone who listens to his words will come to the light.

What does that Light say, then? It says: "I have come to bring fire to the earth" (Lk 12:49). It also says: If you want to be perfect, if you want to see me in glory, if you want your heart to be transformed, go and sell everything that is weighing you down, your selfishness, your useless wealth, your deceitful needs and your self-satisfaction, and follow me. Then your heart will be like a clear mirror and you will see my glory.

The Light also tells us: "Would you bring in a lamp to put it under a tub or under the bed? Surely you would put it on the lampstand" in the middle of the room, to shine in every dark corner (Mk 4:21). I renew the whole earth. I set free every desire. I make everything small grow. I bring to light everything that is fine and beautiful. I make everything that is dull bright.

Finally, the Light says: Be like servants waiting for their master to return. It is getting darker, the house seems to be dead and day is apparently never going to dawn. But you, my faithful servants, have only to wait and watch with your lamps in your hands until your master knocks. He will come, light the lamps and set the table, and there will be a great feast.

So listen to the one who says: "I, the light, have come into the world, so that whoever believes in me need not stay in the dark anymore." Even if you hesitate to go forward, like a man who hardly dares to believe his eyes, you can take the step in the bright light of God himself.

■

Lord, you have come to us in the darkness of our world.
    We bless you for the light
    that has been with you since the beginning.

You have let that light shine out in our shadows,
    and day after day
    the Spirit of your Son transfigures our earth.

We ask you, then:

let the hour of your grace rise over us again
and let your Day come.
May it last forever.

THURSDAY OF THE FOURTH WEEK

LOVE

Acts 13:13–25: Paul here takes over the leadership of the mission. He has changed his name, dropping the Jewish "Saul" in favor of the Roman "Paul" because the Spirit is directing him toward the pagan world. He keeps, however, to the usual practice among Christian missionaries and still addresses the Jews first. Here we see him speaking on the sabbath in the synagogue in Antioch (in Pisidia this time, that is, in southern Turkey). He takes Scripture as his point of departure and recalls Israel's past. Like all Jews, Paul has a keen sense of the unity of history, and for him the event on Mount Sinai and the Easter event form part of the same economy of salvation. God has promised man eternal life, and the same Spirit is at work in history.

Psalm 89 consists of several different elements. The verses that are recited or sung in today's liturgy all belong to a dynastic poem (vv. 2–5, 20–37) recalling God's promises to David and his election and that of his descendants to the throne of Judah. This poem may well be a response to a governmental crisis. Taken in the context of the first reading from the Acts of the Apostles, the poem suggests that Jesus is descended from David.

John 13:16–20: During the last meal that he shared with his disciples, Jesus rose from table and wrapped a towel around his waist in order to wash their feet. Just before his departure from this life, he expressed what had been its very essence in an act of unparalleled depth. For Jesus, living had been loving. Love enabled him to give his life to save others. That same love also enabled him to serve his own in the most humble way. "If anyone wants to be first, he must make himself last of all and servant of all" (Mk 9:35).

Jesus' example and Commandment—these are rooted in the whole of his own life. His most basic demand is that we should love others, even our enemies. The whole of his life can be seen as a commitment to sinners. He invited them before others to share meals, reconciling them in this way with themselves and with God. When he washed his disciples' feet at the Last Supper, he was washing the feet of sinners. On the following day, they would leave him to his fate, for men to do what they liked with him, and he had already recognized at the meal that one of them, Judas, was a traitor. The whole of his life had been characterized by active love of others and it was that love that also inspired his death.

■

He stripped and became the very image of the Servant. He humbled himself and, in his obedience, went as far as death. Passing through death, he also passed through the condition of a slave (see Ps 2:7ff). He performed the humblest of services and loved his own to the end (see Jn 13:1).

"If I, the Lord and Master, have washed your feet, you should wash each other's feet. . . . Now that you know this, happiness will be yours if you behave accordingly." The essential passing through is that of love. When he humbled himself, bending low to wash his disciples' feet, Jesus was already entering his agony. The Son of Man came not to be served, but to serve. As St. Bernard observed, "The measure of love is love without measure."

Anyone who has tried to measure for a moment the passionate love of God for himself can do no more than spend the rest of his life asking himself in great wonder: "Who *is* God?" God has indeed loved the world without ever measuring that love. He loves us boundlessly.

If we try to grasp the logic of the resurrection, we have to let ourselves be involved in the play, the dynamic process of love. Christians are in no sense heroes or especially virtuous. Love is something that the believer expresses as faultily as others who do not believe. Sometimes it is so inhibited or restricted in him that it is no more than a caricature. But he is always aware of the power of God's grace, and the victory of Love is already present whenever he tries to love. Love is a gamble, an expression of faith and a commitment to live like God himself. The only assurance that the Christian who tries to love has is the Spirit of God.

The Servant of God went to the very limit of his life, handing it over completely, and he calls on us to follow him. What is the law of the resurrection? It is simply the law of the inaccessible "as": "Love one another as I have loved you" (Jn 15:12). Those who put that law into practice will be very happy. They will be happy too if they venture to dream that one day their love will be like God's love. Happy too are those who are ready to pay the price required for their dream to be made a reality in the lives of men.

■

Love that is quite immeasurable,
   God overflowing with love,
   God who gives without counting,
fill us with your Spirit
   and we shall be born to the love of sons
   that you have promised us for eternity.

■

You washed your disciples' feet
   and revealed to them the secrets of the Kingdom.
Let us, Lord Jesus,
   carry out in every way
   the law of service and humility,
so that we may be counted
   among the number of your friends.

FRIDAY OF THE FOURTH WEEK

THE WAY
Acts 13:26–33: The promise made to the patriarchs of Israel was fulfilled in Jesus. The unity of the history of salvation is revealed in Jesus' shameful death on a cross which at the same time accomplished the words of the prophets read aloud every sabbath in the synagogue. He was handed over to men—but for the salvation of the world. God himself vouchsafed for that

voluntary sacrifice and raised Jesus from the dead, thus ratifying the work of his Messiah, particularly in the act of placing him on the throne to reign in glory.

The Jews who had come to the synagogue in Antioch to hear Paul were expecting "some words of encouragement" (Acts 13:15), but he gave them words of salvation. When Christ rose again, the Kingdom became part of the history of mankind. The "holy things of David" had for a long time been the inheritance of mankind, but now it was through Jesus "that forgiveness of sins is proclaimed, and through him justification from all sins which the law of Moses was unable to justify is offered to every believer" (13:38). To every believer, the resurrection of Jesus goes far beyond Jesus himself and reaches everyone who believes. It is the work of the Spirit and Paul had received from Christ himself the task to proclaim it.

Psalm 2 is a royal Psalm recited by the king on the day that he was enthroned in Jerusalem. It contains a divine decree ratifying Yahweh's acceptance of the monarch and an oracle defining his destiny.

John 14:1–6: The Sanhedrin has decided to put Jesus to death and he has freely resolved to ratify that human decision. He has been anointed for burial by the woman and Judas has already left to carry out his act of treachery. Already "the Son of Man has been glorified and in him God has been glorified" (Jn 13:31). The passion has already begun, and the Christ who is speaking now is the living Christ who has passed through death and who reveals to Christians the meaning of that crossing.

Christ is going, but his disciples should not "let their hearts be troubled." He is certainly going away, but he will "return to take them with him" so that they will be reunited with him. Jesus' death marks a break in time. Because he is going to the very limits of his self-offering, he is able to reveal the depths of God's love and in this he can also show us the way that leads to God. If we imitate him in the mystery of his death and resurrection and thus enter into communion with the Father, we shall pass from this present life into eternal life.

■

The disciples wanted to keep him with them. We always want to keep a friend with us when he says he has to go. We want to keep God with us, revere what we have left of him. What remains may be relics of his

life with us, but they are in themselves lifeless. They may be words to repeat, but the letter kills the Spirit, or principles to defend, but those may prevent us from hearing or proclaiming the apparently foolish good news. We want to keep something of God. It may not be a real encounter with him, but we want at least to be able to confess his name or a few titles. We want to revere him in a reliquary.

"I am the Way, the Truth and the Life." Jesus replies to those who are so anxious to keep the past imprisoned in terms of life. "I am the Way." He invites us to follow him. He knows that mankind has a long journey ahead of it before it can become really human and welcome God fully. But, if we listen to Jesus, how can we set a limit to our way and become rigid and motionless in a static religiosity? How is it possible to reduce the one who identifies the law with his own person to a formula? If we are really drawn to his way of looking at our own lives, we shall be born of his grace. He is himself the Way and he has been on all our paths. He still walks and will continue eternally to walk along our roads. Because of him, they all lead through the gates of the Kingdom of God.

"I am the Truth." How is it possible to confine a Truth that can always be discovered and welcomed anew to an abstract and inflexible system? We may repeat the words handed down to us by those who bore witness to Jesus' life, death and resurrection, but we do so to make ourselves alert to what they aim to give birth to in us. He is the Word, but his words are simply ours and therefore fleeting. In him, however, they become a vow of love which he is able to make eternal.

"I am the Life." We only have to consider for a moment the violence, injustice and oppression in the world today to become filled with every possible doubt. It has often been said that faith is a dream that enables people to close their eyes to the realities of life and its harshness and run away from their responsibilities. But we, on the contrary, confess that Jesus is Lord and God because we are already in communion with him. He is the Life and he takes the little deaths that we die every day and the great death that we shall die on the last day of our life and sows in them the seed of endless life.

We want to keep him, the living Christ, with us, but he is already on his way toward God's world. Life is ahead of us and him, not behind. God comes from the future.

God our Father,
your Spirit has spoken the truth about our life:
  we are made for you
  and we live through you.

Give us enough breath
  to be able to follow your Son.
  He will let us pass over into a new world
  forever and ever.

SATURDAY OF THE FOURTH WEEK

IMITATION OF CHRIST

Acts 13:44–52: A dramatic event is described here. Paul has just preached the message of salvation to the Jews. He has said that a new future has been revealed to all who believe in the resurrection of Christ. He has also recalled the promise made by Yahweh to Abraham: "All the tribes of the earth shall bless themselves by you" (Gn 12:3). But there is at once a division among his listeners. Some of the Jews reject what Paul has said and insult him.

So Paul declares with great solemnity and in the freedom of the Spirit: "We had to proclaim the word of God to you first, but since you have rejected it, since you do not think yourselves worthy of eternal life, we must turn to the pagans." This is an absolutely critical decision. On the one hand, it marks a provisional failure of the word of God among the people of the promise, but, on the other hand, it shows that the pagans have a legitimate claim to inherit eternal life and that they share that inheritance with the faithful of Israel.

Psalm 98 proclaims the great joy of the disciples that cannot be overshadowed, despite all the difficulties of their mission. It is a hymn of the universal nature of salvation.

John 14:7–14: "Lord, we do not know where you are going, so how can we know the way?" (Jn 14:5). Thomas, in asking that question, is like Philip and even like the Samaritan woman. It is a very naive question—but it is, of course, our question too. How can we know the way? How can we know where Jesus is going?

Jesus is about to found his Church. The decision has been made. He has to die—to go to the very end of his work. Then the love of the Father will appear and Thomas and everyone else will see that God has given his Son for the salvation of the world.

But Christ's work did not end with him. His disciples were to "perform the same works" as he and were indeed to "perform even greater works" (Jn 14:12). Christ was to die, but witnesses were to arise. Filled with the Spirit, they were to proclaim his resurrection and affirm that love is stronger than death.

■

"Have I been with you all this time and you still do not know me?" He was called Emmanuel, God-with-us. He was the Son of the God who is Love. He was in the beginning. He was the Word which gives birth to worlds. But the world was sick because it did not know how to love. Emmanuel assumed the flesh of the world and went so far as to give his life so that love would be born again. His life was an embodiment of life in all its aspects from the beginning to the end.

He taught us how to speak the tender, hidden language of true love. With him, all things were made new, and love above all never ceased to be new. His last words are a unique testament of inestimable value: "I give you a new commandment: love one another" (Jn 13:34). In doing this, he was entrusting to us the history and the future of the world.

"Have I been with you all this time and you still do not know me?" God's only face is the face of love, and the only way to God's country is a heart that ventures to love.

"Believe on the evidence of this work, if for no other reason." Look at the man set free, risen again, revived, and at the world that is beginning to hope. The only evidence that love can offer is its own existence. The face of love is unveiled only when it is caressed. The law of the resurrection is simply this: imitating Christ, the face of love. So, when we meet him, he will say to us: "I have been with you all this time."

∎

Holy God, no one has ever seen you
  except your beloved Son.
The Word hidden in our flesh,
  he discloses your plan to the lowly
  and reveals your name to the poor.

We invoke your name and ask you:
  glorify us in him
  because he gave his life for us.

∎

Fulfill, Lord, what you have begun in us;
  reveal the Father to us.
Following you and listening to your word,
  may we come to know the eternal love
  in which you live with the Holy Spirit
  forever and ever.

FIFTH AND SIXTH WEEKS OF EASTER

THE CHURCH, THE FUTURE OF THE WORLD

In order to enable us to enter into communion with him, God wanted to make himself known to us or, to use the biblical phrase, he wanted to reveal himself. And in order to do that, he followed the instinct of all love and looked for ways of living with the beings he loved. He therefore became a man. He left himself, stripping himself as far as he could of his transcendence. That is the supreme mystery. His foolish but quite rational extravagance is above all what causes us to believe. Our faith is not a merely theoretical consent to an abstract virtue. No, it is more than that. It is a sharing in God's being, given to us in communion with him.

The mystery of the Church has to be understood against this background. Throughout the ages the Church has been the history of the one Word handed over to us by God in Jesus Christ. The Kingdom of God has come among us in that Word of God, who can only make himself heard in the words that men use hesitatingly to speak of the mystery that has been revealed. It is in those hesitant words that the eternal Voice can be heard. The only way in which Love can make its presence felt is by using the vulnerable actions and lives of men and women who are trying to love. It is in those lives, confused and uncertain though they may be, that the great action of God can be detected.

The time of the Church is merged together with the time of waiting and expectation. The Church always points to the future—to Advent and the coming of the Kingdom—and points as decisively in that direction as it points to the past event of Jesus himself. The Church recalls the past. It is memory and its faith is an inheritance. But it is equally turned toward fulfillment in the future. It is conscious of the totality of the mystery of Christ, but it will not experience that mystery fully as a living reality until it sees God face to face. God has revealed himself once and for all time, but the Church's life, long though it is, will not be long enough for it to fathom the depths and explore all the wealth of that revelation. The time of the Church, then, is a time of humble invocation: "Thy Kingdom come." In the assurance that Christ has given to the Church, it proclaims that the Kingdom has already come and is here among men, but it knows that the resources of that Kingdom can never be exhausted.

■

You are the body of Christ—
  you should never misuse love.

You are the vine planted by God—
  you should not drink at dry springs.

You are a holy people—
  you should not go in pursuit of an earlier world.

Lord, have mercy on us!

PRAYING WITH JESUS AT THE LAST SUPPER

We thank you, God our Father,
  because your Son has looked at us,
  chosen us
  and sown in our lives the seeds of eternal life.
In order to complete
  the work of love that you entrusted to him,
  he handed himself over to death
and, by his resurrection,
  he broke down the wall of shame
  separating us from you.
Because he is living now with you
  heaven and earth are joined together
  and we know where the longing of our hearts
  is impelling us to go.

Father,
  hear the prayer of your beloved Son.
Through your Spirit
  make those who share in your body
  see quite differently.
Let us contemplate here and now
  the glory of your Son
  in the mystery of the Eucharist
  and live from his life
  as we dwell in him.

Yes, Father,
  we know that you have sent your Son into the world
  so that we might in him live in your dwelling place.
Your Spirit prays in us
  and when he urges us to say
  "Come, Lord Jesus"
  the table where bread is broken
  becomes a meeting place
  of faith and hope.

We thank you,

tender, loving Father,
for the grace that inflames us
and the source of life that nourishes our longing.
We thank you through Jesus,
the radiant star of the new day
that is already rising over our earth.

With Jesus, who washed his disciples' feet,
shared with them the bread and the cup of the Kingdom
and handed over to them the testament of his love,
we pray:

For all those who are experiencing painful separations:
may they find in Jesus the way
to a dwelling where a place has been prepared for each of us.

For those who are looking for truth, faith and hope:
may they find in the Gospel
an appeal that will lead them
to go beyond themselves in their trust in God.

For those who serve God in their work in the world:
may their faith and the truthfulness of their actions
be visible in the witness they bear.

For the Church, that it may be able to discover
words of hope throughout the centuries
that are always new because they are faithful to the Spirit of Christ.

For those whom Christ has chosen to be his apostles:
may they live their vocation as friendship
in thanksgiving and unfailing devotion.

For all people, that they may discover
that love is like news that they have wanted to receive for a long time
and that it is everything that they want
so long as it is experienced in faithfulness to the Lord's Commandment.

For our brothers who are exposed to persecution:
that they may know that Jesus is at their side
while they are being tested and tortured.

For ourselves, that we may be faithful in upholding the Church
in its difficult struggle

for justice and truth.

*For ourselves, that we may also go through times of crisis
as periods when the future is born
and our faith and commitment are required.*

*For the world, that it may be a place,
in the physical absence of Christ,
where every man's face bears traces of the eternal.*

MONDAY OF THE FIFTH WEEK

GOING FURTHER THAN STATISTICS
Acts 14:5–18: Stephen had been stoned to death by order of the Jewish authorities and the Church had moved away from Judaism. Paul and Barnabas had been fiercely opposed both at Antioch and at Iconium and were tending more and more to evangelize the pagan world. The blood of the martyrs thus became a source of grace and growth.

Like Peter in Jerusalem (see Acts 3:1–10), Paul healed a sick man at Lystra. The crowd was delighted and thought that the two Apostles were gods visiting their worshipers. Even the priests of Zeus were ready to offer sacrifice. But as soon as they realized that they had been mistaken for gods, the missionaries tore their clothes and vehemently insisted that they were proclaiming the one true God who had created man and provided for him. The whole way of preaching had in fact changed—it was addressed to the pagans and no longer contained references to the history of Israel or to the Old Testament prophecies.

Psalm 115 is an unformed composition with verses borrowed from other psalms. Vv. 3–8 clearly express Israel's opposition to idolatry, while v. 15 contains a priestly blessing.

John 14:21–26: Christians not only bear witness to Christ's resurrection, they also proclaim the message that love is stronger than death. In revealing God to the world, the Church follows the same path as Jesus himself, who spent his whole life expressing God's love for men. He expressed that love in many ways—by inviting sinners to share his table, by washing his disciples' feet, and above all by his own obedience.

Christians have also to bear witness to that same love. "By this love that you have for one another, everyone will know that you are my disciples" (Jn 13:35). The Father has revealed his love by sending his Son, and Jesus has manifested that love by giving his life. In the same way, the disciples have to love one another "so that the world may believe" (17:21). God's love for mankind is also revealed today in that love that binds Christians together.

This is what Judas has to understand. Christ manifests himself not to the world, but to the disciples, that is, to those who imitate his love so that the world may witness it. What is Christ's "coming"? What is to happen "after" his death? It is that he will be alive in the Church. He will live in the community of believers when they are living in the love of the Lord. That is the epiphany for the world, and when the disciples experience it, the Spirit will remind them of all Jesus has said to them.

∎

"If anyone loves me . . . ." Whenever sociological surveys are conducted in the Church, the results contain statistics and figures concerning the number of practicing Christians, the number believing in the Church's "traditional" teaching, the percentage accepting the standard of behavior recommended by the Church and so on. But we who believe know the Church goes further than statistics. It is quite a different reality. The originality and the mystery of our faith cannot be reduced to the level of figures. It is not simply a question of practice, behavior or teaching. "If anyone loves me . . . ." Who can really express the secret of faith? The poet, perhaps . . .

"If anyone loves me . . . ." No one can know God unless his heart is profoundly involved. He has to be astonished. Fascination plays a vital part. It is ultimately a question of loving. How many Christians treat God like an object that is part of the world and that they use when they need it and throw aside when it is no longer wanted? Jesus was asked: "Why do you show yourself to us and not to the world?" Why do we try again and again to enter into contracts with God? How is it possible for us to think of our faith as a matter of purely human duty?

"If anyone loves me . . . ." The originality of Christian faith is this: relying on another. Until we learn how to rely on Christ, we cannot begin to be his disciple. We have to be fascinated by God because he has done everything in order to give us a share in his life, including being stretched out on the hard wood of the cross.

"If anyone loves me . . . my Father will love him and we shall come to him and make our home with him." God has chosen to make his home forever in the hearts of those who love him. That is where God is to be sought and found.

■

God, source of boundless love
  and overflowing with love,
  fill us with your Spirit.
Fill us with a longing to look for you
  and give us the joy of knowing you.
Make your dwelling place forever in us.

"This is my commandment: love one another":
  So that your Church's only concern
  may be to love more and more passionately,
  Lord, give us your Spirit.

"I give you a new commandment":
  So that any sign of growing old
  may give way to the love that never grows old,
  Lord, give us your Spirit.

"Just as I have loved you, you must also love one another":
  So that people will know that you are with us
  because we are bold and without restraint in loving,
  Lord, give us your Spirit.

TUESDAY OF THE FIFTH WEEK

OUR INHERITANCE: PEACE
Acts 14:19–28: The people calm down, but not for long. Some Jews arrive from Antioch and Iconium and stir up the people's feelings against the Apostles. The very men who had acclaimed Paul on the previous day now begin to stone him and leave him for dead. The man who had been present when Stephen was stoned to death is himself tortured as a witness to the Lord Jesus Christ, who had been crucified after his triumphal entry into Jerusalem.

A page is turned in the history of the early Church. When they left Jerusalem, the missionaries spoke first to the people of the old covenant, but must of their listeners rejected their message. Then the Spirit led the Apostles into unexpectedly fertile fields. God "opened the door of faith to the pagans." The Spirit "blows wherever it pleases" (Jn 3:8). The Church has now to be recollected and to recognize the work of the one who is filling it to overflowing.

Psalm 145 makes use of previously existing formulae and is usually regarded as a hymn.

John 14:27–31a: "Do not let your hearts be troubled or afraid." Jesus is going away. The Father hands him over to men for a little while, but does not abandon him. God has, after all, never let anyone who is faithful to him remain in need. He will not "allow the one he loves to see the pit" (Ps 16:10). He will raise Jesus from the dead.

So it is peace that Jesus intends to leave as an inheritance for his disciples. It is a peace that the world cannot understand, because it is fullness of life—the pre-eminent messianic gift. It is also the gift of the Spirit that enables everyone to share in the life of God. "I am going away and shall return."

Judas is already on his way and, even as Jesus is conversing with his disciples, the "prince of this world" is coming. But he can do nothing to Jesus. He has no power over the one who is without sin. In complete freedom, Jesus can go forward to meet him. He is able to carry out his Father's will quite serenely.

The Son is going away. There is a festive air—the spirit of Easter is everywhere and it is almost possible to hear a freedom song. Judas is silent, weighed down by the meager payment of silver that he is about to receive for the price of a slave. Priests and Pharisees are waiting impatiently together with soldiers and guards in the temple precincts. The conspiracy will take place that night. "Come now, let us go." The Son goes. The hour has come, marked with blood. The men who are to raise him up from the earth do not know that God is raising him up to himself.

It is the hour of the Son, but it is also the hour of the Church. It was born in that hour marked with blood shed, bread broken and feet washed. The Son goes away, leaving his beloved Bride, and the only inheritance that he leaves her is a blessing: "My own peace I give you."

That peace that is not the same as the peace that the world gives. Men argue about the terms of their armistices, which are often no more than temporary, and their peace treaties, which simply achieve a balance of power and a provisional end to violence. "My own peace I give you." That peace is based on the same birth and the same blood—that of the Son. The Son's blood, shed for many, is the seal of his peace. It is true peace for those who go beyond everything that divides them and share in the communion of the same body in the knowledge, given by faith, that they belong to each other.

That peace is different from the peace that the world gives. Men have, in the course of history, found countless ways of buying favors from their gods and, in so doing, of deceiving themselves that they are getting rid of their guilty feelings without in fact ever getting to the root of their guilt. "My own peace I give you." This is not making a pact with God to get him to close his eyes. That peace is sealed because God has pledged himself not to reject his Son. "God loved the world so much that he gave his only Son" (Jn 3:16). Jesus' peace is unconditional and it is grace.

The Son goes away and the Bride remains behind with her inheritance, his peace, which is his gift of a new era. Throughout history, she will herself have no more than that peace to give to mankind. "Whatever house you go into, let your first words be, 'Peace to this house'" (Lk 10:5). Throughout the history of Christianity, Christ's disciples have never had and will never have any more to say than that to a world that is looking for but cannot find peace.

∎

God our Father, we ask you:
you have formed bonds with the world
   that nothing can break—
Jesus has sealed your covenant with his blood!

May your peace, which passes all understanding,
   be our inheritance
   now and forever.

WEDNESDAY OF THE FIFTH WEEK

THE VINE

Acts 15:1–6: The door leading to faith has been opened to the pagans, but "some men" want it to be closed again. The Spirit opens boundless horizons to the Church, but there are always "some men," in this case from Judea, who want the Church to remain isolated. Here the aim is to keep it restricted to its Jewish ghetto.

A serious crisis is caused by this attitude. There is the question of the difficulties raised by circumcised and non-circumcised Christians eating together at the same table, but there is also the even more fundamental problem that the Church has to resolve: Who is the source of salvation, man or God? Is man saved by his religious practice, that is, by obeying a law, the prelude and symbol of which is circumcision? Is he saved by his own efforts? Or is the source of salvation God himself? Is man saved as the result of bargaining or is salvation a gratuitous gift from God? What use is faith if it is subordinate to circumcision? Is the cross of Christ an unfortunate incident or is it the gate leading to life itself?

Psalm 122 is a pilgrimage Psalm which expresses this same concern for all the churches to be in communion with the mother Church. The Apostles and elders met at Jerusalem to discuss the question of admitting pagans to membership of the Church.

John 15:1–8: "The vine that you uprooted from Egypt . . . you cleared a space where it could grow, it took root and filled the whole country. . . . Why have you destroyed its fences? Now anyone can go and steal its grapes" (Ps 80:8ff).

That vine is Israel, the vine chosen by Yahweh, who surrounded it with care. But the fences were broken down and the vine was ravaged. Does God intend to let this go on? "Please, Yahweh Sabaoth, relent. . . . Look at this vine. Visit it. Protect what your right hand has planted. . . . May your hand protect the man at your right, the Son of Man who has been authorized by you" (Ps 80:14ff).

The "true vine" is Jesus. He is not only the bread of life; he is also the wine of the Kingdom, the "product of the vine." His disciples are the branches, and just as shoots and branches share in the life of the vine of which they form part, so too do the disciples share in Christ's life. They have to remain in him, just as the root of the vine has to remain in the ground. As the eternal Son of the Father, only Jesus can give to what men do an eternal value.

■

What a wonderful thing a flourishing vine is! When its stem and leaves are full of sap and the raisins are swollen and juicy from the sun, so that one can almost taste the wine already, the vine proudly bears the name of the owner of the vineyard. That was the case with Israel, the vine that belonged to the Lord: "My friend had a vineyard on a fertile hillside. He dug the soil, cleared it of stones and planted choice vines in it" (Is 5:1–2). It was in such words that the prophets described the relationship between God and his people. A parable of this kind was guaranteed to evoke a tender response and to make the people think of the Lord's care for his possession.

"I am the true vine and my Father is the vinedresser." The plant chosen by the vinedresser, then, was Jesus, the beloved Son. He was the stock planted by God and he was also the priceless fruit of the vine, the new wine. Who is the new tree of life? Surely the people born of Jesus and united to him as closely as the vine and its

branches! That is the great mystery of the sap that is hidden, but moves and unites the shoots and branches to the stock and enables them to bear fruit. "Whoever remains in me, with me in him, bears fruit in plenty."

What an immense vine, in which men struggle, work and give their lives without ever knowing that the fruit that they bear comes from a sap that is hidden from their sight—sap without a name! The stock has become the food of those who hunger and thirst for justice, the source of life for the poor, the unshakable serenity of the gentle, the magnanimity of the merciful, the strength of those who are tortured and the faithfulness of those who work for peace. "Whoever remains in me . . . bears fruit in plenty." The vine of mankind has become God's vine forever. Happy are those who know that they are the branches, that Jesus is the stock and that the Father is the vinedresser. Happy are those who prune that vine so that it can bear even better fruit; they are themselves the harvest of God's vine.

∎

God our Father,
the earth has given us the best fruit of all—
   Jesus, your Son.
In him, we are already living your life.
   He lives in us
   and we are your possession.
May your Spirit prune us.
Then, when we come to the autumn of the world,
   your harvest will be a good one.

∎

We bless you, our God,
for this cup and for the life given for many.
Make us drunk with your grace,
   for the wine of the new era
   is the blood of your beloved Son,
   celebrating here and now the joy
   of eternal life.

THURSDAY OF THE FIFTH WEEK

DISCIPLESHIP

Acts 15:7–21: It was decided that Paul and Barnabas should go to the meeting of the Christian community at Jerusalem. There was a long debate, and eventually the assembly was addressed by Peter, who told those present about his own ministry among the pagans, which he believed was the result of God's providence. "It was in the early days that God made his choice among you," he said, "the pagans were to learn the good news from me and so become believers." This shows that he understood at the deepest level the meaning of his encounter with the centurion Cornelius, namely that the gift of the Spirit, the forgiveness of sins and salvation itself were the work of God's grace. This applied to the pagans as well as to the Jews. To make the gift of eternal life subject to the practice of circumcision would, Peter claimed, be despising God's work and "would provoke God to anger."

This is quite unambiguous speaking on Peter's part, and later on Paul would speak just as plainly in his letters to the churches. For the time being, however, he takes advantage of the silence to which Peter had reduced the assembly to outline the positive achievements of his missionary activity.

Finally, James speaks to the assembly in an attempt at appeasement. He is a kinsman of Jesus, a leader of the Jerusalem community and respected by the Judaizers. He gives his loyal approval to what Peter has just suggested and even confirms it by an argument based on Scripture. But his own suggestion is a compromise. The Jewish converts should not insist on their pagan brethren being circumcised, he argues, but the latter should conform to certain legal demands. The conclusion, then, of this fierce debate is this: the people of God was in the future to include both circumcised and uncircumcised members, and the uncircumcised Christians from a Greek background were to respect Jewish scruples with regard to purity.

Psalm 96: All the nations are invited to praise God. The framework of this Psalm is the proclamation by a herald that "Yahweh is king" of all peoples.

John 15:9–11: "God is love, and anyone who lives in love lives in God and

God lives in him" (1 Jn 4:16). Jesus bore witness to that love in the whole of his life and in his death. The love of the Father and the Son is only one love, a translucent and reciprocal gift.

Christ's disciples had then, as they still have now, one very certain way of interpreting their lives as believers. They have only to ask themselves honestly whether they are living in love, since where there is love, God is present too. Those who live in love know perfect joy—the joy of a people that is both loved and free.

■

"I am the vine, you are the branches. Cut off from me you can do nothing" (Jn 15:5). Jesus is the whole vine, and we are part of him. Our salvation is only in him: "Remain in my love." That has always been the Church's task throughout the centuries—to proclaim the reality of this teaching. "If you remain in me . . . you will be my disciples." Then the vine will continue to grow and its shade will increase with time until everyone lives in it. The disciples of Christ are not ambassadors, but the vine—the sacrament of the presence of Christ.

"Remain in my love." Discipleship does not in the first place mean doing or saying certain things. It means above all an intimacy between Jesus and his Church. Our spiritual life should not be spent in attempting to escape from or avoid certain things, nor is it an optional extra. It must be the very heart of our being. Discipleship is living in and through Jesus. "Life to me, of course, is Christ," Paul wrote to the Christians of Philippi (1:21). Being a Christian will never be simply a question of accepting teachings, respecting certain morals or acting in certain ways. It will always be this dwelling in Christ's love, which is as essential as breathing. "Remain in my love. . . . Cut off from me you can do nothing."

The second aspect of discipleship is "bearing fruit." "If you keep my Commandments you will remain in my love, just as I have kept my Father's Commandments." The disciple imitates the Master and the branch lives from the sap. Throughout his entire life, Jesus bore witness to what was in his Father's heart, and that was love and mercy. Living Jesus' life can only be bearing the fruit of love and mercy.

"I am the vine, you are the branches." The only future for Christians is to remain in the love of the one who has begotten them.

■

"As the Father has loved me,
so I have loved you."
   May your Church live from love,
   may it speak tenderly
   and breathe charity,
     Lord, we pray you.

"Remain in my love."
   May your Spirit graft us onto your life
   and may our baptism bear fruit,
     Lord, we pray you.

"Keep my Commandments."
   In the secrecy of our prayer
   we bring before you
   everyone who is trying to make the world
   more human, a true brotherhood of man,
   and all who, without despair,
   are working for a new earth.

"May your joy be complete."
   May your prayer, Lord,
   be our blessing.

FRIDAY OF THE FIFTH WEEK

CHOSEN TO LOVE
Acts 15:22–31: The crisis has been settled and the decisions taken at Jerusalem have now to be made known to the churches in Antioch, Syria and Cilicia. It is quite important to note here that Paul takes the new rulings only to the members of the church in Antioch, that is, to the

various groups of Christians who were originally Jewish and Greek. The compromise reached at Jerusalem, then, clearly favored the communion of those Christians who came from completely different environments. It was therefore universal in its outreach. Membership of the Church has always meant respecting the differences of each individual and group. This is certainly what Paul told the Christians of Corinth in the controversy caused by some of them eating food sacrificed to idols (see 1 Cor 8:10).

Paul, Barnabas and other delegates are sent, then, to Antioch to explain the decisions that have been taken at the assembly. They are tried and tested men and they have the common good firmly in mind. Peter is featured no more in the story of the Acts from this point onward. The part that he has always played and will until the end of his life continue to play is to guarantee the universal communion that God has always wanted, since the beginning, for his people. Strengthened by the support he received, Paul is able to include this appeal in his teaching with the help of the Holy Spirit.

Psalm 57: The Church has taken the psalmist's promise to give thanks to God in this Psalm, which is fundamentally a lament. This is also what Paul and Barnabas are doing, surely, in explaining the decisions taken at Jerusalem to the churches.

John 15:12–17: "Love one another; just as I have loved you, you also must love one another. By this love that you have for one another, everyone will know that you are my disciples" (Jn 13:34–35). That is the great sign of the Church and the calling of the disciples—bearing witness to love. The Church is there only for that. During the time of the old covenant, God gathered a people around himself. With Jesus Christ, however, he did more than this—his people became a "communion." Love cannot be expressed fully in solitude, because it is above all a sharing.

The servant carries out tasks for his master, but the friend is joyful when he hears the Bridegroom's voice. His obedience is also a form of communion. He experiences love in order to hand it on to others, so everyone's joy will be complete. It is the fruit that the branches of the vine must bear.

∎

He was called Emmanuel, God-with-us. He was the child of God who is called Love. He was begotten by Love and he was nothing but love himself. He lived love from the beginning to the end. Emmanuel—you

put your arms lovingly around children, looked into the eyes of the woman taken in adultery and formed a pact with Peter. You taught us how to be patient and how to forgive. You showed us the joy of knowing that God loves us and the peace that comes from hope. With you, love is unchanging, yet always new.

You are now ready to say farewell. It is the Last Supper and, like the lowliest servant, you have been kneeling down. "I shall not call you servants anymore . . . I call you friends." Judas has just gone out. But you will go to the very end, as you have always done. Your words have unique solemnity: "I give you a new Commandment: love one another; just as I have loved you, you also must love one another" (Jn 13:34).

Then you went to your death. You handed yourself over. Your very last glance was one of forgiveness. Your last breath was a breath of love. "Love one another, as I have loved you." That Commandment was to be our life. Love is everything. It is God himself.

"I chose you . . . to go out and to bear fruit . . . . What I command you is to love one another." The Church is founded on the action of the Servant. The only thing that I can look for in the Church of Jesus Christ is the joy of loving. The world despises love and conceals its fear of it under a deceitfully clever appearance. But your only Commandment, Church, is: Love! That is the only reason you have for existing and it is what makes you beautiful.

■

God our Father,
   let the disciples of your Servant Jesus
   love as passionately as he did.
May your Church
   have communion every day in your love,
   and she will be as beautiful as a young bride,
   sparkling with happiness
   for the eternity that you have prepared for her.

■

Your Son has made known to us
   the secret of your eternity,
   God our Father,

and in him we know you call yourself Love.
Grant that we may live in brotherly love
  and devote our lives to one another.
Then the world too will know
  who you are, living God,
  a God who loves your work with eternal love.

SATURDAY OF THE FIFTH WEEK

COMMITMENT

Acts 16:1–10: Luke thought of Jerusalem as the place where everything began. The angel Gabriel had announced the coming of the Kingdom to Zachariah in the temple of Jerusalem. Jesus' destiny had followed its course at the gates of the city. It was in Jerusalem too that the Holy Spirit had come like fire upon the Apostles at Pentecost and the new Israel had become open to receive the pagans.

The leaders of the Church had also met in Jerusalem in council and had safeguarded God's freedom there. Paul's great mission also began in Jerusalem. His first recorded action was to recruit a disciple, Timothy, the son of a Greek father and a Jewish mother. Anxious to confirm the continuity between the Church and his own mission to the pagans, Paul had him circumcised. At the same time, he also informed the Christian communities he visited with Timothy about the decisions taken at Jerusalem. The Church was both traditional and open to the future.

Paul first went in the direction of the coastal towns of Ephesus and Smyrna, but turned north. At the latitude of modern Ankara, however, the Spirit of Jesus again directed him toward the coast and he went to Troas. This was the ancient port of Troy, where the east and the west had met in conflict in earlier times. Paul, however, came to the port with a promise of peace for all nations. The Spirit had led him there.

Psalm 100 is a hymn of universal praise.

John 15:18–21: "You are of this world; I am not of this world" (Jn 8:23). Like Jesus himself, the disciples are also not of this world. As branches of the vine, they have crossed with him from death to life and the world does not know them. But, like the man born blind who had been driven out of the synagogue after he had seen the "light," the disciples were to be persecuted. The world was bound to try to harm God by harming them.

■

"You do not belong to the world." That is the truth of the Church and its commitment.

Who, then, has left the world to belong to God? The one who can live every day in the humble knowledge that his life has meaning. The one, in other words, who believes in Jesus as the Christ. "You do not belong to the world because I have chosen you." Who is Jesus? A man among men, a prophet in Judea who came into this world to die here. His story is like all human stories. His death is sad, like all deaths. But those who believe that God has expressed the hidden meaning of life in this heartbreaking story do not belong to the world.

"If you belonged to the world, the world would love you as its own, but you do not belong to the world." The one who believes that Jesus is the Savior is born of God. He is born with Jesus of God. Our faith is that he lives in us and has experienced our human destiny since becoming our way. With him, we can risk everything for love.

Throughout human history, the Church has always and will always be the place where a different message is heard. It shares men's aspirations, searches painfully with them and accompanies them on their often hesitant and devious way forward. All the time, however, it bears witness to another place elsewhere. It is the beacon that lights the haven to which they are driven by the often stormy sea of history. In today's dark world, the Church has a commitment. Its task is to go ahead of man toward the future that God is preparing for man through the slow work of the Spirit in him. The Church is the bridgehead of God's promise in man's slow and difficult conquest of the meaning of life.

"If you belonged to the world, the world would love you." The world always clings to the past. We are reassured by our habits and our earlier ideas and practices. The cross will always be foolishness for human wisdom and a scandal to the hearts of men. But we who are the Church of God bear witness to the fact that the future of the world and its happiness are to be found in the love that goes as far as the cross.

■

Holy Father,
the world does not know you.
Because you have chosen us
  to watch over our earth,
we ask you:
  strengthen our faith
  so that we may be the spokesmen
  of good news
  going further than the limits of this world.

MONDAY OF THE SIXTH WEEK

MEMORY

Acts 16:11–15: Paul's first port of call was Philippi, a town that was part of the Roman world and populated for the most part by Italian people. It was a place that became very dear to his heart.

Judaism was quite marginal in Philippi and the Jewish community gathered for prayer on the bank of a river on the sabbath. Paul went with them to this place, preached there and baptized Lydia, a proselyte "who was in the purple-dye trade." Quite spontaneously, Lydia put her home at the Apostle's disposal. She was, in other words, welcoming the Church into her household.

Psalm 150 is a hymn expressing the joy of those who have been recently converted.

John 15:26—16:4: "Blind? If you were, you would not be guilty, but since you say, 'We see,' your guilt remains" (Jn 9:41). Confronted with the Jewish authorities, the man born blind had pleaded the cause of light. When the Pharisees drove him out of the synagogue, then, it was really Jesus himself whom they were excommunicating. But Jesus reversed the situation and pronounced judgment on the bad shepherds of Israel.

His death was in fact a proclamation of the time of judgment. The disciples were also to be taken to court and put on trial, but an "advocate" would defend them. They had shared Jesus' life since the beginning and would bear witness, but it would be the Spirit bearing witness and giving men's words their full meaning. Now it is the world that is to be judged, but the counsel for the defense is to take the place of the judge. Jesus reassures his followers: when the testing time comes, they should remember this, and they have no need to fear, because the Spirit himself will be speaking in them (see Mt 10:20).

∎

"The Spirit . . . will be my witness. . . . You may remember." The Church is distinctive in that it is founded on words that are heard, experienced and received. At the heart of the Church there is memory.

"You may remember." The faith of the Church is this: a word that it hears and responds to. Memory is an inheritance. We experience our faith and our lives as believers as an inheritance. But as soon as we say this we must also add that the life of faith is not an object that we try to obtain for ourselves, a possession that we defend or capital that we preserve.

The Church is the people of the word and the memory of what God has revealed to men. That memory is subject to the work of the Spirit who bears witness in it. We are a family of co-heirs, but we have done nothing ourselves to be given that inheritance. We are called together to receive it and to hand it on. We are called to share in the generosity that we have received and pass it on to others. "You too will be witnesses, because you have been with me from the outset."

The word exists only as something offered. The memory has to be brought to life in sharing it, otherwise it vanishes. The inheritance cannot simply be preserved. It must either increase and bear fruit or be lost.

"You may remember." When the Church remembers, it turns toward the future. It leaves the past behind and does not try to revive it. We have in fact only received that inheritance on account, as earnest-

money. Both our memory and our faith operate at the level of hope
and expectation.

■

God our Father,
when we remember your Son,
   the Spirit helps us to glimpse our future.

May your Word be our bread for today
   and may it be fulfilled
   forever and ever.

■

Jesus your Son handed over his life as a sacrifice,
   and we have known since that time
   that the greatest truth in your eyes
   is the gift of oneself in love of others.

Holy Father,
   preserve in trust
   those whom you have called to bear supreme witness,
   giving their lives for the Gospel of Christ.

TUESDAY OF THE SIXTH WEEK

COUNSEL FOR OUR DEFENSE
Acts 16:22–34: After exorcising a girl fortune teller, Paul was taken to court with Silas and punished by being whipped and thrown into prison (vv. 16–24). It seems, however, that the privilege of being Roman citizens that they enjoyed secured their rapid release. The account of this event is interrupted by vv. 25–40, which describe how the two missionaries were set free by a miracle. The prison was shaken by an earthquake, making the prisoners' chains fall off. The jailer, knowing that he was responsible, asked Paul and Silas what he had to do to be saved.

This part of the story of the miracle is followed by a series of actions forming a structure that would be very clear to the community for whom the text was intended. There had been a night-long vigil of prayer (v. 25), and in addition to this the word of God was preached (v. 32), the jailer and his family were baptized (v. 33), and a meal was shared (v. 34). This meal must, in accordance with the practice of the Christian community, have been a eucharistic meal. This episode is inserted into the story of the exorcism of the slave girl who told fortunes and is in fact a catechetical instruction on the sacraments.

Psalm 138 is a hymn of thanksgiving and recalls the believer's distress. He is, however, conscious that his prayer is heard.

John 16:5–11: "I am the Way, the Truth and the Life," Jesus replied to Thomas' question: "How can we know the way?" (Jn 14:6). That way was for Jesus the way of the cross, on which he offered himself for the salvation of the world. It was his passover, when he passed from death to life. Here, too, he speaks of "going," and the road will, he predicts, also be hard for the disciples when they are persecuted. It will, however, be an upward road, leading to the Father.

The risen Christ of the discourses following the Last Supper reassures the disciples, however, telling them that, however much persecution they have to suffer for bearing witness, they should never forget that the truth of that testimony comes from the Spirit, who has in fact changed the entire situation. His condemnation by the legal authorities of Judaism would seem to have exposed him as an impostor, but now his crucifixion is seen as something in his favor, since his resurrection that followed it demonstrates the truth and justice of his case. God has acted as counsel for his defense, showing that he was right and the world was sinful. The world and the powers of evil that govern it are condemned. The disciples' sadness should therefore turn to joy.

■

"It is for your own good that I am going." The Church is a people of free and adult children. What has been given to the men and women who form the Church should make them live and grow, not keep them infantile.

We are adult human beings, and all that we need in our confrontation with the reality of life is the word that has brought us into the world. The Church is not a haven from the storms of history. "I am going."

We should never think of Jesus as a mother-hen. Faith should never keep us in a state of childhood. If it does, it is an illusion.

But neither is God a cruel stepmother. "The Advocate I will send to you . . . will show the world how wrong it was." We are not orphans brought into the world by an unknown father.

The Spirit, then, is our "Advocate," the counsel for our defense. Everything may seem to be chaotic, absurd, dull, meaningless, useless or lifeless, but the Spirit bears witness to the fact that Christ has initiated his revolution in the heart of the world of men. We may be deeply disappointed, threatened with disorder and even swept along on the tide of disaster, but the Spirit will always be at the center of time, a living and breathing organism bringing us the odor of the new world. We are bound to be conscious of the divisions between men, but the breath of the Spirit unites the one body of mankind, and the beating of his heart is the beating of the heart of God himself. God may seem to be far from us. He may even be a stranger to us, but we can know something of his mystery, especially if we look at the Gospel.

The Spirit is the counsel for our defense. Our hearts may well condemn us, but God is greater than our hearts (see 1 Jn 3:20). "It is for your own good that I am going." One man has initiated our future. He who was "the eldest of many brothers" (Rom 8:29) has discovered the way to freedom and rebirth. His Spirit leads the people who have chosen his name.

■

God our Father,
  do not leave us to ourselves.
  Go on ahead of us
  along the way that leads to life.

Send us your Spirit.
Let him defend us
  until we find you
  and never leave you again.

■

Lord Jesus,
   when you left your disciples,
   you promised not to leave them orphans.
Look at the faith of your Church
   and give us peace,
   especially now as we hope
   for your coming in glory.

WEDNESDAY OF THE SIXTH WEEK

KNOWLEDGE

Acts 17:15, 22—18:1: Athens, the center of pagan civilization, the focal point of all literature and art and for centuries a seat of learning, was the natural place where ancient philosophy should encounter the Gospel for the first time. Each side was quite friendly and well disposed toward the other. Paul knew that some Jews were open to the religious values of the pagan world and Athenians were clearly eager for every kind of new idea. He was therefore invited by some of the leading citizens of Athens to preach to them.

He begins by praising them for their religiosity. They had even erected altars to unknown gods in order to obtain favors from them. Then without delay he goes on to say that the God they worshiped without knowing him was the God of the Jews, the God of Jesus Christ, the one God who had created all men and who provided for them. Paul's sermon is full of Stoic themes, such as the order of the universe, the unity of the human race and the fact that God does not live in human temples. Those themes are also biblical.

Finally, Paul presents the Gospel within quite a limited perspective. He insists that we are saved here and now, that our salvation is closely connected with the resurrection of Christ, an event that calls our human values into question. His preaching is only moderately successful, and most Greeks, who thought of continued existence only as a spiritual reality, resisted the Gospel of Christ for a long time. Only a few leading intellectuals such as Dionysius were converted at once. Some two hundred years later, another Dionysius, St. Denys of Paris, was also to proclaim the resurrection of Christ on the banks of the River Seine and another metropolis was to be built near his tomb. Paris was to become the new Athens.

Psalm 148: There are several hymns like this at the end of the psalter. They are used during Eastertide to mark out the stages in the process of evangelization.

John 16:12–15: "The Advocate, the Holy Spirit, whom the Father will send in my name, will teach you everything and remind you of all I have said to you" (Jn 14:26). Jesus is now approaching the time of death, a road that will lead him through the tomb to life itself. His disciples, however, are not yet fully able to bear his passion. But Jesus has to experience his passover and glorify the Father by his obedience.

Then and then only, he says, the Father will glorify the Son. Men will then be able to understand, in the full light that they will receive, that Jesus' faithfulness leads not to death as an end, but to his glory through apparent failure. They will then know that God is the only source of salvation. The Spirit of truth will not contribute any new revelation to the Church, but will lead it to the mystery of the incarnate and risen Christ.

■

"I still have many things to say to you, but they would be too much for you now." In other words, you will learn from experience. It took time for the disciples to understand. They really thought that the Kingdom would become an almost instant reality in the popular imagination, and they misinterpreted Jesus when he spoke of passing through the failure of his passion and crucifixion. They would learn from experience. They could not understand the work of the Spirit and wanted to impose ancient practices on the young Christian communities. It was when they were persecuted by the Jews that they began to know how to be really open to the pagans and what the freedom born of the resurrection really meant.

A child cannot possibly understand what it is to be a man. He can only learn from the experience of becoming adult.

"The Spirit will lead you to the complete truth." The Church is still learning how to understand the mystery of God and the mystery of its own life. It is learning by the experience of prayer and contemplation.

In this way, it is coming to know more and more perfectly the inexhaustible richness of the one who is known as Father. It is exploring more and more fully the mystery of what it means to be called the "beloved Spouse" of Christ.

Throughout the centuries, the Church has been able to express the mystery of its hope more clearly in reflection. It has continued to penetrate more and more deeply into the unfathomable secret revealed in Jesus Christ and to interpret what it has been given in the word in faithfulness to that word. In the patient love of those who try day after day to express what they have received from God, it manifests with increasing clarity "the breadth and the length, the height and the depth" of the love that God has aroused in men's hearts.

"The Spirit will lead you." The mystery of God and the Church is like an island—its outline can only be known by approaching it from different sides. One or other aspect of that mystery is understood as a living reality in each century, but it is only at the end of history that we shall know completely the secret of the interior of the island. We shall have learned that from the experience of generations of men and women who have been fashioned by the Spirit to be led "to the complete truth." We shall have discovered the inner mystery of God together, and the Spirit will have led us to shared knowledge.

■

Make what you have sown in us, Lord, grow.
Let your Spirit lead us
 to a knowledge of your mystery
 and communion forever with you.
Lord, do not forsake those
 who have placed their trust in you.
May your Spirit lead us
 to truth and knowledge
 and make us grow every day
 toward eternity.

THURSDAY OF THE SIXTH WEEK

(in those places where the Ascension is celebrated on Sunday)

WIDOWHOOD

Acts 18:1–8: After visiting Athens, the city of intellectuals, Paul went to Corinth, a trading center with two ports that were as famous as its reputation for vice. He arrived there in 49 or 50 A.D. and found attentive and friendly listeners among its dock workers. But, like everywhere else in Greece, there was also a wide variety of philosophies and new ideas. In his preaching, the Apostle did not give way to the wisdom of the world, but stressed the foolishness of the cross.

He was welcomed in Corinth by a Jewish family who had come from Rome. As he did not want to be a burden on them, he worked manually with them, as was the practice among rabbis. On the sabbath, however, he preached in the synagogue, where the familiar scene repeated itself: many of those present opposed him and this led to divisions.

Psalm 98 proclaims the work of the Spirit in the Church. "Sing to Yahweh a new song."

John 16:16–20: Terrible things were soon to happen to the disciples and would make them falter. But Jesus urges them to take heart. "In a short time," he assures them, the Church would be born, like a child born of a mother, and it would live from him. It would have a much clearer vision of him and would "see" him with the eyes of faith, which are also the eyes of the heart. John the Baptist had been glad to be the Bridegroom's friend. What would be the experience of the Church, the bride? Surely they would share intimacies and difficulties. The story of Christ and the Church was surely to be a love story.

■

"You will no longer see me." We talk too much about the presence of Christ. Perhaps we ought to be conscious of his absence. Do we really understand that his ascension has placed us in a situation of faith in which absence is the sign of his real presence?

The Church is a widow, and we who belong to the Church are separated from the one who left these strange words to us: "It is for your own good that I am going." We can still hear him saying what he said to Mary in the garden at Easter: "Do not cling to me."

Christ, then, is absent from us so that we can go toward God. Love becomes dangerous when there is a risk that we shall go to sleep in the safety and warmth of the present moment. Sometimes it is very important for lovers to be separated from one another. Jesus goes away so that we can follow our own way in search of him, and his absence enables us to believe.

"You will no longer see me and you will see me again." Christ's presence is hidden now in his body, the Church. He is with us until the end of the world, because the world is the place where his body is built up until that fullness, which goes far beyond all limits, is achieved.

The Church is a widow. We go along with her and sometimes we are given the chance to hear and understand a little of what she is saying in a mysterious language that does not quite belong to this earth. It is a way of speaking that she learned one day from the man who came from God and went back to God. Sometimes too we can catch a glimpse in her features of the face of the beloved Son.

∎

Let us pray for the Church, the body of Christ,
    that it does not become so down to earth
    and without vision
    that it fails to reveal to those who are in search
    a future that is always new.

Let us pray for those in positions of responsibility,
    that they may not be confined to their own narrow sphere,
    but may go beyond it in an attempt to build a universe
    of human dimensions,
    created in the image of the one, eternal God.

Let us pray for our brothers living in the shadow of death,
    that they may not be crushed by doubts,
    but that their hearts may be filled
    with the breath of God,
    who calls everyone to share his life.

Let us also pray for ourselves.
   We are all invited to be God's guests in his Kingdom.
   May we go beyond everyday signs and symbols
   to an understanding of the hidden God,
   who gives himself to us
   in the Word of his beloved Son.

FRIDAY OF THE SIXTH WEEK

THE BODY OF CHRIST
Acts 18:9–18: For the first time, Christianity is put on trial by the pagan world. Paul is brought by the Roman proconsul Gallio, the philosopher Seneca's brother, before the tribunal. The disputed question covers a very wide area: Is Christianity a form of Judaism or is it an entirely new religion? Paul's enemies claim that what he is teaching goes counter to Judaism. This claim, if it can be substantiated, means that they may win their case, since it was regarded as a serious crime in the Roman Empire to introduce a new religion. The proconsul, however, is less critical and does not share their view. He regards Christians as members of a Jewish sect who therefore enjoy the protection granted to the Jews. He therefore dismisses the plaintiffs. Luke takes advantage of this opportunity to emphasize how impartial Roman justice was—the shadow of Nero's persecutions had not yet appeared over the Church.

Psalm 47 is a hymn. The theme of the conquest of the promised land is linked here with the success of the Christian mission.

John 16:20–23a: A new world is in the throes of being born, like a butterfly emerging from its chrysalis or a child from its mother's womb. Jesus' passover from death to life is painful. He had to become nothing before he could be glorified. The Church is similar—periods of crisis enable it to grow in the breath of the Spirit.

Endurance is necessary in a time of trial. But the mother smiles with happiness when she sees her child, forgetting the pain of giving birth. The leaf bears no trace at all of its slow unfolding from the bud. The builders no longer feel tired when the house is finished. The same applies to the birth of the Kingdom of God—there will only be joy when it is present.

∎

"I am going . . . . You will be sorrowful, but your sorrow will be turned to joy." The Church will weep for her Beloved who has been taken away from her, but she will rejoice too, because she can bear witness to the hidden greatness of the man who has gone.

A man like ourselves has "gone up" to God. Jesus of Nazareth carries with him, in God, man's aspirations and concerns. God is now no longer simply Father, Son and Spirit, but Father, Jesus Christ and Spirit. The Word has become flesh and for eternity continues to be a son of the earth. The tastes, passions and ways of speaking and being of Christ do not merely express something of God—they are God. God's life is made of what was Jesus' manhood.

He is going away and we can be joyful. We are no more than poor, wretched human beings, but we are Christ's Church—the body of Christ. There is no discontinuity between his glorious body, seated at the right hand of God, and his earthly body, living in the Church.

The body of Christ, the sacraments of the Church, are humble and everyday signs, words expressing faith. Every time a believer is immersed in the bath in which he is born again, he is drawn into a marvelous dialogue in which the Son gives himself entirely to the Father and is made joyful by doing his Father's will. Every time a believing community breaks bread and shares the cup together, the Church experiences the love that unites the Father and the Son in one Spirit.

The body of Christ is the love that brings us together into one body. Our loves, our acts of forgiveness, our longings and our sufferings are all made one in the one love that is, quite simply, the name of God. From generation to generation the body of Christ continues to grow through failures and successes until it ultimately reaches adulthood. Then love will be the last word and the highest reality.

The body of Christ is also the very history of the Church. It is the history of those who have a name, the history of the poor, the humble and the lowly. It is the history of God continuing untiringly and the history of Jesus who mediates between God and us and gives meaning to the history of salvation by presenting it to the Father. God recognizes himself in Jesus every time men commit themselves to life according to his word.

∎

Lord Jesus, we pray
that your voice never ceases to be heard in our hearts
and that your love is never blotted from our memory.

Remain with us,
  Word that rises up from our silence
  and Love that satisfies all we long for.
May your kingdom and your glory come.

∎

We are looking for you, Lord,
  wondering who will speak to us of you.
We find hope in you alone,
  because you are love.
Only you can still come to us
  and we are waiting for you.

Send us your Spirit,
  so that we shall not find it too painful
  to wait for the spread of your Kingdom.

SATURDAY OF THE SIXTH WEEK

LONGING

Acts 18:23–28: Paul now decides to go back to Antioch. On the way, he visits the Christian communities in Galatia and Phrygia. Finally, he reaches Ephesus, one of the most important religious and trading centers in the Graeco-Roman world. His arrival there had been preceded by the coming of a Jew called Apollos, who had originated in Alexandria in Egypt. We know very little about this preacher, but it is clear from the Acts of the

Apostles that he knew Scripture very well and that he proclaimed Jesus Christ. His teaching, however, seems to have pre-dated Pentecost, and we are told that "he had only experienced the baptism of John." Luke tells us that Priscilla and Aquila gave him "further instruction" before sending him on to Corinth, where he did excellent work.

Psalm 47: See Friday of the Sixth Week.

John 16:23b–28: Happy are the disciples who have believed in Jesus' words. They are happy because they now have access to the Father. They are happy because they have once again found the paradise that was lost. Jesus' offering of himself in love has opened the gates of the Kingdom and men have found God's way of tenderness, the way that is Christ himself. Asking in Jesus' name is being closely united to the Son in faith and love. It is a certain way of touching the Father's heart.

▪

How long, Lord? How long must our time of testing last? We have suffered so much distress, so much violence and so many injustices—more than enough to make us lose heart.

The time of the Church is a time of waiting and patient prayer. Prayer is what characterizes the time of our widowhood, while we are separated from the one who has gone away. It draws us like a magnet to consider what God has done for us. It is pregnant with the future and brings to life in us what we are to be.

"Ask in my name." When Jesus directs our attention toward the Father who loves us (Jn 16:27), he knows that our existence will be divided by this. "Ask and you will receive": God wants to extend the scope of our lives and make the world wider.

Asking in Jesus' name is praying that we and the world we live in should have the destiny that Jesus himself had. Asking is receiving from him the light and the energy we need to transfigure the world. It is giving ourselves to the future.

The Church of Easter and the Ascension is the Church calling gently on God. As St. Paul said (Rom 8:23ff), the "Spirit groans in us." Christians will always persist along the often painful, difficult way of love. They will always be on the lookout for the guiding light in which they believe. Nothing will ever prevent them from waiting in love.

"Ask and you will receive." In the silence of prayer, they are already looking forward to tomorrow, and in the meantime they will go on their way, as though they were able to see what cannot be seen.

■

Lord, teach us how to pray.
  Give us your Spirit—
  may his new word revive our drooping spirits
  and his consuming fire make us burn
  with a longing to look for you.

May our lives be given entirely to love
  today and every day
  forever and ever.

■

It is really good to glorify you, Lord,
  every day and in every season,
  but even more especially today,
  when your Church is celebrating
  the glory of your beloved Son.

Raised high into your glory,
  he intercedes without ceasing for us,
  and to fill his Church with joy
  he has sent the Spirit of truth,
  to be the counsel for our defense.

Faithful to the end to your commandment,
  he has overcome death
and, raised to life, he lives with you
  and enables us to live your life.

Together with all those who have believed in your promise
  throughout the centuries,
  God, our hope, we praise you.

SEVENTH WEEK OF EASTER

CALLING ON THE SPIRIT

"I will not leave you orphans.... I will send you the Spirit" (Jn 14:18; 15:26). At this time, the time of the ascension, we read Jesus' farewell discourse in the liturgy and we notice that it is a prayer to the Father for those whom Jesus has received from his hands.

His disciples are to receive the Spirit. The Church, in other words, is going to receive its constitution, which is not a legal code consisting of Commandments, but rather an inner law that the Spirit is constantly rewriting and bringing up to date. Again and again throughout history, the Church is born again of the Spirit and is called to rediscover the source of its life. The Church continues in this way to live from the Spirit and to be on fire with love.

The disciples will receive the Spirit. Throughout the centuries, the Church is to be the sounding board of the good news in the world. It is to be the meeting place of everyone and everything in the Father's love.

"I will not leave you orphans. "The Spirit, the Easter gift of the Lord Jesus, is the one who makes the Church. Pentecost, the feast of the Spirit, is not celebrated as something quite different from Easter, the feast of Jesus, but we do celebrate it as the flower and fruit of what Jesus sowed when he overcame death. The fifty days of Easter will not have been spent in vain if we have looked forward to welcoming the living Spirit of Christ.

We should have all this in mind when we take our place in the upper room this week with Mary, the mother of Jesus, and the Apostles and ask for the Spirit to be poured out on us. There is a certain monotony in the passage of time, and our celebration of the liturgy can often be seen as an attempt to let God's own time break into our lives so that his great Easter gift can be renewed. It is particularly meaningful to ask again and again for the gift of the Spirit during this week. To repeat again and again "Come, Holy Spirit" is the same as declaring our firm faith that he will certainly come. Our prayer for the Spirit is not a senseless cry. Yes, he will come, but his coming is always in our asking and our submission to him.

Mary was also present in the upper room—a discreet presence. She was present then as she has always continued to be present with the Church, as an icon of welcome and fertility. In her, the Word was made flesh by the Spirit, for "nothing is impossible to God" (Lk 1:37; cf. Gen 8:14). In the Church too, the Word becomes the flesh of men by the power of the Spirit as long as we, like Mary, welcome God and his quite astonishing grace.

There have been many rather sickly devotions to Mary in the past, but they should not prevent us from letting her discreet presence during this time before Pentecost give a distinctively Marian flavor to the month of May in which it falls.

COME, HOLY SPIRIT!

Send your Spirit, Lord,
and the face of the earth will be renewed.

We are so withdrawn and weighed down with trouble
that our hearts have become dry.
Spirit of God, flowing from the depths of Love—
come, Spirit of God.

Silence weighs us down
and we must talk and sing.
Spirit of God, you make the dumb sing—
come, Spirit of God.

The earth is cold
and man, the enemy of his fellow men, is cold.
Spirit of God, fire and heat for our earth—
come, Spirit of God.

The feast is beginning, our hands are stretched out,
water flows from the spring and the fire glows again.
Spirit of God, you bring together those who are scattered—
come, Spirit of God.

Our silence turns to happiness,
peace and smiling on our faces.
Spirit of God, you give birth to new life—

come, Spirit of God.

The Spirit is power and strength
   and love that overcomes our sense of defeat.
Spirit of God, you are the cry of death that is conquered,
   the cry of the child that is born—
   come, Spirit of God.

Come, Spirit of God.
Come, Father of the poor,
   come, quench our thirst,
   come, make us bolder.
You who are the wind of peace and the breath of fire,
   come and widen our horizons;
   create a new heart in us.

Come, Spirit of God,
   give us the breath of morning,
   burn us with the fire of midday
   and be our peace during the night.
Every day we shall rise again
   to praise you for marvelous deeds.
   Our thanksgiving will be heard
   at the ends of the earth.

∎

The life that you have given us, Father,
   cries out to you.
Pour your Spirit out on us again,
   as you did in the beginning
and, astonished by our own renewal,
   we shall once again be able to call you
   our Father.

∎

Father, you gave us life—
   a life overflowing with your love
   and abounding with your Spirit.
Let that Spirit turn us toward you in praise
   and toward our fellow men in love.

■

*Where two or three are gathered together in Christ,
   the word of the Lord can bear fruit—
   holy God, put your Spirit into us.*

*Anyone who remains in the word
   will know God and grow in love—
   God of peace, put your Spirit into us.*

*Whoever believes will see God's glory
   and God's light will shine upon him—
   living God, put your Spirit into us.*

MONDAY OF THE SEVENTH WEEK

THE HOUR

Acts 19:1–8: "He will baptize you with the Holy Spirit and fire" (Lk 3:17). While he was staying at Ephesus, Paul met several Christian disciples and asked them if they had received the Holy Spirit. They were very surprised and said that they had received John's baptism, but they had not apparently heard of the event of Pentecost.

Who were these disciples? Probably, like Apollos, disciples of John the Baptist. They knew Jesus of Nazareth, but they had not followed him in his Passover experience and, like the disciples on the road to Emmaus, they had in a sense lost their direction on the way, because they had not understood the meaning of the events in Jerusalem at the deepest level.

Paul opened their eyes to that reality, proclaiming Jesus Christ as the one who died and had been raised from the dead, and giving them a Christian baptism. They were illuminated. For them it was like a new Pentecost and they received the Spirit and "began to speak with tongues and to prophesy."

Psalm 68 is difficult to classify. It consists of several early poems drawing attention to God's power and glory as attributes in which believers place their hope.

John 16:29–33: The hour has come. It is a crucially important hour for Jesus, because it is the hour for which he has himself come. It will also be crucial for the disciples, who were to be blown about like straws in the wind. It is also the hour of victory for Jesus, who has already overcome the world.

It is finally the hour of faith. The disciples declare that he has come from God. After Easter they will discover that he is the only real answer to their questions and they will know peace.

The hour of faith is also the hour of dispersion and the hour of the Church. The Church was born at a time of faithfulness—God's faithfulness to man and man's uncertain faith in God. It was born in the hearts of insecure men and women. The Church was really what Christ was going to make of it and of those people, who would not forget him throughout the centuries.

■

"The hour is coming." Jesus did not, of course, think of that hour simply chronologically, as a point in time. For him it was the time of fulfillment that had come. The whole of his life was to be recapitulated in that hour. It was to be summarized and presented as a final and definitive synopsis.

Jesus welcomed the coming of his "hour." He was, during that time of suffering and death, to give glory to the one he called quite simply "Father."

"The hour is coming." God, who will change the face of the earth and make human history follow a new direction, is coming. The glory of God will arise, not in power, but in a body marked by wounds, a swollen and unsightly face and a man who has been tortured.

"The hour is coming." The Jesus who died on the cross was the same man who associated with the sick, the rejected and the poor. He was the man who found God's traces in the whole of mankind and even in the heart of a prostitute or the appeal of a Roman soldier. God's glory began to shine when the carpenter from Galilee called blessed the poor in spirit and those who hunger and thirst and wait for God's coming. The same light continued to shine for all men and women, from Lake Tiberias to Golgotha.

"The hour is coming." That hour becomes the whole of time whenever men and women give themselves to death and to life. St. Irenaeus declared: "God's glory is man alive." The light of that hour can never be enclosed in a temple built by human hands, because God's dwelling place is living men and women. "The hour is coming" surely means that the Kingdom of God comes whenever men and women follow the way that will lead them through death to the garden of the resurrection.

∎

Father, the hour has come—
   the hour for him to go to the very end
   and love until he dies of it.

We bless you, Father, for Jesus' hour—
   he handed himself over so that we should live.

We ask you:
   let us follow him in faith and love,
   because our hour has also come.
   It is for today and forever and ever.

∎

The world is in great distress, Lord Jesus—
   come and give us peace.

Do not leave those who believe in your words
   scattered and alone, Lord.
Bring together in the unity of the Spirit
   those for whom you have prayed
   when the hour came
   for you to conquer the world with love.

TUESDAY OF THE SEVENTH WEEK

A TESTAMENT
Acts 20:17–27: Paul had broken bread with the community in Troas. Then he left in order to be in Jerusalem on the day of Pentecost. When he arrived in Miletus, "he sent for the elders of the church of Ephesus."

He knew that his end was near and he thought of himself as on reprieve, waiting for death. This prospect did not deter him in any way, however, because he was conscious of the Spirit leading him on. Like Jesus, he "set his face" to go to Jerusalem (cf. Lk 9:51, 54).

Like Jesus too and in common with many others in the ancient world, he bequeathed a spiritual testament to those who had worked with him, reminding them of his ministry. He had "served the Lord" with many "sorrows and trials." He had called on the Jews, both in public and in private, to believe in Jesus Christ and on the pagans to turn to God. But now the hour had come for him to bear supreme witness. He had to run his race to the end and conclude the ministry entrusted to him by the Lord. So he bore witness once again to the good news of Christ.

Psalm 68: See Monday of the Seventh Week.

John 17:1–11a: Jesus has washed his disciples' feet so that they might have part in him (Jn 13:8). He is about to communicate life to them in his total offering of himself on the cross for the salvation of the world. His crucifixion was the expression of his self-giving in history, but that gift also became a reality when he knelt down to wash their feet to give them life.

Christ raises his eyes to heaven and prays. He is therefore already with his Father, or, rather, he "raises" himself to the Father, bringing after him those whom he has made his friends. His prayer is his ascent to the one who will glorify him.

The hour has come (see Jn 16:32)—the hour to give life to those whom the Father has loved since the beginning of the world, the hour when man is born again to the life of God. The hour has come to contemplate the depths of God's love, the love revealed by Christ, who alone loves as only God can love.

Christ prays for his disciples. They have believed in him. They have trusted him and given him their lives. They are no longer servants, but friends (see Jn 15:15). They belong to God as they belonged to Christ. That is the mystery of love.

■

"I pray for them." Jesus' concern for his own is expressed in the form of a prayer. At the very time when they are about to face the test of being separated from him, he prays for them. "They belong to you . . . and in them I am glorified." The Church is from generation to generation to be the face of the one who was sent. He, the Son, is to be glorified in what the Church says and does.

Jesus has already said: "It is for your own good that I am going" (Jn 16:7). The others rely on him as long as he stays with them. But as soon as he goes away, the disciples have to take their task seriously. "I am not in the world any longer, but they are in the world."

That is the mystery of the Church—it is expressed when Christians try to live the good news. Their living the good news is the mystery of God among men. He, the Word, has, since his going away, only had our words that are so quickly lost to proclaim the coming of salvation. Those are the only words that he has for eternity, but, however fragile they may be, they bear, in his Spirit, love that fills them with God's power. He, the Life, has also only our lives, marked by sin and death, to make the flowers of tenderness spring up in the desert. What we do, however, is, in his Spirit, filled with infinite life. Since his going away too, he, the Way, has only had our modest longings to stimulate a thirst for something else, and this will be so for eternity, but, in his Spirit, our hopes are already a way to great hope and, with him, we shall pass through the doors of the Kingdom of God. The Church is already shining with a secret light. There is nothing showy on the outside, but the Spirit dwells in the depths of the Church's heart.

The Church lives from those who believe in that hidden seed, each member welcoming the word of God in order to share it with others and each one letting himself be raised up by the Spirit in order to form one body with the others. It is the Spirit who keeps the Church faithful to the name of the Father, revealed by the Son. "I pray for them. . . . They are in the world . . . so that they may be one like us."

Holy Father,
your Son prays for those
   whom you have given to him.

Fill us with a new fire
   so that we may know the glory that is in us.
Hand us over to undivided love
   so that we may know perfect joy.
Let us sink down into the death of your Son
   so that we may be reborn to Life
   by sharing in his resurrection.

WEDNESDAY OF THE SEVENTH WEEK

FOR THE WORLD

Acts 20:28–38: Before he died, Jesus had entrusted the flock to Peter, and the college of the Twelve had been formed with the task of bearing witness. They had filled up their number by choosing Matthias and had given themselves over to prayer and the ministry of the word.

Paul was now about to "go away" and the dark clouds were gathering over the Church. False apostles had slipped among Christians, like wolves among the sheep, and the message of Christ was being distorted by heresy. But men were still continuing to do the work that had been commenced and true shepherds were acting under the guidance of the Spirit. It was to them that Paul, who had so far had the care of all the churches, entrusted the "Church of God which Christ had bought with his own blood." They would in their turn be the ministers of "the word of his grace that had the power to build them up."

Then we read: "When he had finished speaking, Paul knelt down with them all and prayed." It was for him, as it had been for Jesus in Gethsemane, the hour of sorrow—the hour of the prince of darkness.

Psalm 68: See Monday of the Seventh Week.

John 17:11b–19: "Holy Father, keep them." Christ has gone back to the Father, but his disciples are still in the world. He consecrates himself for their sake. He gives his life for them. After his self-offering, however, there is acceptance by the Father and the gift of the Spirit.

The Spirit "consecrates them in the truth," placing them in a position where they will discover true values. Although they are in the world, Christians are not of the world. "They do not belong to the world." They are not seduced by its attractions. They live in the light that reveals to them the secrets of God's existence.

They no longer belong to the world, but they have been "sent into the world." Jesus bore witness to the Father's love and, like him, they also proclaim the good news of salvation. Their preaching is confirmed by the Spirit who confirmed Jesus' preaching. But "the disciple is not superior to his teacher" (Mt 10:24; Lk 6:40). Because they are one with Jesus, those who believe in him will inevitably share the effects of the world's hatred of him.

■

"Holy Father!" About to leave this world, Jesus prays for those whom he has chosen. It is a moving prayer with a strong flavor of the earth—a prayer for the world. It is also a prayer with a taste of eternity—the prayer of a world turning toward God.

A prayer for the world. The word "world" occurs no fewer than nine times in this short passage. The world was the work of the Creator, but it is also a rebellious and sinful world. It is the world that the Son made into his dwelling place, but also the world that condemned and crucified him. It is the world forming the very fabric of the Church, but also the world that is hostile to the good news. "You sent me into the world," but "I am not of the world." Praying for the world, Jesus is unable to reject the bonds of flesh, because he took manhood onto himself. He cannot forget his origins—he was born of God. God cannot reduce himself to the level of the world, yet he is not hostile or indifferent to it—in Jesus, what is incompatible is combined. In Jesus, God is both the heart and the distant horizon of the world.

A prayer for the disciples—they too will combine what is incompatible. They are of this earth—they are made of clay—but from now on they will breathe the Spirit of eternity. They will be "holy"—

sanctified by sharing the destiny of sinners. They will inherit life even if they continue, like all men, to be marked by failure and death.

"Holy Father . . . while still in the world I say these things to share my joy with them to the full." Why should the world be contrasted with the holiness of the Father? Jesus is, after all, the way from the one to the other. But the joys and sorrows, the suffering and the longing of the world will always form the fabric of the Church. The Church has always been and will always be the hidden, secret warp and weft giving meaning and direction to the cloth and taking history to its end. But, then, Christians are not of the world, and this is because he has made it possible for them to see the end of history. "Father, I want those you have given me to be with me where I am" (Jn 17:24).

∎

Lord our God,
  so many prayers
  and so many requests come from our hearts.

We ask you:
  May your Kingdom come
  and your will be done
  on earth as in heaven.

∎

Holy Father,
  keep us true to your name.
  You have given us forever to your Son.

Let us live in unity,
  in trust and in joy.

Consecrate in the truth
  those who bear witness to your word
  in this world in which we make our pilgrimage every day.

THURSDAY OF THE SEVENTH WEEK

UNITY

Acts 22:30; 23:6–11: Paul had told the members of the community at Ephesus that his aim in life was to "finish his race and carry out the mission the Lord Jesus had given him—and that was to bear witness to the good news of God's grace" (Acts 20:24). During the last stage of his life on earth, he was no longer concerned with the need to establish Christian communities. His task, as he saw it, was to give thanks for what he had experienced—the grace of God revealed in Jesus Christ. He therefore felt compelled to do more than simply defend himself when he was taken before Jewish or pagan tribunals. He was the spokesman of the Gospel of Christ and spoke in defense of another. He did not merely explain the truth of an argument. His whole life bore witness to Jesus Christ.

In Jerusalem the same accusations were made against him that had been made throughout his whole missionary career. Both the Jews and the Judaeo-Christians complained of the same thing—Paul did not respect the law of Moses and preached salvation by faith alone. The question confronting the Church and the people was this: Was Paul an apostate? In other words, was the foundation on which many of the Christian communities were based the work of a renegade? It is true to say that the very existence of the Church, as the new Israel and the heir of God's promises, was at stake.

He tried to make clear to the Sanhedrin, then, that faith and resurrection from the dead were in accordance with what the Pharisees believed. He did not stress the differences between the Pharisees and the Sadducees, nor did he insist that salvation was the consequence, not of good works, but only of faith in God's gift. He was not to die in Jerusalem, but in Rome, the capital of the Graeco-Roman world.

Psalm 16: The structure of this Psalm is not at all clear, and it should perhaps be regarded as one of the individual laments. It is, however, a very suitable Psalm for Holy Saturday, because it expresses man's hope in the face of death.

John 17:20–26: God has visited his people in Jesus Christ. That is a cause of great joy not only for the disciples, but also for everyone who welcomes God's gift.

Christ now prays for all who will hear the message of the Christian missionaries and will unite to form his body. "May they all be one." That is the only way in which men will be able to experience the love of God. Love is never easy, because it comes from another world. But if Christians, thanks to the Spirit acting within them, live from that love despite all the difficulties confronting them, then the world may come to recognize that God has visited his people and to know that Christ's mission is authentic.

■

To make sure that the family or the group to which they belong sticks closely together, some people insist on a strict uniformity of customs or behavior and sometimes even that all members should share, privately or publicly, the same convictions.

"May they all be one." We know how often the Church has been guilty of this insistence on uniformity and how it has all too frequently been totalitarian. But such an attitude shows an ignorance of the true basis of our unity. We are one body, but only because the same life supports our lives and the same blood flows through our veins. Unity is a matter of life and breath, not of doctrine or rules. The Church should never be a club or a chapel.

"May they all be one. Father, may they be one in us, as you are in me and I am in you." The model on which our unity is based is simply this: the love that unites the eternal Father to the Son.

When we say that our unity has these deep foundations in love, we are bearing witness to the fact that it is impossible to exhaust the truth of God and his birth. No individual can do that, and we are dependent on each other in discovering, experiencing and testifying to the mystery revealed to us by the Spirit.

Our unity will be a gift when we all come to experience fully, in a clear vision of the Kingdom, the mystery of God. We shall only be one body in that ultimate communion which we still have to receive, when Christ will be "all in all" (see 1 Cor 15:28).

"May they all be one." In prayer we try to see the face of God. In meditation we learn how to give flesh to the love dwelling in our hearts. We gaze into the depths of our longing to express God in truth when we practice contemplation. In all these related activities, we

are secretly tying together the threads that form the fabric of the great cloak which God will one day wrap around the great body of the whole of mankind.

■

God, our only Father,
we ask you:
let each one of us be fashioned by your creative breath
and lead us forward in love.

Give us your Spirit
and we shall become the one body of your Son,
united to each other forever and ever.

FRIDAY OF THE SEVENTH WEEK

LOVE
Acts 25:13–21: Paul's trial continued, but, despite its reputation for impartiality, the Roman law could do no more for him as the Apostle of Christ than the law of Moses. Claudius, Felix, Festus and Agrippa all recognized that he was innocent, but they had to yield to his appeal to resort to the emperor's judgment. Paul appealed to the emperor in order to avoid being summoned before a Jewish court.

All the judges who were confronted with the problem recognized it as a theological argument between the Jews and the Christians. What divided the two groups was "some argument or other about a dead man called Jesus whom Paul alleged to be alive." The philosophers whom Paul had addressed in Athens had fought shy of the question of the resurrection of the dead, and the Roman politicians at once ceased to be interested as soon as their authority was called into doubt by Christian teaching. They were apprehensive when the disciples of Christ refused to regard the emperor as sacred and therefore called the whole social order of Rome into question.

Psalm 103 is a hymn to God's goodness experienced by an individual.

"Bless the Lord, my soul!"

John 21:15–19: The last chapter of John's Gospel is generally regarded as an appendix and its origin is widely disputed. It is almost certainly a supplement edited by the evangelist's disciples after Peter's death. It contains the most recent evidence of Johannine thought regarding the structure and task of the community as entrusted to the first of the Apostles.

There was an urgent need to define the hierarchical structure of the various communities of the Church in Asia at that time of conflict with the Gnostic heresy. Peter's investiture as shepherd of the flock after the Easter event is clearly very important, and the reference to his martyrdom emphasizes the essential condition of the one who is devoted exclusively to caring for his sheep.

Jesus asks Peter three times "Do you love me?" and the Apostle's affirmation of his love not only functions as a counter-balance to his threefold denial before Jesus' trial, but also stresses the trust and even the complicity that unites the two. The bond of affection between Jesus and his disciple, then, is clearly the source of Peter's pastoral ministry. It is revealed as a very exacting task, occupying him for the whole of his life until he is very old and possibly ending in violent death. "You will stretch out your hands" (v. 19) may indicate crucifixion. That is what is meant by "following" Jesus.

■

There is an element of overstatement in this account of the meeting between Peter and the risen Christ. We cannot quite accept it as reasonable.

"Do you love me more than these others?" Such a degree of commitment would never have been required if no more than a business transaction were involved. But the Church is founded on the Spirit who is always excessive. Faith and love that are kept within reasonable limits are always caricatures.

Three times the question is asked: "Do you love me?"—a heartbreaking question, opening an old and barely healed wound: "Before the cock crows twice, you will have disowned me three times" (Mk 14:30; Lk 22:61) and "I do not know the man you speak of" (Jn 18:17, 25–27; Mk 14:68–72; Lk 22:55–62).

"Do you love me?" It is not a reproach, but a friend's prayer. Jesus loves Peter. He entrusts his sheep to him and expects him to go ahead of them. He who is to lead them will himself be led by the Spirit. He will be led by the love of the shepherd who hands over the whole of his life. "Follow me!"

Only love can come close to the mystery, and it can only do that when it has been made pure in the crucible of forgiveness and faithfulness. "Do you love me?" "Lord, you know everything; you know that I love you." The meeting is summed up in those simple words.

Meeting the risen Jesus means that we must be open to the foolishness of the Spirit. We will then expose ourselves quite spontaneously to love—unreflectingly, foolishly and without any certainty as to what will happen. Love has never been reasonable.

■

"Do you love me more than these others?"
"Lord, you know everything:
　you know that we love you!"
Let us, then, love you even more
　and make our shortcomings
　the foundation of a new Church.

We pray for the Church and its pastors:
　may they overflow with love
　for you and their brethren.

We pray for those who have betrayed you and their fellow men:
　may an excessive love
　be the place of their reconciliation.

We pray for those who are dying:
　may your Church lead them
　to resurrection with your living Son.

SATURDAY OF THE SEVENTH WEEK

FIRE

Acts 28:16–20, 23b–24, 28–31: Paul eventually arrived in Rome, where he was to stay for two years, free but under supervision. As always he turned his attention first to the Jews and spoke to them about "the hope of Israel," which he interpreted as the resurrection of the dead anticipated in Jesus' resurrection. Once again, however, the Jews were divided in their opinions.

It is also the hour of judgment. Paul has come to the end of his travels. The good news has reached the "ends of the earth" (Acts 1:8). The apostle "welcomed all who came to visit him," both Jews and pagans. Some Jews, rejecting the fulfillment of salvation in Jesus, are regarded by Paul as guilty, but those who are converted to the word are regarded as justified by the Lord. They are the Church—Israel restored—and will be united to the pagans who will later receive the message of Christ in great numbers.

The proclamation of the Gospel to the Jews ended with Paul's mission to the Roman Jews, and from that time onward all peoples and nations were to hear the Christian message. Through the faithful people of Israel, the words of grace of the risen Christ were sent to all men. That was the ultimate and true judgment.

Psalm 11 expresses the believer's trust in God's protection.

John 21:20–25: The tradition of the "disciple Jesus loved" was preserved in the Church of Ephesus. He had been the perfect disciple. He had knowledge of faith, he was devoted to Jesus, and he was intimate with Jesus. These were all characteristics which gave him a higher status than the other disciples, including even Simon Peter. What is stressed at the end of the Gospel, however, is that those who inherited his tradition had no intention of setting him up against Peter. Their attitude toward Peter was simply one of critical appreciation, which can only be explained on the basis of the special position that he occupied in Christianity.

Christ does not reveal in these concluding verses what the ultimate destiny of the beloved disciple was. That would have been useless, since Christians would not have been able to follow him, however much it might have cost them. Later, when they were able to follow Jesus in his passion, they would discover that his was the only way that led to the Father.

∎

"There were many other things that Jesus did; if all were written down, the world itself, I suppose, would not hold all the books that would have to be written."

This statement brings us right back to the question: "But you, who do you say I am?" (Mt 16:15; Mk 8:29; Lk 9:20). All this has been written down so that you may believe that Jesus is "the Christ, the Son of the living God." A man appeared in human history—"he came to his own domain" (Jn 1:11). "He lived among us" (1:14). He was life, light, salt and leaven. With him our whole being as men and women was changed. "To all who did accept him he gave power to become children of God" (1:12). All this appears at the beginning of John's Gospel, and the end of the same Gospel brings us back to ourselves, to our own hearts and to the breathtaking suggestion made to us.

"There were many other things that Jesus did." Men had seen his body hanging from a cross. They had witnessed his painful death and had learned that his life had been able to conquer that death. They had also rediscovered in their own hearts everything that they had received from him. After experiencing all that, they had been able to say: "God loved the world so much that he gave his only Son" (Jn 3:16).

This news seems to have survived the wear and tear of centuries of use, but its explosive power has been neutralized in many ways. Yet, even now, it can still act like the wind of the Spirit at Pentecost, completely upsetting us and giving our lives, both individually and collectively, a much wider perspective.

"What does it matter to you? You are to follow me." The condition of faith must always be the fire that the Spirit kindles in us and burns us so deeply that we are eventually consumed by love. The Christian is not someone who clings to certain teachings. He is not just a decent person. He is possessed—possessed by the Spirit and totally dedicated. "Follow me!" Irresistible appeals are made to our hearts.

∎

Come, Holy Spirit,
  bathe us in your light
  and fill us again with your life.

Guide us in the footsteps of the beloved Son
  so that we are led
  to the love that will never cease.

■

Your word could never be enclosed
  within the pages of a book.

Lord Jesus, make your Church
  an open book until the end of time—
  a book in which men will be able to read
  the astonishing history of your endless love,

good news and hope that never tires
  forever and ever.